letters to Tiptree

edited by
Alexandra Pierce
and Alisa Krasnostein

First published in Australia August 2015
by Twelfth Planet Press

www.twelfthplanetpress.com

Design and layout by Amanda Rainey
Typeset in Sabon MT Pro

National Library of Australia Cataloguing-in-Publication entry

Title:	Letters to Tiptree / Alisa Krasnostein, Alexandra Pierce.
ISBN:	9781922101259 (paperback)
Subjects:	Tiptree, James--Correspondence.
	Authors, American--Correspondence.
	Science fiction, American.
	Letters.
Other Creators/Contributors:	Krasnostein, Alisa, editor.
	Pierce, Alexandra, editor.
Dewey Number:	826.92

Table of Contents

Introduction

In 1967, James Tiptree Jr. was born, named after a jar of
marmalade in order to be forgettable to editors on rejection.
His first fiction sale was in 1968 and 1969's "The Last Flight
of Doctor Ain" caught the world's attention. Ten years later, with
two Hugo wins and three Nebulas under his belt, he, along with
Raccoona Sheldon, was outed as Alice Sheldon, born in 1915,
"one aged suburban matron" as she described herself. *In Letters
to Tiptree,* we commemorate Alice Sheldon in her centennial year,
celebrating her achievements and contributions as James Tiptree
Jr.; remembering her amazing life outside of her writing career; and
reflecting on her ongoing impact on the science fiction community,
both in terms of her fiction and what it means to reflect on gender
and identity.

We asked writers, editors, critics, and fans to write a letter to
Alice Sheldon, James Tiptree Jr., or Raccoona Sheldon (or any
combination thereof). We asked them to celebrate, to recognise,

to reflect, and in some cases to finish conversations set aside nearly thirty years ago on Sheldon's death. We're very pleased with the responses. Our letter-writers have engaged with specific stories—and which of Tiptree/Sheldon's work has made the most impact will quickly become obvious. Others explored what it meant that a woman was behind James Tiptree Jr., and what that therefore means for other women who want to write science fiction. Still others have reflected on Sheldon's gender and sexuality.

This book is presented in four parts. Section one, "Alice, Alice, Do You Read?", is composed of letters written to Alice Sheldon, James Tiptree Jr., or Raccoona Sheldon (or all of them). The second section, "I Never Wrote You Anything But The Exact Truth", presents selected letters exchanged between Sheldon and Ursula K. Le Guin, and Sheldon and Joanna Russ. Sheldon had had a long paper relationship with both women as Tiptree, and this continued well after the revelation of Tiptree's identity. We have chosen to include letters primarily from 1976 and 1977 that illuminate aspects of Sheldon's identity and relationship with her two friends, as well as their reflections on Tiptree/Sheldon and his/her work. The letters have been reproduced with spelling mistakes and the occasional typewriter malfunction in place, to help preserve the sense of their immediacy and intimacy. We have included these exchanges partly because reading these letters is a wonderful privilege—a glimpse into a passionate friendship always is—and because we wanted to give Sheldon the opportunity to speak for herself and address some of the questions left unanswered. We especially wanted to know *how* (or whether) the revelation of Tiptree's persona changed the close relationships s/he'd developed in the science fiction community.

In "Everything But The Signature Is Me", we have reprinted academic material on Tiptree's work and identity. Ursula K. Le Guin's introduction to *Star Songs of an Old Primate*, written soon after the revelation of Tiptree's identity, is an exploration of Tiptree's writing, as well as the question of his identity. Michael Swanwick's introduction to the 2004 reprint of Tiptree's 1990 collection, *Her Smoke Rose Up Forever*, provides further biographical detail on Sheldon for the unfamiliar as well as the experience of Tiptree being exposed as Sheldon. The excerpt from Justine Larbalestier's excellent *The Battle of the Sexes in Science Fiction* also examines Tiptree's identity and work, while Helen Merrick considers what makes something a "tiptree text" in light of the creation of the James Tiptree, Jr., Award. Wendy Pearson considers Tiptree's work within the context of reading the author as trans, and what it means for Sheldon to "be" Tiptree. Together, these pieces provide some context for understanding James Tiptree Jr., his work, and his relationship to/with Alice Sheldon. And, finally, Alice Sheldon herself writes about who she "really" is in the titular essay.

Editing this book together has been a remarkable experience. The honesty and enthusiasm evident in the modern letters has been startling and humbling. They inspired us to write our own letters to Tiptree, included in the afterword, "Oh Joanna, Will I Have Any

Friends Left?" We also enjoyed the unexpected commentary on the *act* of writing a letter. Perhaps letter-writing is an art that needs to be revived. Additionally, the experience of reading the Sheldon/ Le Guin and Sheldon/Russ correspondence was a remarkable and thought-provoking one. We are both intensely proud of the book that you're reading, and hope it will inspire and bring joy.

Alexandra and Alisa,
August 2015.

Alice,
Alice,
Do You Read?

Dear Tiptree

They say a field, but really it's a spaceport,
we cobbled it together out of dreams
we had assembled from popular mechanics
and broken hearts,
our yearning for stars, distance, escape,
for there to be something
out there,
something more,
cradles for spaceships patched up
from a carton of spark plugs.

There you came striding,
disguised
through our field, our spaceport,
looking as though you owned it,
swinging your new tool kit,
a wary awareness,
of edges of longing
your careful reflections,
your pulsing heart,
the honed lines of your craft.

You rocked our spaceport,

left it changed, wider,

more solid, more open,

stranger, expanded,

containing doors undreamed of,

marked "men", "women", "other".

Now, each reaching out,

shall we walk forward

step into "other"

to see where it takes us?

Jo Walton

Dear Dr Sheldon,

I wondered, when I planned writing this letter, how should I address you? Maybe I'm just British, but it worried me. I can't call you "Alice"; or "Tip". That would be rude; I never even met you. "Dear Tiptree" seemed like a possibility, but though "Tip" may have been your handle, among friends, "Tiptree" was never your name. "Mr Tiptree" sounds ridiculous, "Mrs Bradley Sheldon" anachronistic. You were Major Bradley in the US Army; I suppose you were *Agent* Sheldon in the infant CIA? You had so many titles; so many brilliant careers you seem to have sampled and tossed aside... Then I remembered you had a PhD in Psychology, and I felt my path was clear.

Anyway, the first thing I need to say is what every writer wants to hear: I love your writing. I loved your writing before I had any idea you were a secret agent. I should explain that I've read science fiction all my life, but I've never been a fan in the technical sense. I had no idea the Science Fiction Community existed until my first novel was "hailed" as sf, back in the eighties. I knew nothing about the controversy around dazzling, honours-laden, "ineluctably masculine" "James Tiptree Jr" until it was long over, and you had been unmasked. I have to confess something: I was disappointed. In the seventies I had found plenty of sexual-revolutionary US female sf writers to admire (Ursula Le Guin, Suzy McKee Charnas, Joanna Russ, Vonda McIntyre ... for the genre, it was a crowd!). There were men who were okay, doing their best according to their lights (Chip Delany, Fred Pohl). But James Tiptree was different. I remember reading your first novel (*Up The Walls of the World*) when it was new, in its yellow and red Gollancz jacket, and thinking: *at least there's one*. Tiptree gets it, he sees what the problems are... And you were gone. It was a shame.

If I was completely fooled, I was in good company. When someone reads the transcript of *Khatru 3* (a free-ranging discussion of sex and gender issues, organised by fanzine editor Jeffrey D. Smith, in 1975) it's clear that Ursula Le Guin, Joanna Russ *et al* never doubted that Tip was a male fellow traveller—although they took issue with his effusive, *dear lady* manner, and his tendency to put Woman on a sentimental pedestal. You were having fun, I suppose. But I sometimes wonder, were they disappointed too? Did they wish "Tip" could have been the man they thought he was? The proof that science fiction could change? That *male* science fiction writers could be everything the sf world wanted, and win all the prizes, and still didn't have to be sexist?

How did you ever get away with it? The short answer is that you didn't; not for long. You were Tiptree for nine years: heaped with praise; the man of the moment. But your failure to appear in public had quickly attracted attention, and there *were* doubts about your sex, based on your preferred themes. Your fans, bless them, felt they had a right to know who you really were, and were soon trying hard to find out. Meanwhile, you were playing with fire. You must have known that discovery would cost you your place at the top table, yet you formed intimate, confessional friendships by mail. You shared personal data in correspondence. You didn't say no when you were invited, and expected, to play a prominent part in the big science fiction/sexual politics debate—an issue that was so important in your work, and so vitally interesting to the real Dr Sheldon. Something had to give.

The other answer is that you were a natural for the role. You were a skilled writer with a science doctorate. You knew science fiction: you'd tried writing it already, but without the help of "Tiptree" garnered only a handful of rejections. You'd been testing the limits of what a woman could do and be in a man's world (a succession of male worlds) your entire life, if we count the childhood adventures with your redoubtable mother in Africa. Journalist, Intelligence Officer, Experimental Psychologist, Spy ... you were protected, I'm sure, by the sense of entitlement that children of privilege never lose, but you'd had to learn to hide in plain sight, like the escapologist mother and daughter in "The Women Men Don't See". I suspect you'd learned to enjoy the danger, too. And the timing was perfect. Science fiction, primed by the New Wave, infiltrated by the ferment of sixties and seventies radical movements, was open as never before to the challenges you had to offer.

You wrote other stories (cover stories, maybe?), that were polished, competent, and unthreatening: like your family-values Scientific Apocalypse tale "The Man Who Walked Home", but ironically it was probably the hard-hitting feminist material that sealed the success of your masquerade. You wrote about brutal rape and brutish lust, with considerable style and in shockingly candid language. Sometimes blackly comic, sometimes deadly serious, you portrayed *man*, the male of the species, as a tortured soul, helpless in the grip of his urges. Man, the slave of Life's meaningless, never-ending expansion-drive; the monster who can't be tamed... And while your female colleagues saw other nuances, male writers and critics simply loved you for it. They felt recognised: vindicated by a fearless older brother.

The shock value of your sexual imagery has faded. Today, the famous lust scene in "And I Awoke On The Cold Hill's Side" (one of my favourites) reads like a sideshow in a powerful story that uses sexual excitement *as a metaphor*, in a savage critique of US imperialism. But your preoccupation with sex-as-death can't be deconstructed so easily, and your profound pessimism about the human race is as haunting as ever. You said once in an interview that "the birth and growth of Nazism" was your "central generation event". I believe you, but I think it went deeper and wider than that. Nagasaki and Hiroshima, and the madness of Mutually Assured Destruction, were probably also entries in the catalogue of horrors that made you see your own humanity as the stuff of nightmares. Maybe your lab work didn't help, either. Experimental Psychology can be a nasty business, and a dissertation on "*Responses of animals to novel stimuli in differing environments*" sounds a bit sinister to me. Not much fun for the white mice, I'll bet.

You were a child star, *Alice in Jungleland* with your picture in the papers, before you were nine years old. You first tried suicide when you were a teen. Many child stars find celebrity a hard act to follow; many celebrated artists have struggled with depression, as you did all your life. But you were not a quitter. You kept going, having a wild time, a tumultuous life full of triumphs and disasters, and for your swansong you blazed a remarkable trail, in the quintessentially US American literary genre of science fiction.

The last thing I want to do is be one of those people who lay claim to the dead: I'm not going to speculate on your "real" sexuality. But I do feel personally proud of you, and enduringly grateful for what you achieved when you decided, for such pragmatic and insouciant reasons, to *game* your science fiction career. You didn't prove that science fiction can change. But you *did* make any bloke who says women can't do it look like an idiot. Permanently. And that still makes me grin.

I wonder what you make of the fact that we've survived, despite all our awful faults, into another century? You'd probably tell me nothing's changed. We're still well on course for annihilation, doomed by our biology to destroy ourselves and take the living world with us. And I'd have to agree, you could have a point. But if you were still writing that "Last Flight of Dr Ain" kind of story, and if I could talk to you, I'd tell you my own motto is never say die, and *la lutte continue*. There's more to life than a giant penis, piercing the heavens in search of its doomy, Wagnerian love-death. The future's not out there, it's right here on Earth, all around us, and full of surprises.

Well, that's all for now. Thanks again for the stories. Thanks for your wildness, and your *wicked* sense of humour.

All best,
Gwyneth Jones

Neat Things

Dear Mr. Tiptree:

I thought a lot about that salutation, because the discovery that you were a woman changed my world when I was fourteen years old. But I first "met" you as a man, and so it seemed appropriate to address you that way. You were one of the kindly uncles and beloved teachers of my childhood, back when I was a gawky, confused girl in glasses too big for my face, reading everything that I could get my hands on, soaking it all in like a sponge.

I might have missed you if we hadn't been so poor. My reading material was often a decade or more out of date, dictated by what people with disposable incomes decided to get rid of. My mother, a connoisseur of yard sales and flea markets, came home one day with several boxes of back issues of *The Magazine of Fantasy and Science Fiction*. Thousands of short stories, novelettes, and novellas were suddenly dropped into my hands, and I read them all with the unthinking voracity of the starving bookworm. I didn't really keep track of authors, except to note whether the story was by a man or a woman—and almost always, when it was the sort of thing I wanted to write someday, the sort of thing that spoke to me on a level so deep that it was difficult to put into words, the story was written by a man. I couldn't decide, at that age, whether women didn't write science fiction, or whether science fiction by women just didn't get published. At the same time, writing seemed like such a big, difficult, *holy* undertaking that I couldn't imagine that many people did it. So women probably just didn't write science fiction very often. That was too bad. I would have liked to do that someday.

I kept reading. As so very often happens to children, various of my possessions disappeared every time we moved, until my entire precious run of *F&SF* vanished into the ether, never to be seen again. I cried. I complained. And one day, I realized that if I didn't have the magazines, I didn't have those stories anymore either, and that I couldn't remember the name of the author, only that they—like every other story I had ever loved—had been written by a man.

I began describing them to other people I knew who liked science fiction. "It was about a little girl and an alien who lived in her brain and also there were cows," I would say. ("The Only Really Neat Thing To Do")

"It was about two spiders in love only they weren't really spiders and maybe they weren't really in love, I don't know," I would say. ("Love is the Plan, the Plan is Death")

"It was about a man who loved a mermaid and then he realized that men were bad for mermaids and so he tried to go home," I would say. ("The Color of Neanderthal Eyes")

"It was about me," I would say. ("Houston, Houston, Do You Read?" and "Your Faces, O My Sisters! Your Faces Filled of Light!" and so many others; so many, many others.)

Eventually, someone knew what I was talking about. "That's by James Tiptree," they said, and "That was the penname of a writer named Alice Sheldon," they said, and the world turned upside down.

You were my superhero, Mr. Tiptree, because you were also Alice Sheldon, and that meant that a door I had always presumed was closed to me was open: girls *could* write science fiction, and sometimes when they did, they were so good that everyone believed them when they said that they were really boys. Maybe that's a common story, and I think that's a good thing. You weren't just my superhero. You belonged to every girl I knew who aspired to someday be allowed to write science fiction, who thought that the words in her head were more important than her gender.

Maybe that sounds silly now, but when I was fifteen, sixteen, seventeen, and all the names on my book covers were male, and all the boys I knew said "girls can't write science fiction" and "A.C. Crispin and Janet Kagen don't count, they're exceptions, they're not as good, this isn't for you," knowing that you were out there, that you were a girl like me … it meant the world, Mr. Tiptree. It meant that I had a chance. And then I learned you were also Raccoona Sheldon, and that changed everything all over again. I could write my stories without hiding behind a male name. I could be me, and I could still belong.

You had your reasons for the pseudonym you chose. I wish I'd had the chance to know you, to ask what those reasons were, to hear them in your own words, but at the end of the day, your choices were your own. I am so very glad you made them. I am so glad you were a revelation, a surprise that couldn't be dismissed as "girls writing science fiction for girls". You paved the way for so many of us, and you did it one beautiful, surreal, world-changing story at a time. Maybe you didn't mean to. I don't think that most of the people who change the world for the better ever really *mean* to—they just do it. It just happened.

So thank you, Mr. Tiptree. Thank you, Mrs. Sheldon. Thank you for showing me that there was a path to the mountain; thank you for pressing the rope into my hand and telling me that I was allowed to make the climb. I never met you, but I have spent my whole writing career trying to make sure that if we had met, you would have been proud of me and the things that I had achieved. You helped me find the strength to pursue science fiction. You were part of the reason that I shrugged and said "sure, that's not too confusing" when I had the chance to become Mira Grant. You were, and are, and will remain, my hero.

Yours always, thankfully,
Seanan McGuire.

Dear Alice,

I was talking about you just recently.

I write to you as Alice, rather than Tiptree, because I'm writing not only to the mature author, but also to the young girl who, like that other Alice, went down a rabbit hole and experienced the strangeness of Wonderland. When I talk about you, it's as Tiptree of course. That's how I'm used to talking about authors: Le Guin and Russ and Tiptree, all of you so important, all of you creating the world that came after you, which is the world that allowed me to write.

I was talking about you, as Tiptree, on a panel at the Stonecoast MFA (Master of Fine Arts) Program winter residency. The panelists were me, Nancy Holder, James Patrick Kelly, and Elizabeth Hand. We represented a range of ages, genders, and genres. Each of those genres, fantasy, science fiction, horror, had been influenced by you in some way. You had dipped your finger into each, as into a witch's cauldron, and stirred. (What is "Love is the Plan the Plan is Death"? Fantasy? Science fiction? Horror? *Romance?* I have no idea. It's a story that stands outside of genre. You can see genres in it, mixing as in a magical brew, but it is also *sui generis*.) Sitting in the audience were Stonecoast students, mostly studying Popular Fiction. They all wanted to become writers, hopefully successful writers. Maybe even important writers. We had assigned them your biography (about five hundred pages) and a selection of your short stories (another five hundred pages). A thousand pages of you. We had questions we were trying to answer: Who was James Tiptree, Jr.? Who, for that matter, was Alice Sheldon? And more importantly, what could we take from the stories? Could they still speak to us, and if so, what did they say?

It's a little dangerous, I think, showing your stories to aspiring writers. They are so very themselves, from the first story we read, "The Last Flight of Dr. Ain," published relatively early in your career. They reveal your concern with the fate of individuals and humanity itself. They are deeply philosophical, while using the apparatus of science fiction and fantasy, the voice of popular (even pulp) fiction. And those elements merge seamlessly, to create stories that are intellectually complex, in which every conclusion is ambiguous, every victory also a loss. What is an MFA student to make of "The Women Men Don't See"? That sort of subtlety seems beyond reach, impossible to learn. Yet there we were, trying to learn from it anyway.

One lesson, I think, is cautionary: the future never looks the way you think it will. Visions of the future themselves become dated. In "Houston, Houston, Do You Read?" humanity has ventured into space, but attitudes toward gender have not changed. Your male astronauts lost in space and time seem to come from the 1970s, not the future we inhabit. Confronted with a world of cloned women, they go mad and must be put down, for humanity's and their own sakes. Science fiction often anticipates technological change without imagining social change, except as a result of apocalyptic catastrophe. And yet our world, in 2015, is so different from the one you grew up in, where you became tired of often being "the first women to…" So yes, sometimes the stories seem dated, particularly in what they were most celebrated for: their discussions of gender. And yet, the central problems they present are still and always will be with us. How do we express our full humanity? How do we find love, which is our only way to bridge the gap of difference? How do we avoid destroying our common heritage, including this planet we still haven't gotten off? Sometimes your stories do seem prescient: "The Girl Who Was Plugged In" is almost a description of our plugged-in 24/7 celebrity culture, with its tweets and instagrammed selfies, its lifestyle brands. It shows us one human being, lost amid the machines of hypercapitalism, trying to live the only life available to her. And yet, science fiction is always necessarily writing about its own time, creating a projection of contemporary concerns onto the future. What remains relevant is the individual attempting to find or forge an identity in the midst of social conventions and proscriptions: that, I think, is at the heart of your work, and the reason it endures.

But we were learning as writers, not scholars: what could we take from the stories in more practical terms? First, that we should not fear complexity: great stories contain their own contradictions. Love and death are not mutually exclusive; joy can be found in defeat. You never provide what we might call a "happy ending," and yet your endings often fill us with a sense of triumph, a sense of something overcome or fulfilled. Second, to aim for lean, clear, sophisticated prose, in which not a word is wasted. The beauty of your prose is that nothing in it is deliberately beautiful: everything communicates. And yet it achieves a lyricism that comes from, not despite, clarity and tensile strength. And third ... there is something under many of your stories, a sort of platform on which they are structured. I think that platform is anger. Not an impotent raging at the world, but the anger of someone who sees the world clearly and wants it different—and then writes it different, whether that involves explicitly focusing on issues of power or telling human stories that turn out to be stories about humanity. We tend to think of the writer as somehow impartial, a Keatsian god of negative capability. But you, and Russ, and Le Guin, show that stories can also arise out of a political point of view; they can be stories of both engagement and literary achievement.

When I think of Alice Sheldon, I think of the little girl in Africa turned into a literary character, the heroine of her mother's children's book *Alice in Jungleland*. Or the debutante wondering what she should do with her life and the husband she married at nineteen. Only after that marriage ended could you start creating yourself, and there is a sense in which James Tiptree, Jr. is another one of your stories. Virginia Woolf implied that all women writers must undertake such acts of self-creation. I don't know if that's as true now as it was for you, but to the extent we must all make ourselves, you serve as a model: you show us how to create rooms and identities of our own. In "The Women Men Don't See," two women leave for the stars: alienated on earth, they have chosen to become actual aliens. Your biography tells us how to stay home and claim a voice.

It's not as easy finding your stories as it should be. I think it's time for a *Complete Works of James Tiptree, Jr.* Where's the Library of America compilation? There should be one. I write to you as one of the women who followed you: who is also trying to remake the world, as you and Russ and Le Guin did. The three of you are my Macbeth witches, showing me how to stir the brew. In your stories I hear what the incantation sounds like. If I can bring some attention, by teaching a seminar or by writing a letter like this one, well, it's part of my duty to a foremother—my way of bowing down to an ancestress. Who was James Tiptree, Jr.? After a thousand pages, we could not come up with a satisfying answer. Which I think is as it should be: you are too complicated to categorize, either as a human being or a writer. And that, I think, is one of the most important lessons you taught, and continue to teach.

Complicatedly but most sincerely yours,
Theodora Goss

Dear Tiptree

I knew your story before I read your fiction.

One of the most eye-opening experiences for me was picking up a copy of *Women of Other Worlds*, edited by Helen Merrick (now a very dear friend) and Tess Williams. The book was something of a scrapbook of feminist SF and its history, revolving around the community of fans, professionals and academics that Merrick and Williams had discovered at the Wiscon convention.

All at once, I learned about Joanna Russ, Kelley Eskridge, Nalo Hopkinson, Katharine Maclean, Karen Joy Fowler and so many amazing women in science fiction's past and present. It's a good thing that it blew my mind so thoroughly, because that made space for all the new reading lists.

At the centre of it all—the book, the convention, the community—was Tiptree. Tiptree meant an award, it meant bake sales, quilts, honour lists, winners, art, chocolate.

I know that the Tiptree Award is not you, that it came along after you were gone, but the story of you and the story of the award are woven together so tightly now. It will always form part of your legacy.

Names matter. Remembering important writers matters. Maybe it's not great that what most people remember about you is that you wrote science fiction under a man's name, but on the other hand … there are worse legacies.

It's amazing how many female writers miss out on the tradition of having a legacy at all.

While I had been reading science fiction and fantasy for more than a decade when I discovered you, the history of the field did not especially interest me until I discovered the feminist lens offered by Merrick and Williams. I expanded my reading from there, following up with Pamela Sargent's anthologies that I discovered in a bookshop in Rome, and *The Battle of the Sexes in Science Fiction* by Justine Larbalestier, which Justin Ackroyd put into my hands at Aussiecon, and through to Joanna Russ and Aqueduct Press.

Maybe it skews my vision of the science fiction community and its history, that I have studied it entirely from the perspective of feminism, gender and other "Tiptreeisms", but I'm completely okay with that. Too many female authors I loved in my teens are all but forgotten now. How does this even happen? Why is it that their names fall away, no longer brought to mind when current writers and fans are citing their influences? Why does the field constantly want to announce that diversity is something we've only just discovered in the last twelve months?

Your story, at least, is loud and brash and just plain interesting enough to stick. And with an award attached to it, surely it will be remembered.

Like many modern Tiptree readers, I never had the dual experience of reading your works when you were a male author, and then again after you were revealed to be female. As the decades wear on, that experience is going to become rarer and rarer in our community.

I read "The Women Men Don't See" almost simultaneously with Karen Joy Fowler's "What I Didn't See"—and I knew why I was supposed to experience those two stories together. I never had the experience of reading your fiction outside academic or feminist context, simply because I wanted to read a good SF story. My experience of being a Tiptree reader has been thoroughly, entirely political.

I'm okay with that, too.

Some authors are terribly dull, compared to their fiction. Some of them have biographies that offer no extra breadth or depth to their bodies of work. This is not true of you, Tiptree. I thought I knew all about the author of "The Smoke Rose Up Forever" until I read the amazing Julie Phillips biography and came to the stunning realisation that writing science fiction under a male name was quite low down on the list of interesting things that Alice Sheldon did, said and was.

But here is what you did for me:

Almost as soon as I started thinking about science fiction academically, and intelligently (instead of merely wondering where my next reading book was coming from, which is also a valid worldview), I was thinking about gender.

I don't know whether I would ever have sunk myself so deeply into the SF genre if it hadn't been for that open door connecting me to conversations past, present and future about feminism, gender, bias, legacy, and how it actually matters to people who wrote the words.

I was ready for the other conversations that sparked up in such interesting ways in the genre: about diversity and intersectionality, about race issues and trans issues and cultural appropriation and so much more, because you got me in from the start, and it never occurred to me that science fiction was not a place where we could have those conversations.

There are times when I feel guilty that when I think of "Tiptree", the first association my mind makes is not the author at all, not the real woman who wrote science fiction (or who actually spent most of her life not writing science fiction) or the kindly avuncular figure that you pretended to be. Instead, my first association with the name "Tiptree" is the community that I longed to be part of as soon as I found out it existed: of women and their allies coming together to bake chocolate chip cookies ironically, to celebrate those people who make art that interrogates gender, and to commission chocolate typewriters.

But "Tiptree" is more than the legacy and the award that you gave your name to—let's face it, no one is going to write letters like these about that bloke the Oscars are named after.

One of my favourite things about your story—the detail that always stuck with me—is how disappointed many fans of your work were to discover that James Tiptree Jr. was a woman. Not because being female made your work less in their eyes—though perhaps that was true of some readers—but because the idea that a straight white male science fiction author could be so expressively feminist, and be celebrated for his artistic exploration of gender, was incredibly empowering. Losing the idea of 'Uncle Tip' was a bit of a blow...

But the Alice/Raccoona Sheldon/James Tiptree Jr. who has replaced that fellow in the history of the field is such a fascinating, complex and meaningful figure. I am not remotely sorry to have you in his stead.

With fond regards
Tansy

Dear James/Alice (and sometimes Raccoona),

The two of us could not ever have spoken, given that we weren't even close to living on this planet at the same time; I was born in 1990, three years after your death. So, I'm afraid I might be presumptuous in using your given name(s)—but I am writing with the utmost respect to commemorate a one-hundredth birthday that you are not here to celebrate. It *has* come around for the rest of us, though, the writers and critics and fans who knew you—or not—who read you in the prime of their own lives or grew up reading you or have, perhaps, at just this moment happened upon your work. And as one of those people who grew up with your stories—and, just as important to me, stories *of* you—I'd like to thank you for the things you continue to offer us: compelling stories, sharp critiques, and on a more intimate, personal level, a difficult and complex relationship to gender and the performance of self.

It isn't all that common to write letters, for folks of the generation I happen to be a part of. We write to each other, sure, but there's a certain brevity that's encouraged in digital communications. However, it seemed important for me to attempt to tackle the form and offer some account of the affinity and admiration I've felt for your life and your work—because despite that gap of time between our respective existences, I would say that I feel strangely close to the *figure* of James Tiptree, Jr. &/or Alice Sheldon, even if not the real person I will not ever be able to meet or speak to.

Maybe it's the depth and intimacy of the published letters I've read; it might also be thanks to the biography by Julie Phillips, and it possibly also has something to do with feeling a sort of doubling myself in terms of gender, performance, and identity. Regardless, this letter feels like writing to a friend of a friend, or possibly the friend of a grandparent—from a different time, but somehow quite familiar.

On the one hand, I've been reading Tiptree stories since I was a teenager; Sheldon (in this case, Raccoona) too. I have a particularly vivid memory of reading "Houston, Houston, Do You Read?" and "The Screwfly Solution" back to back—which was certainly different for me than for readers at-publication, since I was aware from the first that both were written by the same person under different identities. There seemed to me to be a complex approach to the idea of masculinity in each piece; however, I wasn't aware until later on that the complexity I saw there was also present in the life of the person writing those stories. Reading the Phillips biography in particular was moving for me. She argues that "Tiptree" was more than just a casual nom-de-plume but likely a valuable outlet for an expression of your (perhaps) dual or fluid or at least complicated sense of gender—something that I, as a young writer struggling with issues of complex gender identification as well, resonated with intensely.

I'm often curious—and perhaps this is untoward speculation, but if you'll allow me to consider it: if Alice had been born perhaps fifty or sixty years later, we might have never read a story with

James Tiptree Jr.'s name on it. All right. But would that shift in time, that opening up of potential opportunities, have made a profound difference in your life? I've read the selection from one of your letters that your friend and colleague Joanna Russ published after your death, where you say, "Oh, had 65 years been different!" and lament having never been able to share a love-relationship with another woman. I wept a little, reading that the first time. It broke my heart, and more so did reading that biography, which delves even further into the difficult and complex ways you dealt with both gender and sexuality.

I cannot imagine the restrictions that you grew into yourself under. I wonder if, were you right at this moment here with us, you would feel an affinity not just for the identity of "lesbian" but "genderqueer"—that liminal and complicated gender space that occupies the spectrum between male and female, shifting and radical and hard to pin down. I wonder if perhaps, then, we still would have seen James Tiptree's name on stories and if we also would have seen Raccoona's and Alice's—if the world would have been kinder and let all those selves coexist as equal and relevant and significant to your personal being.

It is in part because of stories like yours—and life-stories like yours—that a person like me can feel less alone, or less marked out as different. The letter you wrote to Russ about identifying as a lesbian came, you said, after reading a book of coming out stories. Having the word accessible and having other people's stories to draw on might have been, then, what gave you the courage to speak up about it—that's something I understand, and a role that some of your work has played for me over time. I also feel a deep affinity and empathy for the difficulties you had when people discovered that James was "really" Alice—though it seems, to me, that perhaps it was the other way around at least some of the time. And all of this, too, seems potentially even prurient; the biography was written with information that became available only after your death, information that was private and personal and often painful. So I also feel conflicted about assuming a level of connection with the individual that people have speculated you might have been, being unable to ask your opinion on the matter or hear the answers.

Nonetheless, I thank you for being there—for writing, for speaking, for telling stories that mattered and for being brave in the face of a life that did not necessarily allow you to be or experience the things you wanted. It's unacceptable for me to call the suffering of another person inspirational; but, I'd say, it isn't the fact that you suffered hardships with your designated-female-at-birth self and your love for women that makes me admire you. It's the fact that you made people understand what it was like to be so trapped, so complicated, so in-between. The stories that you wrote often deal with that sense of not-quite-right-ness, and while in them it might be alien or otherwise in nature, the truth is much closer to home: the space of one's love and one's body can be an in-between or contested space, and reading narratives that explored that affectively was important to me. Still is, even.

The courage and the cleverness and the sharp-edged critical voices of the people who came before us are vital, I think. Remembering and respecting those people for their contributions, their struggles, and their unique individual experiences is also vital. Your irrepressible talent and willingness to tackle hard social/cultural issues in your stories have been, unmistakably, of great importance—and, I would argue, have helped to change the world that I live in at least in some measure. Certainly without the complex trio of Alice, James, and Raccoona, the field of science fiction would be narrower and less challenging and less thoughtful. Ideas about masculinity and femininity in prose would have been shaken up less; people's understanding of what makes a man or a woman came under a bit of fire thanks to your simply being who you were and writing as you would, living the life that you did. I regret that you had to go through the difficulty of losing James as an outlet and a private masculine self, if that's what you would have considered him; I also think that, for someone like me, the fact of Alice being James being Raccoona was a deep and personal comfort. And I can't thank you enough for that—and for the work you did, have done, and across time will continue to do.

Yours sincerely,
Brit Mandelo

Dear James Tiptree / Raccoona Sheldon / Alice Bradley / Alice Sheldon / others,

So here's a strange thing—when your secret came out and it turned out that you were a woman, I wasn't even all that surprised. (Thrilled, of course, but not all that surprised.) After all, the idea had been suggested, played around with, endorsed, negated... No, what surprised me was that you turned out to be in your sixties. I mean, so old, man. Like wow.

Yeah, I was an ignorant little pup. And now, when I'm the exact same age as you were when your identity became known, I burn with embarrassment just thinking about it.

But even as a sixty-one-year-old, I have to say I can understand where I was coming from (as we said then). Your vibrant and energetic writing, your ability to take off in six whole new directions at once—it's something you'd expect more from a younger person.

But, as I said, I was also thrilled. I'd wanted to be a science fiction writer from the moment I started reading the stuff, at fifteen. So it was disappointing to find so few women writing science fiction, and more so to discover that a lot of people (men) thought women weren't even capable of writing it.

Ursula Le Guin was the first writer who saved me, and I think many other aspiring female writers as well. At the time I thought of sf as a sort of game—start off with some difference in technology or biology or social structure and move out from there, changing what needs to be changed, keeping what should be kept. It was an inspiration to see her playing the game I loved, and doing it better than anyone else in the field.

But you—you took the game and tore up the instructions and substituted a Cubist painting for the game board, and halfway through you turned half the players into goldfish, or butterflies... And yet you too were playing, and you did it, whatever it was, better than anyone else. It was eye-opening. It was a revelation.

Yeah, I was ignorant, but I did manage to figure some things out eventually. Your work taught me that science fiction could be far more than a mechanistic, rule-bound genre. That it was, almost by definition, about anything in the universe, and then even beyond that.

(And later, as my mind stretched even farther, I realized that Le Guin was doing this too, that her writing opened up the more you thought about it. That I could put her stories in my little boxes, but that they worked much better outside, in the air and light.)

And you taught me other things as well, not just about the games but the pieces within them. In most of the sf I had read up until that point those pieces, the characters in the story, weren't considered all that important. They were ciphers, there simply to follow the game to the end, to discover what needed to be discovered, explain what needed to be explained.

But in your hands those counters became actual people, people we cared about. People who were in pain. The pain of being alive was a subject you had carved out for your own. I won't speculate about how you understood it so well—I know you hated people prying into your life, and anyway that was the least interesting thing about you—but I will say that your understanding of human nature was often breathtaking. I wish I knew how you did it.

In some ways, the Three Wise Women of science fiction—you, Le Guin, and Joanna Russ, all of whom showed up at around the same time—were so good you put those of us who followed on notice. Sloppy writing wouldn't be tolerated; neither would sloppy thinking.

Le Guin and Russ had to be that good; writing under women's names, they had to prove themselves to the (mostly male) gatekeepers at the time. You, on the other hand, with your marmalade pseudonym—you could have sailed in under the radar. You could have taken it easy, had a decent career writing unremarkable fiction. The fact that you didn't, that you wrote the stories that you did, was (and still is) an inspiration. Thank you, from the bottom of my heart, for all of it.

With gratitude

Lisa

Dear James Tiptree & Alice Sheldon,

When I first read "Houston, Houston, Do You Read?", I was twenty-one years old and you were a man. The story disconcerted and amazed me. I had never read anything so mind-altering, frightening, disorienting, and downright amazing. That story took my mind and shook it —rearranging my reality, shifting my perceptions.

A few years later, I found out that you were not just James Tiptree, you were also Alice Sheldon. That's how I thought of it then and think of it still: James Tiptree and Alice Sheldon. Both of you are real, as far as I'm concerned.

To me, your very existence seemed like a wonderful joke, a cosmic prank. Like your stories, it rearranged reality in an interesting way, shook up the fabric of the universe. Such a lovely surprise.

I'm writing because I thought you'd like to know that your joke lives on in a new form. Back in 1991, Karen Joy Fowler and I founded the James Tiptree Jr. Memorial Award, presented for speculative fiction that explores and expands gender roles.

Karen and I really had no business starting an award. Usually awards are started by organizations or people with lots of money—and we didn't qualify on either count. All we really had lots of was attitude.

It seemed clear to us that most science fiction lacked imagination when it came to gender and sex. (Your work was an exception, of course.) Karen and I wanted to encourage stories that explored new social rules, new ways of living, new attitudes toward gender and sex. I figured the first step in changing the world was imagining a new one. That's the job of science fiction writers. We imagine new futures, create new stories to live by.

Ultimately, Karen and I wanted to change the world. But I'll freely confess that I had another motive that was not nearly as high-minded. I wanted to piss some people off. Specifically, I wanted to piss off those people who kept complaining that women's writing was ruining science fiction.

So at WisCon, a feminist science fiction convention, I announced the creation of the James Tiptree Jr. Memorial Award. We planned to finance the award through bake sales—that was Karen's idea and a stroke of genius, I think. After all, if you can't change the world with chocolate chip cookies, how can you change the world?

I think you understand, perhaps better than anyone, how something that starts as a joke—a lark, a prank, a laugh—can dream its way into reality. You wrote some stories, slapped on a name that was lifted from a jar of preserves, and sent them off in the mail. Then, in the way of these things, one thing led to another and you found you had become famous in a strange community of science fiction writers and fans, people with wild imaginations and boundless enthusiasm.

I should have learned from your example. I should have anticipated what might happen to a joke created in your name. After the speech, I found myself surrounded with people volunteering to hold bake sales. And things started to happen.

The Tiptree Award has made me feel a bit like someone at the top of a mountain who idly tossed a pebble downhill—and started an avalanche. A group of fans raised funds by creating and selling cookbooks titled *The Bakery Men Don't See* and *Her Smoke Rose Up From Supper.* Fan artist Freddie Baer created a series of t-shirts, one for each year of the award. An annual auction at WisCon, emceed by SF writer Ellen Klages, raised money each year.

Today, more than twenty years after Karen and I joked about starting an award, the James Tiptree Jr. Memorial Award is still going strong. Each year, a jury selects a winner or winners and an honor list of recommended works. The winner receives a check for $1000. There's a ceremony involving a tiara (worn by the winner), chocolate, and boisterous singing. The award and the community of people who work to make it possible remind me of the women's spacecraft in "Houston, Houston, Do You Read?" We are untidy, with redundant bits and a great deal of cheerful enthusiasm.

Of course, like all jokes, this one had a bit of blow-back. I had thought that bake sales were an amusing concept, but I was never much of a baker. Yet as a founder of the award I found myself whipping up desserts for the bake sale. I don't sew, but an enthusiastic group of fans proposed the Tiptree quilt—and I found myself carefully stitching a quilt square.

I suppose the joke was on me in the end. But I don't mind. I still think that science fiction can change the world. You see, most people don't take it seriously. In the eyes of the world, science fiction is goofy, fun, entertaining, silly stuff, really. As such, it flies beneath the radar, seeping into people's minds below the level of conscious thought. And that, I think, is part of its power.

The stories we read and the stories we tell shape who we are. Stories shape our assumptions, our expectations, our understanding of the world. They get under our skin and show us how to behave, what to expect, who we can be.

Your stories snuck into my unconscious many years ago, and they've never left. And I thank you for that.

Pat Murphy

Sheldon was an outside reader for my first novel, Pennterra, and wrote a wonderful letter in support of it to my editor at Contemporary Books. It was among the very last things she did before her suicide; by the time I had seen the letter, she was gone. I've always felt awed that among the final pieces of business she completed before her death was that letter in support of my book—that she felt it important, even at that time of crisis, to do as she had promised.

Judith Moffett

Dear Tip,

I never met you. But I've read some of your work; I've also read some of your letters, and I know that you liked to mail authors you didn't know in person to express your admiration. By your own admission: to place people on your own custom-made pedestals. When they responded, at first you were often too hesitant to reply in kind.

This is why I dare to write to you, sight unseen; it's as difficult for me as it used to be for you, before you became the prolific letter-writer you were in your later years. But I would love to have a conversation; even if it is a time-delayed, one-sided, sending-messages-to-Proxima-Centauri kind of conversation. What little we can do, we attempt. I attempt.

Just a few words of introduction: I'm Hungarian, Jewish, and I was born in 1983—when you were already preparing for your death. I read some of your stories in Hungarian, on yellowing pages of *Galaktika,* exhaustively collected by my dad. I still remember an illustration by László Ámon, an artist from my then-hometown, that he drew for "The Man Who Walked Home". If there were any biographic words attached about your identity, any always-imperfect approximations of your gender, I don't recall them. Maybe they were there: at that point it was already known that James Tiptree, Jr. was the same person as Alice Sheldon. But *Galaktika* was always spare on author biographies. I can't check; my dad's collection that he later gifted to me remains in Hungary, across the globe. I only brought a suitcase and a carry-on with me to the US, the bare essentials—I counted on Hungary being Hungary, part of Eastern Europe (cue the stereotypes), where everything can be found on the Internet. Not everything can be found on the Internet.

Galaktika was amazing in that time—stories handpicked by repressed intellectuals who were glad the government allowed them to retain their lives, if not their literary careers. And yet, the febrile intensity of your prose that later captivated me in English, did not always make it across the language gap. You melted into the *Galaktika* crowd: you were a white American man, with the ultimate white American name—James Tiptree, Jr. (The "Jr." was sometimes left off; incomprehensible or simply irrelevant? I'll never know.) The usual *Galaktika* lineup: American men, Soviet men, even more Soviet men, Hungarian men, various men from the Eastern bloc and sometimes from Western Europe. The occasional woman author or remote-country special issue.

I wrote an article about you for another Hungarian magazine in 2010, rereading all the Hungarian material. But I didn't have the whole picture: I read your anti-colonialist stories more recently, in English—I assume they were off-limits in the heyday of *Galaktika*, censored alongside a wide variety of authors from Heinlein to sometimes even the Strugatskys. There were the right kind of Soviets and the wrong kind of Soviets.

But I read your "We Who Stole the Dream" in 2015 in small-town America, in the kind of Midwest that people on the coasts would often call flyover country, accompanied by a sneer. The place where

I now live, work, study. And I wondered, why was making an anti-colonialist statement ever important to you? You had been white. Rich (I assumed). American. By that time I'd learned the hard way that even left-wing, progressive-intellectual Americans often did not care, that even activists could conceivably have no idea what went on beyond the country's borders, or how immigrants in their own country lived. Why did *you* care?

So I investigated. I read a biography of yours, I read about your childhood travels to Africa, you a kid in tow just because your parents wanted to show that they could, the self-declared explorers that they were. You saw. You remembered. And what struck you possibly the most was the constant change, that when you returned to the same places later, and again, almost nothing remained. Progress, whatever it was, swept away everything. While the center appeared to stay still, the periphery foamed—rotated—as if a giant mixer agitated cream in a bowl. All the detail was gone from one visit to another.

And this is what I'd like to tell you, this is why I'm writing you a letter: I understand this. I understand because I experienced the reverse.

I'm not from Africa and I can't claim that in any way. But whereas for you this constant change was a mind-shattering experience, for me this was the baseline, the norm. I grew up in Communist, then post-Communist Hungary: I lived through a regime change as a child, then several turbulent governments each with their own ideals—invariably, ideas of dramatic change.

When I moved to Iowa City, I read the travelogues of Ágnes Nemes Nagy, a Hungarian writer who spent a semester in Iowa City several decades ago, in the International Writers' Program, at that time funded by your own dear spooks. She wrote about all the small, glimmering fragments of everyday life, and I marveled at first, then froze in shock.

In the Iowa City of my time, everything was as it had been: the street sign on the corner that showed the time and the temperature. The riverside, with no banks to constrain the spring flood. Ágnes Nemes Nagy thought the river must never flood. At that point, Iowans must have assumed so themselves; this was before the great floods of the early 2000s. Even as the weather patterns changed, the city seemed constant.

The businesses: "Est. 1956". "Since 1969". How many revolutions, how many upheavals in my country of birth since then? How many nationalizations, how many shops shuttered? How many economic crises? How many "temporarily occupying forces"? Unthinkable. And here, at the center of Empire, the heartland, proud declarations for me to read: "Smalltown Plumbing—Our family serving your family, for four generations". I cried. Three generations ago: the Holocaust.

I had to travel back and forth a few times between Hungary and this cozy semi-rural America, Iowa and Kansas, visa regulations being what they were—I trust I don't need to explain this to you, you who spent so much time working in basement offices, producing reports. And every time I returned to Hungary, more and more was gone, the constant change suddenly more noticeable because I had been away from it for a few months: my favorite tree, well over a hundred years old, cut down. The park I played in as a child, demolished. Innumerable shops, closed. Fewer new shops; empty storefronts. People leaving. (New people arriving? Not so much.) When I finally went to the municipality to turn in my ID card, a requirement before leaving for a country outside the EU for an extended time, the line snaked along the corridor. How far can we go to leave the periphery behind?

Your sympathies were with the peripheral, the occupied, the colonized. But these people, the marginal, were often aliens in your work, in the literal sense. Extraterrestrials, as in "We Who Stole the Dream". I'm only an alien in a figurative, government-speak sense of the word, a "legal alien" as Customs and Border Protection would have it.

For you, I'd be an outsider. An outsider worthy of attention, perhaps; worthy of being defended, worthy of your sympathy.

But could I be a peer? Or rather, due to the age difference, a younger writer who awakens your protégé-instinct? Could I share a community with you—you who seldom shared a community with anyone? Could we talk, could we exchange letters about all the vagaries of life? Could we commiserate about "the field"—it seems to me that SFWA had no fewer controversies in your day—could we talk about all the impossible, to tackle vagaries of gender, how I am situated in the neither-land between male and female while you yourself seemingly occupied both? Could we discuss power, the many uses and abuses thereof, often invisible even to professional SF writers whose bread and butter would be the disassembly, the deconstruction of societal norm? Because you saw. You understood.

Could we have been two outsiders, together? Colleagues? Friends? Nemeses-in-cheek, as is in fashion these days? Aliens of different sorts?

We missed each other due to multiple kinds of happenstance: age, culture, geographic location. I would have loved to talk. We had much in common, and much else was different, and there would have been volumes to share.

Thinking of you,
Bogi

Dear Alice Sheldon,

I have always held your fiction in such high regard that I can easily imagine writing you a fan letter with the simple object of expressing my gratitude and admiration for your work. But another kind of letter demands to be written. I will admit up front that it is the kind of letter I would never even have considered writing to you while you still lived. But death, like publication of one's words, changes everything. Just as your published fiction must always be a fit subject for public discussion, so certain facts and speculations about your life must be as well. In your *Contemporary Authors* interview, you said, "there is a certain magic in writing, and there is no magic in writers. I have a very strong feeling that the writer's life and the writer's work should be kept separate, especially in writing that carries some sense of wonder." And you quote lines from a Kipling poem, "The Appeal":

> *And for the little, little, span*
> *The dead are borne in mind.*
> *Seek not to question other than*
> *The books I leave behind.*

You were replying, in that interview, to a question about whether the revelation of your "real personal identity" changed your feelings about your writing. I imagine there was more to your desire to keep the writer and the writing separate than the wish to preserve the magic of the work. You would, of course, have long since understood that to write well, one can hold nothing back.

I know from my own experience that holding nothing back from the writing generates a deep, almost irrational need to keep trivial aspects of oneself private. For years I avoided meeting people in the sf world, although (like you) I happily corresponded with them. During my first few face-to-face encounters with editors, fans, and other writers, I felt naked and exposed. I had no particular secret to conceal, only that fierce wish to maintain a separation between the work and the writer. As a woman writing and insisting on taking herself seriously, how could I not feel that separation to be crucial?

Women writers have traditionally been unable to keep the fact of their gender from influencing how their work is read and judged. Knowing we're marked, doesn't it make sense for us to seek ways to keep consciousness of that marked-ness at bay? And so when the sf world discovered that James Tiptree, Jr., was Alice Sheldon, you discovered that possessing a marked gender (in sharp contrast to "Uncle Tip's" male privilege of being unmarked by gender) necessarily meant that when the writer is known to be a woman, the work will never enjoy the privilege of being judged without reference to the writer. But I suspect that even before you were subject to that harsh lesson, as a writer burdened with a heavy secret that began life weighing less than a feather more apt to tickle than crush your spirit, you always understood the impossibility of maintaining a clear separation between the writer and the work.

I doubt you'd appreciate knowing that feminist sf fans of a certain age sometimes reminisce about where they were and what they felt when they discovered that James Tiptree, Jr., was in fact Alice Sheldon. I have heard some say that they were delighted to learn the news, others that they were shocked and disappointed— disappointed, that is, to learn that there was no such exceptional man as James Tiptree, Jr., appeared to be. I had barely begun reading sf at the time of the revelation; I lacked fan connections and read and knew your fiction in a strictly private way. So I don't recall how I first discovered you were both Tiptree and Sheldon. Probably I read it in an article about your work, or in a head-note to one of your stories, or even in the intro to one of your books. But the fact that I don't remember the moment and context of my discovery tells me that the revelation did not have the same impact on me as it did on so many others.

What strikes me most forcibly all these years later is that the greatest effect the revelation of your gender had on your work was to render it all but invisible even as it led to your becoming an icon. Shortly before the revelation, Gardner Dozois wrote a long essay about your fiction. He proclaimed your significance:

> *Who is James Tiptree, Jr., and why should we care about him?*
>
> *We should care about him because, at his best, he is one of the two or three finest short-story writers in science fiction; because he has produced a body of work almost unparalleled in the genre for originality, power, and consistent quality; because he has managed to be a literary synthesist as well as*

a trailblazer, bringing together disparate—and often formerly
hostile—traditions to produce viable fictional hybrids; and
because, perhaps most important, he is one of the most
influential of all present-day SF writers in terms of his impact
on upcoming generations of authors—much of the future of
science fiction belongs to Tiptree, both through those shaped
directly by him and those who will—perhaps unwittingly—
follow his well-blazed paths, and if we are to understand that
future it first behooves us to make an attempt to understand
Tiptree.

Did anyone, after the revelation, characterize you as a trailblazer? As a "literary synthesist" producing "viable fictional hybrids"? Or as an influence on the future of science fiction? Alas. As you and I both know, the revelation swamped the fiction, and the issue of your gender took front and center stage. And the only people who devoted themselves to writing criticism of your work were feminist critics. I discovered this myself only recently, when Karen Joy Fowler's "What I Didn't See" became a *cause célèbre*, and I learned that many sf professionals were unfamiliar with "The Women Men Don't See,", which John Clute characterizes as "your most famous single story."

Though you were dismayed to discover that being identified as a woman meant that your female status would become scandalously visible and your work all but invisible, I don't believe you could have been all that surprised. You soon came to articulate with painful clarity certain aspects of that invisibility that very few writers, critics, or readers are aware of taking for granted. In "Zero at the Bone," you wrote:

As Tiptree, I had an unspoken classificatory bond to the world of male action; Tiptree's existence opened to unknown possibilities of power. And, let us pry deeper—to the potential of evil. Evil is the voltage of good; the urge to goodness, without the potential of evil, is trivial. A man impelled to good is significant; a woman pleading for the good is trivial. A great bore. Part of the appeal of Tiptree was that he ranged himself on the side of good by choice.

Alli Sheldon has no such choice.

What evil can a woman do? Except pettily, to other, weaker women or children? Cruel stepmothers; male fantasies of the Wicked Witch, who can always be assaulted or burnt if she goes too far. Men certainly see women as doing many evil things—but always nuisancy, trivial, personal, and, easily-to-be-punished-for. Not for us the great evils; the jolly maraudings, burnings, rapings, and hacking-up; the Big Nasties, the genocidal world destroyers, who must be reckoned with on equal terms.

Always draining us is the reality of our inescapable commitment. Whatever individual women may do, it is we who feel always the tug toward empathy, toward caring, cherishing, building-up—the dull interminable mission of creating, nourishing, protecting, civilizing—maintaining the very race. At bottom is always the bitter knowledge that all else is boys' play—and that this boys' play rules the world.

How I long, how I long to be free of this knowledge!

As Tiptree, this understanding was "insight." As Alli Sheldon, it is merely the heavy center of my soul.

In other words, under a masculine name, you could write as a man of the world—and be taken seriously. (Interestingly, you came to feel that though the view allowed to a man of the world was extraordinarily expansive, it was partial, excluding a part of the world you did not consider insignificant: which is how you explain why the Raccoona Sheldon pseudonym came into existence. And Gwyneth Jones later commented that your contributions to the *Khatru* Symposium, which drew flak from participating feminists, were written in drag—not from the perspective of a woman. And I think she was right.) Sadly (and predictably), when you lost the masculinity of the name, the worldliness of your work lost all credibility. Worldliness in a woman, after all, means something entirely different than worldliness in a man. In 1977 there could be no equivalence. As there cannot be now in 2005, for that matter.

Dear Alice Sheldon, your insight about women's lack of moral credibility is not one that many of us ever get. And what's worse: though I get it every time I read that passage above, it always slips away from me. See, I just can't stand to believe it. If I believed it, I'd have to realize that my writing will never have any chance of rising above the private and trivial, even if I did somehow manage to write to the level of my ambition. And yet I know that it's true. It's not just me, of course, who falls continually into denial. You reveal in your *Contemporary Authors* interview that despite your insight, you too continued to deny it on at least some level when you remarked:

*And then there were the male writers who had seemed to
take my work quite seriously, but who now began discovering
that it was really the enigma of Tip's identity which had lent
a spurious interest—and finding various more-or-less subtle
ways of saying so. (Oh, how well we know and love that
pretentiously aimiable [sic] tone, beneath which hides the
furtive nastiness!) I'd been warned against it, but it was still
a shock, coming from certain writers. The one thing I admire
about that type of male hatred is its strategic agility; they
soon got their ranks closed. Only here the timing was so damn
funny, the perfect unison of their "reevaluation" of poor old
Tip rather weakened the effect.*

Dear Alice Sheldon, I believe they *did* take your work seriously
(for as long as they thought you were a man of the world). Yes,
they loved the image of that man of the world, but the image of
the writer didn't interfere with the reading of the fiction until the
image became that of a "little old lady in McLean." All women
writers have to at least *functionally* believe they are an exception
when their fiction explores the "unknown possibilities of power."
And of course sometimes there's some recognition—from men
as well as women—and the thought occurs that maybe this time
a woman's work will be perceived as powerful. But this fleeting
perception of the exceptional woman writer has risen repeatedly
over the centuries. Margaret Ezell has described the process in her
book, *Writing Women's Literary History.* Any brief exception to the
rule is fleeting precisely because it's an exception, for if the work
of enough women were visible, there would be no exceptionality
in the first place.

But reviewing again Dozois's praise of you before the Awful Truth came out, my mind blossoms with speculation, conceiving forking paths of possible histories that might have been. In one possible history, you wrote under the name Jane Tiptree—choosing a pseudonym for the same reason you said you chose the James Tiptree, Jr., pseudonym, but without concealing your gender. You might well have produced much of the same work and probably been able to sell most of it, but it would have been quietly admired and perhaps won an award or two and would not have been seen as "trail-blazing" or powerful. I conjecture that it would have been categorized as "soft" sf and been lumped together with the work of other brilliant women so gloriously illuminating the seventies (which decade is now regarded by some people as having been a mediocre one for the genre). Remember how when in January 1977 *Locus* in a news item headed "Tiptree Revealed" reported that Theodore Sturgeon had commented in a recent speech that "nearly all of the top newer writers, with the exception of James Tiptree, Jr., were women"—only to add that "The exception is now gone"? On the upside, though, had you written as Jane Tiptree, because you wouldn't have suffered the blow that followed the revelation of your gender, you would likely have continued to produce more work at that same amazing pace with steadily growing confidence. Who knows how far your work might have gone?

In another version of history, you wrote as James Tiptree, Jr., and no one ever found out, not even after your death. Perhaps you retired him and let Raccoona take on more and more of the work. In that version of history, following the path Gardner Dozois marked for a future that he judged "belonged" to Tiptree, you would have been regarded as one of the principle influences on the genre, and scholars would now be studying that influence. There would, of course, be no Tiptree Award. (There might, instead, be an award for fine feminist sf, named, perhaps, for Naomi Mitchison or Katherine Burdekin or Charlotte Perkins Gilman.)

As an sf writer, you would understand, of course, why I entertain such a fantasy. It is not wishful thinking, but a desire for insight into why the history of which we are a part is taking the shape it is. History is what hurts, *n'est ce pas?* And so dear Alice Sheldon, history is what we must understand.

With love and respect,
Timmi

Dear Mr. Tiptree

I am writing to you from the future.

I know you will not be surprised at this causality-compromised event, happening as it does, or did, or will, on an early summer morning, full of sticky Virginia sunshine and the dusty attic smell of dogwood blossoms. You are the sort of person who can receive a letter from a ways upstream on the white water rapids of time/space continuity with total grace. It would never trouble you to discover this single squash-colored envelope in your postbox, addressed to your pseudonym, bearing the signature of a writer who was born the year after the publication of your first full-length novel. A science fiction writer never *expects* such things, but somewhere, deep down, they always hope. They keep an extra mug in the cabinet, just in case.

So, here we are. My name is Cat. I began writing science fiction and fantasy in earnest in 2002. I was young, ambitious, stubbornly convinced of my own abilities, and in many ways an idiot. I remain ambitious, stubbornly convinced of my own abilities, and in many ways an idiot. But it is now 2015 and I am thirty-six, which can only be described as young by one's grandparents.

I have often wondered how my career might have gone had I chosen a male pseudonym back in 2002. Or used my initials, as many women did and do—so many that initials now *mean* a female author to most book buyers. For, much as your prose was called "ineluctably male" before everyone knew that James was

Alice, I have spent eleven years hearing critics discuss, in wide and varied terms, the elemental femininity of my work. It matters little whether my stories involve rocketships or fairies, explosions or stepmothers. That I am a woman has always been a point of discussion. On the occasion of my first novel, one of the questions in the first interview I ever gave was:

Ms. Valente, do you think there is something essentially feminine about the way you write?

I said no. Of course I said no. On my floweriest, most adjectively promiscuous day, I could never out-frill Shakespeare or Byron or Keats. I said no, and thought of you. I said no, and thought that the idea that style could have a gender, that specific words and structures and syntaxes were somehow owned separately by men and women was so strange and absurd as to be almost science fictional. I said no, and thought that Delany or Le Guin or Russ or Tiptree would (and did) create worlds where language was a territory to be divided and defended by corps of sexually-stratified grammar shock troops. I said no, and understood, in 2004, why you made the choice you did in 1967. Perhaps if I had put Christopher Valente in the top right corner of my manuscripts, I wouldn't have had to say anything. Perhaps it would have made no difference. You knew to your bones what a difference a James could make. Perhaps the fact that I do not know is a victory of its own.

I want to tell you that it's better now. That there are no longer any women men don't see. That no one needs to use a name as a mask anymore.

And it is better. It is somewhat better. It is a little better. It *is* better ... as long as you keep your eyes straight ahead, on your own paper, and hear no evil. Publishing is an industry overwhelmingly led by women. All of my major novels have been edited by women. My first big New York book was agented by, edited by, and copyedited by women. Science fiction and fantasy are dominant in our popular culture. Every dream of a geeky kid to see their obsessive interests normalized and cheered has seen the light.

But the readership/viewership of science fiction and fantasy is still assumed to be overwhelmingly male. Male taste (the simplistic formula that is assumed to be male taste—violence, science, profanity, unclothed women, the id given free reign) is considered mainstream. A male protagonist is normal, literary, serious, even edgy. A female protagonist is YA or urban fantasy. The level of abuse and humiliation piled on women in movies, video games, and television was once reserved for exploitation flicks. Now it is prime time.

I wish I had better news than that.

But women write. Boy howdy, do we *write*. In every genre, at every level. We tell our stories and mostly use our own names and inch by bookshelf inch, we are becoming less and less unseen. And women who write ... oh, James. Oh, Alice. Oh, Raccoona. How we long for foremothers. How we yearn to be part of a long line of women like ourselves, to have a past, to not be alone. And as Joanna Russ said on many a day when the sun in Virginia felt like syrup drenching hotcakes, the world forever wants to take that past away. To say that science fiction has always been a "Boys Club" and only recently have women stuck their fingers in a previously pure and beautiful pie of masculinity and robot parts. To say that we are intruding now where we were never wanted or accepted, that we are trying to take something from men by merely existing and thinking and writing those thoughts down. To say that we are ruining media by asking to be included in it, and setting it on fire by pointing out, as no one has ever dared to do before, how often it has failed to treat half the human race as anything but a power-up at the end of a level. To say that something has changed in the last ten or fifteen years and now women are rudely taking over where before, when the world was young and innocent, ladies kept their peace and knew their place, which was certainly not in front of a keyboard and definitely not in the guts of a spaceship.

And so I reach back to my foremother. A word that my computer's dictionary doesn't recognize as English. I reach back through the fishing net of time and space and death and grief and fame to say that I have not forgotten that you lived and wrote and showed a large number of people that language is not male or female, that stories are not, that history is not. Some of those people have let it slip their minds again, back into an intellectual oubliette. But many have not forgotten. We have always lived in a world of women. Women have always spoken and written and stood up. Women have never known their place or kept their peace.

It's only that some of them have had to do it in drag.

Letters from the future cause little disruption in the continuum. Words travel forward and backward constantly without incident, so long as they keep their chapters and paragraphs inside the covers and envelopes at all times. Letters are small and unassuming and can easily be mistaken for coupons advertising 20% Off All Dresses at the local department store. Most letters from days yet to come are, in fact, tossed in the wastepaper basket with the odd credit card offer or alumni fundraising plea. But I feel confident you won't consign this to such a graveyard. You were always a great writer of letters. When you've finished reading it, slip it back into its envelope and place it in a drawer. Go out into the dogwoods and the sunshine. Prune your roses. Count the ants on the driveway. And know that the world knows all your names, and the future loves you, and partly because of you, at least one girl, whose career took off when she won an award founded in your honor, has been able to be Catherynne and not Christopher from the moment she put two sentences together and thought they were pretty all right.

With warmest regards,
Catherynne M. Valente

Deception in Six Parts

Dear Alli,

Thank you for teaching us that deceit starts early.

As children we are told not to lie. Our parents or guardians ask us to play games of imagination, but also instruct us in the vital importance of telling the truth. They indoctrinate us in their charming lies about supernatural creatures—Santa Claus, the tooth fairy, a fair and just god watching over us—yet hold us to high standards of being truthful: *Did you steal that cookie? Did you hit your brother?*

You don't have a brother, but you understand my point. Your exposure to the vast world of falsehoods and odd practices, garnered through harsh travel across Africa, India, and Indo-China before you even began menstruation, goes well beyond one jolly man riding a sleigh across the moonlit sky.

All children experience deceit, on issues ranging from very small (*a stork brought you*) to much larger (*we will love you no matter what*). Not just from our parents, but also from teachers (*your art holds such promise!*) and doctors (*this will only hurt a little bit*). But the only ones consistently punished for lying are the children, particularly girls.

Girls bear several burdens. Although required not to lie, we are also carefully taught the value of little white lies (*you look lovely in that*), the importance of rejecting suitors with finesse (*it's not you, it's me*), and the dangers of romantic deceits that might leave us infected or pregnant (*he said he'll call*). Standing at the intersection of competing cultures with little firm ground to stand on, little Alli was asked to balance many fanciful lies and half-forged truths. Before you even board your first train to Sarah Lawrence you understand how dangerous intersections can be.

Being the daughter of a storyteller doesn't help. Your mother Mary—prolific, talented, distinguished—lives a towering creative life that you cast yourself against fruitlessly. How can you not? In the winter of 1970 you will write that the story is the realest part of the storyteller, and for decades your mother's stories overshadow everything you have to say.

After you slit your wrists that first time, you tell Mary that you are recovered. This is a deceit unprecedented, and comes back to you on a spring night in 1987 when you pick up a gun.

Dear Mrs. Davey,

The worst deceptions are the ones we tell ourselves.

In Yonkers, surrounded by the lovely young women of Sarah Lawrence, you engage in many small eccentricities (your attire, your study habits, your reading habits (Lovecraft, *Weird Tales*, *Amazing Stories*)) but can't escape societal and parental expectations that you will marry and reproduce. The women at Sarah Lawrence, you quickly surmise, are spending time in academia only to prepare themselves for white gowns and church altars.

You know the world is wider than an aisle and there are many other colors than white. You can dream of defacing chapels with the stark black lines of your drawings. But you can't express to the world your blossoming desire to bring your pretty classmates to your bed, and in a spurt of rebellion run off with a man who makes for a very poor husband indeed.

You tell yourself it is love. When he is drunk and shouting, when he fires that gun, it is love. When you are drunk and shouting, when you cheat on him in brothels, that is love. When your mother arranges the operation to remove the child that neither of you are ready for, that is pragmatism. But it is all also deceit based on your desperate desire to fit in, to pass as "normal," to achieve artistic and career success in a world you already know is hostile and violent to women.

It is all something else, also, something that ensures your literary legacy and makes you a role model for many writers today.

It is fodder.

Dear Captain Davey,

To win a war, we must hide our secrets and trick the enemy.

After all, one doesn't telephone the opposition to share plans of an impending invasion, nor publish in the newspaper the latest strategies for taking back the hill, the village, or the fortress. Fresh soldiers march to battle filled with false ideas of their own courage. Grizzled veterans march home hiding the secret wounds festering inside.

When you enlisted, you believed you could make a difference in This Man's Army.

They tricked you.

When your unit marches to an inspection by Eleanor Roosevelt, the men catcall and jeer. When a soldier spits tobacco and declares he ain't taking no orders from no women, his superiors agree. When male officers put their uninvited hands on unwilling bodies, the chain of command looks elsewhere.

So you make your own path to success in military intelligence. You take to your heart and your bed sheets only those who earn their way in. You write out your frustrations and ire in prose. When those stories fail to sell you bury them in that private pit of night soil where you keep your old fears and new humiliations.

You marry an army man who is good at love but terrible in bed. Together you step through the rubble of Europe into the moonlit ruins of Germany. Amid the horrible shortages of food and medicine you meet three terrified survivors of Hitler's reign. Later you write about them for *The New Yorker*. The editors cut out the part where the girls had been used by German troops for "service". Omission is a form of deception.

The story is published under the name Alice Bradley. A pseudonymous slight of hand.

We don't hear from you again for twenty years. The next trick makes you immortal.

Dear Dr. Sheldon,

You're tired of undergraduates and teaching, and your academic interests in psychology are not lockstep with those of the university. You feel the eyes of the male chancellors on you all the time. Your scalp itches from their attention, or maybe that's the amphetamines singing in your bloodstream.

You wish you'd never popped those first pills. Was it in the CIA? No, the army. Sometimes it's hard to remember. The uppers that keep you going through gruelingly long days. The downers that help you sleep at night. The other pills that you use to try and break out of black moods. The painkillers you borrowed from your ailing mother, hoping to block out the bleak prospect of losing the one who loved you first and most.

You can't sketch. The charcoal sticks break in your trembling hands. You can't paint. The dark blotches won't stick to the canvas. But at least you're writing again, casting back your dreams to those pulp magazines you first read as a child. Your typewriter is not far from the television where you watch *Star Trek* each week in technicolor, and your visions burst out faster than you can type them.

You need camouflage, for certainly the university wouldn't approve of your writing *science fiction*.

You pick a male name in order to deceive editors and readers. It's a brilliant strategy.

Dear Mr. James A. Tiptree, Jr.,

They love you.

You're a man who writes with a keen and sympathetic eye toward the plight of women. You're a man from the CIA, and your hard-won expertise lends your stories an imposing authority. You're a former army man who brings a distinctly male perspective to storytelling, like Hemingway.

Hemingway is dead, of course. Loaded up a twelve-gauge shotgun and blew his brains out.

Guns have always been your favorite weapon. That spring night in Virginia is coming more quickly than we'd prefer.

But you don't think about Hemingway much. You are far too busy being published and winning awards. Yes, you're reclusive. You don't attend the major conferences or events in the science fiction community. Your peers attribute this to your top-secret occupation. You correspond with many brilliant writers in the field and sign your notes "Tip". They respond to a mailbox in Virginia and your cover remains concealed.

Everyone knows that you are chatty and intelligent. They admire you for being charming and avuncular. They don't suspect you wore nylons with your olive drab uniforms and that your cigarettes have always born lipstick stains.

How ironic that your greatest success in writing about gender and prejudice is under a man's name. Yet as Tiptree, you can rage with authority about the environment that is being destroyed around you, or the systemic and cruel victimization of women, or the sour reality of growing old and useless. A man's name opens doors that might otherwise be shut, and through those portals other women follow.

Including Raccoona. She is another necessary deceit. She is the little sister writer who can be, as you put it, more sentimental. Tip's protege. She doesn't always succeed—she is a woman facing institutional bias in a male-dominated business—but she wins some honors in the field before all the masks are stripped away.

In 1976, your mother Mary dies. You are sixty-one years old. She is ninety-two. She didn't really know, at the end, what validation you had finally earned. She didn't understand that her little Alli had grown into a formidable storyteller whose acclaimed work would eventually inspire an award. Mary won an O. Henry Award but the Tiptree Award will eventually lift up to the light many deserving works about gender and identity.

Mary's obituary forces the dissolution of Tiptree and the reluctant emergence of Alice. But ten more years will pass before spring comes to Virginia and you pick up a revolver.

Dear Alice Hastings Bradley Davey James Raccoona Sheldon,

You deceived us with those gunshots.

After you fired into the brain of your ailing husband and then turned the muzzle toward your own skull, fulfilling a pact of no more fear and no more infirmity, we believed you were dead. The evidence proved it: the police report, the obituaries, the late-night drinks raised in your honor. Even those who had turned against you for not being a man found reason for sorrow.

But no writer ever dies, not while their stories continue to dwell in the world and its collective consciousness. Your texts are instantly retrievable. Your ideas continue to be examined, discussed, and reflected upon. Although you no longer have a say in how you, your masks, or your writing will be received, the illusion of control was never anything more than a wisp of smoke over a ruined German village. Like the people you wrote about in 1946, you have become displaced. Unmoored from mortal life yet living onward.

You were always on the outside, Alli. Set apart and gazing gloomily at a world that didn't know what to do with you, your pain, or your frustration. You had to trick us to teach us. You turned your eyes starward and found a place for your art and vision. In doing so, you changed the gender landscape of science fiction in ways that continue to dazzle and instruct.

You taught us so much, for so little reward.

It is a spring night in Virginia, and your decision now has been a long time coming. The woods outside the window are quiet but for crickets. Is there a moon? Look for the waning moon, Alli. Let the white light guide you to a land where every soul flies free. Let it bring you peace.

Yours truly
Sandra

Dear Tip,

You don't know me. If we had coincided in time, I doubt I'd be writing to you. Perhaps our paths would have crossed on Twitter, where diffcrences in citizenship, age, class, respectability, and the number of awards would have mattered much less than our common preoccupation with gender, the fact that both of us seem to identify strongly as both a man and a woman. We'd have Twitter conversations, and that would help me, perhaps, to overcome my mistrust of you. Mistrust? Yes. I don't think you'd like me to sugarcoat this. Mistrust for two reasons. First, the privilege differential. Second, you're supposed to be in my personal canon, and that's a demand that others have placed on me.

Yes, this is not your regular fan mail. I am angry. I'm not angry with you, dear Tip, because your work means a lot to me—means a lot to me *now*. Earlier this year, we shared a table of contents for the first time in *Sisters of the Revolution*, an anthology of feminist fiction edited by Ann and Jeff VanderMeer; it meant the world to me that my little story was printed between your own "The Screwfly Solution" and Octavia Butler's "The Evening, the Morning, and the Night." But I cannot stop being angry. I hope you can bear with me.

Let me unpack. First, the easier issue. The privilege differential is something I grew to mistrust over the years. You grew up with wealth, in the US. I grew up in the Soviet Union. Your parents took you on a hunting tour of Africa; my parents had to flee

Ukraine because of KGB persecution and resettled in Vorkuta, a former GULAG site beyond the Arctic circle. I was raised by my grandmother, a retired math teacher who taught me, then aged six, how she calculated her budget. I never asked for an ice cream again. You traveled, but you could always come home, back to the West, the center; your citizenship protected you—not from everything, but it still protected you. Me? An immigration awaited me at fourteen, a second one at twenty-four. I came to the US with two changes of underwear, and cried when I finally, finally could afford to buy a few more pairs with my graduate scholarship. Not quite a grand tour in which two hundred people are hired to carry your family luggage. I still don't have citizenship. I know many, like me, who fear deportation, who are trying to flee the disintegrating landscapes of their childhoods, who cannot even hope to immigrate because of religion, skin color, disability. I know some who did not want to go anywhere but were cast out—for queerness, for transness, for the wrong political opinions; those who do not want to and did not go anywhere, but whose lives and whose countries are warped by colonialism. We're taught to desire the center as the ultimate moral value, even as the center continues to corrupt us, even as the center is a construct that does not exist for many if not most of the people who actually live here. But it had existed for you. You came from it.

What way is there to disavow that? You worked hard to acknowledge and counteract your privilege, and you wrote about colonialism with power and insight, but I have come to mistrust.

Where the voices of those who had an upbringing rooted in economical security are able to rise up and speak truth, a hundred, a thousand voices who never had privilege will struggle mightily to speak and to be heard. Reading your work, I came to value your voice, your truths, the power of your stories. I just wish that more of us had a firm foundation.

Yet, after all, I think the issue is pedestrian. We talk about power endlessly, about who gets to talk about power, how much we already need to be holding some kind of power in order to be heard when we speak about power. Yet, once words are out into the world, their weight is the weight of truths. You wrote unflinchingly and brutally about gender and colonialism and there is no escaping the weight of your truths.

Or is there?

Yes, there is—simply by not being able to read your work, and the work of others.

Let's talk about canon. When I arrived to this country, it took me seven long years to begin writing creatively. I was not comfortable writing in English until that point—nor in Russian, Ukrainian, Hebrew, Yiddish, or any of my other languages—I did not deem myself proficient—but when I did, I wrote feminist SFF in English. By trial and error I stopped hanging out with people who thought it gross that I wrote about lesbians, and started hanging out with fellow feminist SFF writers. That's when I noticed that I am simply not one of them because I don't have the same canon. It seemed to me that English-language feminist SFF writers find their forebears in Butler, Le Guin, Tiptree, and Russ. I felt that the knowledge of these writers and their work was expected; only an ignoramus, or a non-feminist, would not know. I felt self-conscious. I had become an English-language feminist SFF writer, but I was only familiar with Le Guin. More than familiar; Le Guin was definitely in my canon. At thirteen, I read *Krylja Nochi* (Wings of the Night), a newly published anthology of translated English-language SF which included two stories by Le Guin. I read the book furtively in class, while covering it with a textbook. I became a fan for life, sought out every work I could lay my hands on. Quite a few books were translated into Russian after the fall of the Soviet Union, in the early 1990s, including *The Left Hand of Darkness* (translated in 1992). I wish I'd had a similar introduction to your books, or Russ's, or Butler's; if I had, I'd have written unsent letters to you in my teens and illustrated your work with my somewhat clumsy gouache. As is, I only did this with Le Guin.

What happened to you, Butler, Le Guin, and Russ in the Soviet and post-Soviet landscape? For all the professed interest of the Soviet regime in the literature of the marginalized and in African-American experiences in particular, Butler had zero works translated in the Soviet Union. Some works have been translated recently, from 2008 onwards (*Clay's Ark*, *Wild Seed*, and *Dawn*). As far as I know, *Kindred* and other major works remain untranslated. A few of Le Guin's works were translated in 1980, published in a small number of copies under the title *Planet of Exile*; I have never seen that one. Russ? No translations that I know of before

1990, then a few short stories were translated in the early 1990s, mostly in large anthologies of American SF classics, such as the *Fata-Morgana* anthology series. As far as I know, *The Female Man* remains untranslated. And, finally, you. I think you fared better, though truthfully, I have no idea how you fared. I know there were two samizdat books at some point, two collections of short stories—one titled *Hjuston, Hjuston, vy nas slyshite?* (*Houston, Houston, Do You Read?* —after the novella, though it also included other stories), and the other *Devochka, kotoruiu podkliuchili* (*The Girl Who was Plugged In*). I am not sure when this was done. Other people have seen these books. I never saw them when I was there, even though I read my share of samizdat, and samizdat SF in particular. There are post-Soviet translations. I found a story of yours translated in 1988—"I'll Be Waiting for You When the Swimming Pool Is Empty"—but I don't know if anything else was translated during the Soviet period.

The Soviet regime professed gender equality, pretty much from its inception. Women could and did receive excellent educations, and had numerous opportunities for employment. Women could and did become scientists, engineers, architects, cosmonauts, famous scholars. Why, then, would the Soviet regime repress the translation of feminist SF writers? Why? The Soviet regime promoted SF as the literature of the future, and yet when we try to simply find *women* authors of Soviet SF, we come up with only a handful of writers, none of them as prolific or famous as you or Russ or Le Guin. Not translating these works, these authors, was part and parcel with Soviet rejection of Western-style feminism; what need did Soviet women have for feminism when gender equality was, ostensibly, the reality? But of course, it was not the reality. Soviet women experienced massive systemic inequalities and sexism, just in ways different from their Western counterparts. And it was swept under the rug, silenced, forbidden in original and in translation.

When I joined the American SFF writers' community, and the feminist SFF community in particular, I felt the lack of canon, of my own foremothers, forebears, very sharply. I read. I filled in the blanks. I filled them with the work of Butler, Russ, your own, and that of many, many others—but later in life it did not have the same effect as reading it in my teens would have done. I would have felt reassured. I would have been upheld. Instead, I am a hopeful stranger to this literature which is native to many, if not most of my peers. And I have no native feminist forebears who wrote in Russian. I'd love to have had them growing up—them as well as you. I'd like every non-Western person writing feminist SFF in English to be able to say, "I have such forebears, I stand on the shoulders of my own giants—I, stifled behind the iron curtain, colonized, exiled, ostracized, othered—listen, I grew from these people, here they are, learn from them, read them—and let me read yours" instead of living on other people's borrowed feminist timeline.

What would it take? Do you know? Is it needed? Do you know?

With very best wishes,

Rose

Dearest Tip,

I want to call you that. Unknown though we are to one another, you're dear to me. I can never be dear to you, I know. Life has moved on, taking me with it, leaving you behind. I send this message backwards to you, against the current of life, back in time. And I call you Tip, your most intimate nickname. And dearest.

Dearest is as dearest does, and what you've wrought is precious, and daring, and wild. All those words mean what is dearest to me. Open up your imagination and stretch out the wings on which your mind soars, flying free above what you thought could become true. Above life as it was ever and always lived. From that perspective you'll see me, surrounded by the many wonders you've made possible.

Here's one: an award called by your name. Given to an author whose work "expands or explores our understanding of gender," the James Tiptree, Jr. Literary Award consists of $1000, a piece of original art, an apron, chocolate, and of course a beautiful commemorative plaque. I received one in 2009—it changed my life! Pat Murphy and Karen Joy Fowler, the Tiptree Award's founders, changed my life! The judges for that year, K. Tempest Bradford, Catherynne Valente, Gavin Grant, Roz Kaveney, and Leslie Howle changed my life! And you changed my life by providing a model of what could be accomplished, an inspiration for the award's existence—and for my work, and the work of thousands of others. Who have received the Tiptree Award in the years since its 1991 inception. Who have been nominated. Who have dared to dream of sharing with readers the precious, wild, stories we're brave enough to create. We might have been brave without you, true, but your example has made it easier.

Another wonder: the Tiptree Fellowship. Again named in your honor, and new, new, new! Born in 2015, one hundred years after you were, the Tiptree Fellowship will provide two people every year with $500 each. This is not a "beautiful reward," which is how your old pal Ursula K. Le Guin referred to her 2014 National Book Award. It's going to be given not in recognition of accomplishments but as a signal, a sort of buoy indicating that these are waters to watch. Tiptree Fellowships are about making Tiptree Award-level accomplishments possible. And they are so constructed as to include endeavors outside traditional literary modes. They can go to songwriters and game designers and performance artists as well as authors and editors, because that's how storytelling is done these days: in various and multiplex ways.

Intersectionality is explicit in the Tiptree Fellowship's initial mandate. I think you'd like that.

To my delight I've just today, this very afternoon on which I sit to write you, been invited to serve on the first ever Tiptree Fellowship jury. We will make you so proud!

And yet another wonder: the changing way the dominant culture thinks about gender.

You came into this world in a female body. So mostly you lived as a girl and a woman, wearing lipstick and dresses and high heels.

Though of course there were times when you could put on jeans and mess about with boats.

But you wrote as a man—and according to Robert Silverberg's introduction to your collection *Warm Worlds and Otherwise*, your writing was "ineluctably masculine". Hee hee hee! Yet... maybe Silverberg wasn't so wrong? Maybe your writing *was* masculine? And maybe you were, too?

And feminine. When you wanted to be.

It's a real possibility. I mean, in the near thirty years since you left us, Tip, a serious effort has gotten underway to think and speak and act as if gender, sexuality, and self-identity were fluctuating and non-binary. We're treating them like the nuanced expressions they actually appear to be. Which is a wonder to me and would be a wonder to you if you were here to experience it.

The beautiful rewards of bravery aren't always the winner's to enjoy.

Not everything is so sweet. Of course not. Maybe you already know how bad some stuff has been. Nobody listened to the warnings about melting ice caps. Bees are dying en masse. Innocents suffer impoverishment, devastation, torture, execution. Advances—same sex marriage approved in more than half the United States, for instance—are met with backlash like certain U.S. laws guaranteeing bigots' right to discriminate.

Those are the realities I try to deprivilege by rewriting the future the way you could. Those are the concrete uglinesses I have to acknowledge as I construct my elegant alternities.

What are they to you? What could they be? Nothing to flinch from, nothing to ignore.

Tip, if only. If only. If only you had not stepped out of life's stream. But by now you would almost certainly have left it in one way or another, anyway. As a teenager I myself often contemplated suicide. As an adult, too. I simply wanted my pain to end.

You, as far as I can tell, were much more logical about killing yourself. You put yourself down like a sick dog. You killed your husband the same way. The future you made viable for others was not for you.

Were you depressed? There are medicines for melancholy. Half the country has decriminalized marijuana, and in the state of Washington, where I reside, it's recently become so legal we're allowed to consume it just for fun.

Were you wary of becoming one of the women men don't see? I have joined that far from exclusive club myself. It's unpleasant in some ways—being ignored can make one feel useless and abandoned. On the other hand, being invisible is sort of secret power. Maybe you would have enjoyed that, once the fading had fully set in.

However you felt, whatever you went through, it's over now. All over but the wonder.

Wonder on. I do.

Love,
Nisi Shawl

Dear Mr Tiptree

It's difficult to know where to begin. I'm writing to you after many years of knowing your science fiction writing and only the merest smidgeon of your personal life.

I used to think you were just a pseudonym for Alice Sheldon and there was no more to it than a desire on her part to stay out of the boring fuss that might follow on from her being identified as female. Lately though, I've read that it was more than just a name and a desire to avoid becoming the next act in the gender roadshow. I don't know what to believe, since I can't ask you. My research on the subject has been deliberately skimpy. I figured that if you wanted it that way then it was fine that way and, other than using the fact of things to point out the futility of gender-based claims to whatever-the-hell-they're-claiming-only-men-can-do-this-week, I should respect the choice and let it lie. However, I heard Ursula Le Guin on the radio today say that she was a man.

Le Guin went on to say that when she was born all people were men. Those who weren't men weren't really people. That hits the nail on the head very neatly in terms of summing up the gender situation and sadly, it's a nail you can still hear being hammered to this very moment, although it's quieter than it used to be in this neighbourhood. But the noise means I can't bring myself to let it alone. So I'll write to you man to man.

I didn't come across your work until late 1996 when I went to the USA to study at Clarion West, the SF and Fantasy workshop. As soon as I did, your titles had me hooked. I didn't even need to read your stories to be inspired; in fact I put off reading them because I didn't want to spoil the feeling of having my mind blown. I have since read the stories and they didn't disappoint me. I just had to get those titles up to full evoking capacity so I could always have them in there as part of my conceptual battery. I still use them whenever I need a hit of the inspiration juice. I'm the kid that used to stand in the bookshop and the library getting high on titles and covers. I read a lot but it was the titles and the illustrations that made me want to start writing.

I used to throw books across the room if they didn't fulfil their packaging promise. I didn't throw yours.

Having read *Her Smoke Rose Up Forever,* I felt properly put in my place; not in a bad way, but because I could see the benchmark for the industry right there. The collection is outstanding in its breadth, depth and consistent high quality production. The scope of subjects and the execution—because they were mercilessly executed—put the mark fiercely high. I've enjoyed taking a jump at it ever since.

I think that part of the conviction most people stuck to—that you must be a man—was your cold-blooded killer style of story-telling. You never pulled a punch. In becoming you, Alice Sheldon became able, MAYBE, to write what Alice Sheldon as herself would not have written. That kicks a hole in the fence, now, doesn't it?

I know that you wrote as a man in the way that men write. Let's be clear as Hemingway about this: you wrote within the accepted male vernacular that men create and which creates them, in which they must be incisive, decisive, rational, and whatever other qualities define Man in that moment. Brief, declarative sentences of exacting precision. (I was originally going to pack all of that into one sentence to stick it to them where the sun don't shine, as basing an entire literary culture and identity around one style choice is damnably ridiculous and has done nobody any favours—yes, I am looking at you down the sights of my drama-hunting rifle—but then I decided I couldn't be bothered to keep finding yet more fractals in this demon-ridden enterprise and anyway, it's too silly for words though it does lead to the next sentence). It seemed in 1988 when I began to write what would be my own first published Science Fiction, that these qualities of Man were those that also defined Literature and Science Fiction and particularly Science. Men wrote these things, and those that were not men who wrote these things were writing *other things* that were *not important.*

This on-the-face-of-it-insane view persisted, I think, because of the shared pool of qualities which had accreted at that point around the concepts Man, Science, and Literature. The categories overlap so much that they seem equivalent to the uncritical eye, as if memetic ownership is a one-time deal. But, as luck would have it, anyone can be a man and anyone can write any genre in any way they want, they shall merely have to run the gauntlet of unreconstructed rubes criticising their every fucking breath as the ossified synapses of said rubes explode and pave the way for the entry into the world of the elder gods. *Pass me my Chthonic Portmanteau, O Beholder of All That Is, I must weave yet more words into super-massive mega-terms so that the specific gravity of the situation warps into a more favourable topography.*

Sorry, where was I? Oh, yes. I was hoping to be an example and make the case that Science Fiction can equally well overlap with the set that is Women, but there's a problem with that because Science has had such a big overlap with Men that it prompts an identification crisis. I think that the feeling of anxiety caused by that categorisation collision is what causes people to go on such vicious, insane rampages about what it means to be A Man. However, I'd be an idiot to think that anyone's going to buy this version of human gender (and other) identity being conceptually superfluid while we're all physically bound in binary and while the drawing of the boundary lines has such significant social and financial power. On the other hand some daytime TV chat shows are getting quite open-minded these days.

I really hope that your persona was an enabling device as I like to imagine. Because there's a man in every woman and a woman in every man, and probably a load of other identities there too, each useful and adapted in its own way to its own path. I think we use them all the time, quite naturally, depending on the task at hand. People get bogged down in whether or not they are 'real', these suites of skills, aptitudes and emotions that we assemble and use like suits, like overalls, like shoes. We walk and talk and play in them and when they've done their work we tend to forget they're only tools. We mistake them for ourselves. Perhaps if you give them a name they become someone—a secondary self, a ghost, an angel: I have several of these, of different genders.

Good luck with getting identified or non-identified with INVISIBLE things, though. Bodies we can see. And colours. And shoes. The immanent real can never be a social power without using physical semaphore; for gods' sakes woman, are you crazy? Thank you, now stop interrupting my letter.

After a lot of thought I published under my given name and that person has done the writing, though she wasn't always best suited for it. I did that because I want the world to change to a place where everyone is counted as a person. I feel like I have to stand up and be whatever I apparently might be for the sake of advancing that cause a bit.

I'm not sure your way wasn't better. If the story matters more than the writer, and it does, then your method for securing readers who would not switch reading mode to Written-by-woman-must-make-allowances was a huge success. I am actually forced to conclude, rather confusedly, that your work was written by a man. Mine was written by me. When I write I'm not sure what I am; I just know that whenever people do special reading that 'makes allowances' or some such shit, it makes me want to morph into a rabid werewolf, rip them to pieces and then *not even eat them. I would put the pieces into a meat grinder and make them into cat food so they can never, ever return as something as magnificently special as a werewolf.*

Sorry about that. Inasmuch as I am a woman, I'm full of permanent rage at the injustice in the way anything that's not a man is treated. I mean person. You know what I mean.

And now I'm haunted by visions of juddering cat food tins trying to reunite and reassemble their spooshy, stinky contents before invading the nearest library as a warped monstrosity formed from the mewling, clawing madness of a clowder of living cats all trying to write death-threats to Kirkus from the same Twitter account—@MrTiddles.

Perhaps I should drink a glass of wine instead of pursuing social justice. *Yes, that is what you should do, Mistress. Let someone else hold the fools to account. You have important business elsewhere.*

Anyway—Cthulhu aside—beneath all our conceits nature lurks, driving everything, demanding everything. The viscera commands and the ephemera follow. I love the way you examined that through your stories. When I was young I resisted this truth fiercely, as if mind were the driver in life. But now I've become old enough I have to hand it to you: that's really not what's going on and while we're at it, I don't think the mind is a ghostly inhabitant of the brain either—I think it's the eternally surfacing and refolding emergent executive of the whole thing. But memory gives you the illusion that you're actually consistently you. As the sages say, it's probably better to abandon the whole idea of being something and enjoy yourself instead. This is anathema to the social human world which relies very much on identifying everything ad infinitum. And here we are again in another iteration of the eternal sublime conflict at the edge of the immanent and the real.

I wouldn't have thought these thoughts this way or seen these things as I see them, if not for your work. *Thank you, Mr Tiptree, you have done the world a great boon in opening the lids on so many worm cans, as you can see.* You made a great contribution to my awareness of just how wide the sky really is and how deep the blood runs. Sometimes men are physically female. Vice versa applies of course, but that's a whole other essay about uptrading and downtrading in social status—fie, if you were a male author who used a female persona to write a romance, you'd probably get a bigshot literary prize!

hands inverted prize across the spiritual plane Thank you, O Unspeakable One, that was very uncharacteristically generous of you. *It was nothing. I like the one about "Love Is the Plan, The Plan is Death."* Yes, it's very good, isn't it? *Yes.*

In one thing, however, I do find your work as Tiptree a little bit deceptive. Your social awareness-and-gender-fu and the desire to write about such subjects, somewhat out you as a woman. You have Austen's love for the smell of conventions being napalmed in the morning.

Your admirer, Justina Robson
admirers.
OK, admirers.

Dear James Tiptree et Alli-ae[1],

You have owed me a ruby for about twenty-five years.

I first read *Tales of the Quintana Roo* in the early '90s, when I was, academically, well prepared for you. My PhD on feminism(s) and (partly) SF had immersed me in Marxist, post-colonial, and especially feminist theory, from destabilizing binary oppositions to valorizing women; I could wield the shibboleths of the fragmented or discourse-based post-modern subject, and the favoured non-linear, fluid and ambiguous narrative, while Samuel Delany and Joanna Russ had worked me into LGBT-soon-to-be-queer and fledgling race theory. And internet research acquainted me with notions of online personalities and avatars.

Unlike Delany and Russ, almost all of whose current work I'd read, James-et-al, I had not read everything of yours. Only so many people would fit in the PhD, and they best suited its parameters. I *had* read most of your landmark stories, from "The Women Men Don't See", to "And I Awoke and Found Me Here". I knew about the Great Unveiling, when despite "his" true credentials, the "ineluctably masculine" James Tiptree Jr. turned out to be "an old lady in Virginia"; a friend in the SF community shared first-hand the disappointment, not of finding Tiptree was a woman, but that "he" was not, as her cohort had hoped, a feminist *man*.

So your double title, "Lirios: A Tale of the Quintana Roo", then "What Came Ashore At Lirios", matched your reputation and, knowing the "alias", I could appreciate the double "performance", to echo Judith Butler, of masculinity: a male Narrator of age and experience, even bilingual, purporting to speak as Tiptree's own avatar at last, while you are already Alli's avatar. But "he" seemed at home among the slope-foreheaded, cross-eyed Mayans of Yucatan, which the introduction sited as an exotic, mysterious, at once archaic and thrilling Somewhere, almost another planet.

As a fiction writer, I admired your deft set-up and data dumps, locating Yucatan four hundred miles from Cuba, foregrounding the blazing, turquoise-and-lime-and-white sea, smoothly glossing the Narrator and Maya's Spanish with an English explanation of "Caminantes". Half a page, and the two main characters were already established, one of them still a distant speck striding up the beach. Retrospect gives you even higher marks for that first ground-shifting simile, the Caminante as a "skeleton" who might admit sun between his ribs: striking image, subtle foreshadowing, brilliantly invoking "The Ancient Mariner's" ghost-ship, whose "strange shape drove suddenly/ Betwixt us and the sun."

Then came the perspective drifts. The Maya dismisses the Caminante as a "gringo". The Narrator subtly judges him a "newbie", especially once he opens his mouth and a Mid-West (American) accent comes out. Then, nicely underlining the Tiptree avatar, his comments on the Narrator's "weighty" psychology books produce wariness. But his sandals, brand-name water bottle and belt-knife, counter *Not a crackpot*. The view broadens from sublimely ridiculous—the guy is a swimming pool contractor from Des Moines—to the ridiculously sublime. He has walked this coast every year, right down to Belize. He has come thirty miles on that bottle of water, he knows the old Caminantes and outré landmarks, like the "Pickle Factory", and his sophistication shows as he judges it "really lovely... Nineteen-thirties art deco." He is, the Narrator judges, "more competent [in the Yucatan] than me."

Whereupon the story up-levels to an inner narrative: a virtuoso gender performance, two interleaved masculine voices now, overlaying your own avatar. The Caminante's tale is also the heart of the story, first because it introduces the supernatural—"*What Came Ashore at Lirios(?)*"—and second, because it presents the main characters' encounter. A third title might have been, "The Young Man and the Sea". This variant is driven home by a neat segue, as Narrator and Caminante swap anecdotes of madly desired objects left by the sea that, another ominous foreshadowing, "brings you everything you need."

What it brought the Caminante turns out to be—well, what? A bobbing mast that might be a valuable drifted buoy. Then a foundering boat. Something tied to the mast. A lot of bobbling white. A face, with what seem open, "huge, shining" eyes that make him think it's a woman. And alive.

After an epic struggle the Caminante gets them both ashore, grasping a "tiny waist" before they collapse beside his canteen at the "trash-line": where the story goes adrift from time as well, for in a careful dialogue insert, the trash-line is noted as "different". No modern debris.

The major shift, your vintage Tiptree shift, so to speak, comes as the Caminante surfaces to a "perfectly beautiful" contralto voice swearing in Spanish, the world's most inventive profanity. Fragments of backstory about "pozo dorado"—fountain of gold—treasure, a perfidious crew, evoke every romantic cliché from the Spanish Main: Ponce de Leon, Conquistadores, buccaneers, ship-wreck and treachery, up to *Treasure Island* and beyond. But simultaneously, "contralto" prepares the (first) gender shift: for the Caminante opens his eyes on a beardless youth with clouds of dark hair tied back from "white silky stuff" that is now an enormous Renaissance shirt. There are huge black eyes and "sensuous" lips and nostrils, sure enough—and tight black breeches with a huge cod-piece "right in my face".

It's a brash, almost coarse insistence on masculinity. But the figure is myth and legend, Errol Flynn as a young pirate, rather than any survivor from a foundering boat. And the Caminante wishes "him" back on the boat, since he "wanted [his] woman back so bad."

You almost amused me with that over-confirmed straight masculinity on both sides. When the castaway demands "vino", again performing the cliché Spanish hidalgo, the modern American responds predictably; but the "hidalgo" has a sense of humour, and eventually the Caminante is "starting to like the little son-of-a-bitch." The story's basis, the reason both Americans are in the Yucatan, slips by under the reason for that liking: "he'd found a key to some life way out, free…"

Next comes the ghost-story essential, the material token

that remains afterward. This one is spectacular. The stranger offers to pay for water, whips a stiletto from his boot, and slices himself "under the ribs". The Caminante passes it as concealing treasure under the skin, but the returning reader finds all sorts of resonances. Two huge gems, one green, one red. The colour of the sea, of ship lights, of safety, of danger; the product of what body, James, legendary or otherwise?

So, the ruby tucked in his shorts pocket, you send the Caminante off for water; a handy interlude to enforce the time-shift, as Lirios' well has vanished along with the modern ever-present radio. The Caminante lets readers catch these clues, only much later wondering if he really travelled in time. Back on the beach, he's ready to pull up that shirt to reach gender certainty, when the flotsam wakes, with an "innocent beautiful smile" —that becomes "the furious aristocrat" at sight of the foundered boat. But gender is wavering in earnest now, as the Caminante falls asleep himself, and the body of the "person in [his] arms" begins to "soften and fit" so he is "absolutely convinced" he is holding either a woman or "the damnedest gay earth ever created."

Again, it's a gay-and-gender play that your modern readers might find both too apt and overwhelmingly obvious. But the supernatural strand overrides, as the Caminante struggles to return the ruby, which like its giver's hand seems to elude his search. He finally gets it pushed into fingers turning oddly hard and cold under his, before he passes out with his nose "in her cool dark hair". Which implies that at the last, the gender decision has favoured his heterosexual desire.

This tale ends in classic Belle Dame fashion: the Caminante wakes alone on the beach in a litter of modern trash; no footprints, only one tiny sign to indicate the interlude's reality. The pocket is unbuttoned on his shorts. Tying up ghost ends, you let the Caminante add that an old *ranchero* told him the gap in the reef at Lirios ("lilies," in Spanish, not incidentally) is called "Paso de los Muertos" because dead ships and their crews wash ashore there. The *ranchero* stresses that you should only pass at the full moon, and asks more forcefully, if "anyone had given [me] anything there." Told that the Caminante gave it back, the *ranchero* adds the traditional detail: "If you had kept it, you would be *perdido*."

Seems clear enough: the Caminante has met some dead, almost been ensnared, should be safe. But far back, the Narrator saw the Caminante as "marked" by some obscure powerful force waiting ahead "along the beautiful sand." Now the Caminante himself tacitly explains his call on the Narrator, asking the psychologist, "Am I crazy?" Did he time travel, or just make it up?

He leaves without awaiting a reply, basing his decision on the memory of a strange, sentimental Spanish song he now mentions for the first time. "I didn't make up that song." So he strides off into the sunset, with the first-time reader, at least, fairly sure of his fate. But there is one more twist.

With a classic ghost-story meme, the Narrator never sees the Caminante again, and next year, asked if he has gone back to "Norteamerica", the Mayans answer, No. But the Narrator constructs his own conclusion: *I don't believe the Caminante was out of his head, but nor do I believe some "life-hungry succubus" or ghost of the Main took him. It was something older and far deeper.* As clinching detail, he offers the grammatical oddity of Spanish, where "mar", the sea, can be masculine or feminine "indifferently and alike". If the Sea came, no wonder it came in "double guise".

Beside an almost perfect gender-bender, it's a fine ending; having had the cake of a Hollywood Conquistador and renovated all the Spanish Main cliches, "Lirios" does not so much resolve as raise the ghost-story to a new level. And as a Tiptree story published in 1981, James, it's as much a masterpiece as *The Importance of Being Earnest* was for Oscar Wilde, as he simultaneously flaunted and concealed the secret of his own "Bunburying".

Yet still, some untied ends remain.

Firstly the song, which seems a clumsy patch in your general deftness. When, precisely, did the Caminante hear this, and why do we only learn about it after his own narration ends? And more contradictorily, the gift. How was the Caminante "enslaved", if he came at full moon, and he gave the ruby back? Well, perhaps the Sea doesn't operate on those simple terms.

But then there's the desire. The Sea might swap genders to suit one who seeks/is sought by it, but if so, though the rescuee first seems and is desired as a woman, why is the bulk of the Strange Encounter with the hidalgo male? Especially since the desires of Caminante and Narrator, and presumably yours, James, should all have focussed on the woman. And as we (now) know from the letters, so could those of Alli behind you all, for once legitimately.

Theory offers multiple explanations. My mind, though, has kept a much tinier burr. Given the context, the emerald is fine: emeralds were the richest Spanish plunder of South America. But the ruby? Red for portside lights, red for danger. But rubies come/came from Burma. And when the Caminante holds it up, it flashes "red as the light on a squad-car". But I learnt in India that light through a genuine ruby flashes murky blue.

Did you know that about rubies, James? If so, did you deliberately falsify? Because if the hidalgo's coin was false, and meant to be known as false, that re-lights the entire encounter. It may even tip the scales to a simple hallucination. And that question has kept this story, out of thousands, lingering in my mind for about twenty-five years.

Do you owe me that ruby, James? Or do I owe you?

Sylvia

Dear Alice Sheldon,

It's been a decade since I last wrote to you. In that decade so much in the world around me has changed at such frenetic pace that I sometimes feel like John Delgano, your man who walked home. The world around him changes dramatically while he, attempting to travel in time, becomes to them a monster all but suspended in time. I first read this story in my late twenties. It was poignant, I thought, but my appreciation of that image of the world changing at unfathomable speed whilst the self moves only in the tiniest of increments was strictly intellectual. Forty years later, I'm acutely conscious that it is in fact impossible for a self to change at the speed the world is changing whilst remaining true to a remotely recognizable self—that is, to remain oneself and yet remain in the world at its most immediate and be and feel oneself to be an active part of that world. These days I consciously strive to change with the world, but as age takes its toll, I know that if I live long enough, I'll inevitably fall too far behind to have even the illusion of being part of it. And so the image of John Delgano "walking home" haunts me. Dear Alice Sheldon, I love that your work has spoken so differently to me at different times of my life, so unpredictably to my reading self of decades past. Its power, for me, lies not only in the sense it helps me make of my own experiences, but also in how particular individuals relate to our ever changing world.

Did you, I wonder, read Storm Jameson's *Parthian Words* (1971), which I myself only recently read? Jameson was about a generation older than you, and English, with a worldview dating from before the Great War. *Parthian Words* exemplifies a writer confronting her own anger and despair at having fallen out of synch with the world. The contemporary novelist, Jameson wrote, lives in a world that has seen Hiroshima, the death camps, wars in which children die of hunger or seared with napalm. She lamented that something like a rupture of the past of human life on earth had occurred, rendering all instability and uncertainty. The novelist's task, she asserted, is to confront our formidable reality, which will require reinvention of the novel, something which, she argued, no one had to date done. I wonder: would you have felt impatience with her, or sympathy? You, after all, used your pessimism to create powerful, sublime works of art.

The problem of maintaining a self in the midst of change that one can only ever be partially aware of first confronted me in 1990/1991, when the world I was living in underwent a full-scale epistemic shift, as shocking as the one that rocked US culture in the 1960s, as deep and irreversible as the one that occurred in England in the 1660s. As a teenager in the 1960s, the shift felt natural and right—so much so, that as red lipstick and high heels became associated with old women and only the dowdiest young women, I sufficiently internalized the shift in aesthetics that decades later I found it impossible to see these accouterments as even remotely attractive when that taste returned with a vengeance. But in 1991, in the face of a new rupture, at age 40 my shift to altered uses of language, aesthetics, and priorities took conscious effort and struggle and careful moral consideration. If I had been ten years younger, I might have shifted without much noticing. Not everyone my age or older adjusted themselves to such changes; some of those who did not lost the ability (and sometimes even the will) to engage expressively with the world, while others continue to speak but are often misunderstood, as slowly, relentlessly they slip further and further out of synch. Since that great shift, we've suffered other convulsions. But the speed at which technology is changing us is now so accelerated that the ground the living stand on never stops trembling, as though our world were being constantly fracked.

I try to imagine how you would see yourself in this world, one hundred years from your birth. John Delgano, though he doesn't know it, will never make it home, but will always be in the process of trying to reach it and his Kate. Your work, and our memory of you, is always caught in those only slowly shifting moments of time. In that story, he is at first taken for an evil monster; later, a monument is erected to him—telling his story, as his brother has pieced it together—and, eventually, a tent put around the lifeless patch of ground on which he annually appears, where watching crowds assemble, scientists prepare their instruments to record what they can. The process is inexorable. And no matter the lens through which his appearance is understood and examined, what the ever changing world makes of him will always be imperfect, speculative, and often fabulated—a signal so confused with noise, so broken up as to require supplementation by extrapolation, that it will always be subject to revision.

Your sense of irony, it has always seemed to me, threads everything of yours I've read, so I can easily imagine your appreciation of the gap of incomprehensibility that manifested in the midst of a feminist science fiction symposium in Eugene in November 2013, as a bright undergraduate reported on the pleasure she experienced reading correspondence between you and Ursula K. Le Guin. She marveled at being given access to such immediate, spontaneous exchanges and said that reading them was like eavesdropping on two writers texting one another. They didn't have texting back in the twentieth century, of course. Even as recently as the 1980s, many people—and not only writers—watched eagerly for the mail carrier's arrival, bringing letters from one's numerous correspondents, and spent a certain amount of the day (or night) writing letters, which one needed to do in order to receive them. Recipients of letters read them over and over again; I often carried letters in my bag, everywhere I went, reading them on the bus, poring over them in a coffee shop, thinking them through, puzzling out the elusive and elliptical, mapping my own replies, silently addressing words to a correspondent for hours before actually writing them down on paper. Some letters were so precious I kept them close, treasure I couldn't bear to be parted from. Letters were carefully crafted (except for the notorious middle-of-the-night indiscretions, which were sometimes rashly dropped into collection boxes before one's body dropped into the sleep that would bring normal inhibitions back into play). Letter-writing wasn't just for writers and academics. My father, who never finished high school, wrote me often when I went off to college, charming and entertaining letters. All that is gone now. I occasionally write a letter the old way, and occasionally read one, but such are exceptional and bear the clumsiness and consciousness of that exceptionality. People say technology has made letters obsolete, but in fact, many of us used each new advance in technology for writing and sending letters—until we suddenly didn't. The real point, I suppose, is that few people want to put that much effort into writing something intended for an audience of one, and probably just as few people are likely to re-read writing written just for oneself. It is too soon to say, but I wonder whether we aren't losing interest in the interiority intrinsic to personal epistolary exchange.

So, faced with that young woman's naïve idea about letters, what could one possibly say to breach the gap? Still, I felt it necessary to point out that each of your and Le Guin's letters had been written by a writer for a writer, which meant that their composition had to be a highly conscious affair. When I said so from the audience, the student only stared dumbly at me, and the friend seated beside me whispered "scold" in my ear. That sealed my sense that few people looking back at letters written in the 1960s and 70s would, unless they'd been alive at the time, grasp even the conditions of their composition, much less understand the gender issues (as we say now: and that expression, too, marks another gap in comprehension) either explicit or implicit in your letters. You would laugh, I suppose, at the anachronisms saturating *Mad Men* and scoff at the nostalgia it evokes in the young for the sensibility it projects onto its staging of the past as spurious as that of any sitcom of that day. But I suspect you would be baffled at the shift in the meaning of words and phrases you and your correspondents used with such confidence. When I read my own letters dating from the seventies and eighties, I doubt whether I'd be able to say the same things so articulately in the language we use now. At first I thought it was because I was so much smarter back then, but now I think it's just the slippage of time, located on the other side of the great rupture.

Is there an irony in my talking about the generic incomprehensibility of letter-writing in the twenty-first century when I'm writing this "letter" to you? The irony, I think, lies only in the fact that epistolary fantasies remain a viable genre when audience-of-one letters are withering and soon to have vanished from the vine altogether. Many of us still love reading the collections of letters by this or that literary person or celebrity of pre-millennial centuries, not so much for the intimate details they reveal as for the intense immediacy delivered through the distinct grain of the personal voice, the turn of phrase crafted for the pleasure (or discomfiture) of a single person, of thought distilled to engage the heart and brain of the correspondent. Correspondent: a beautiful word, no? So in a sense, that student in Eugene was correct to talk about immediacy, however little she understood about the material conditions in which letters were written or even what they meant in their day, to the writer and her correspondent, given how far discourse has shifted over the decades.

Your correspondence, as much as your stories, were all about being in the world, making and keeping connections--which is precisely what John Delgano cannot do as the world speeds by around him. Do you remember the word *reification*? Popular among graduate students and academics in the 1970s, it's nevertheless gone out of style. The difference between you and your work on the one hand and John Delgano on the other is that your man walking home has been reified. Within certain parameters, he has become static (even if he is moving in tiny increments). His brother has told his story and sketched the trajectory of his movement "walking home".

Dear Alice Sheldon, a wonderful aspect of your having put your prose and poetry out into the world is that as long as anyone is aware of it, it will continue engaging with the world, likely in ways you never imagined. It looks static, but as long as it is read, it continues to live, breathe, and engage with the world. I know this through my own experience with it. My essay on "Your Faces, O My Sisters! Your Faces Filled of Light", another story whose meaning has changed for me with the changing of the world (and myself), is all about that engagement. And for you, who felt despair for what you believed were flaws inherent in our species, you saw fiction as the way to understanding our formidable reality, not as an art that had lost its way.

Thank you for reminding me that I too believe that, dear Alice Sheldon.

Your ever appreciative admirer,
L. Timmel Duchamp

Dear Tiptree

What first drew me to you was the titles—*his* titles. "The Snows Are Melted, The Snows Are Gone", "Mother in the Sky with Diamonds", "Love Is the Plan the Plan Is Death", "Her Smoke Rose Up Forever". It has happened only twice before (Zelazny: "The Doors of His Face, the Lamps of His Mouth", "The Teachers Rode a Wheel of Fire"; Ellison: "The Beast that Shouted Love at the Heart of the World", "I Have no Mouth, and I Must Scream"). It was the poetry that is inherently part of SF for me. But of course, as for Zelazny and Ellison, there were the stories themselves. After two or three (read in French translations), I knew that you, the writer, would be one of my favourite *auteurs*. It's a masculine word in French. There is no feminine for "writer", "*écrivain*" in French. We French do have genders, very much so, even now, though *écrivainE* is almost accepted in France, I mean, not laughed at as much as in the '70s. But I have been living in Quebec for more than forty years now where *écrivaine* was accepted much earlier. Thank the goddess. It means slightly less of an identity problem.

So from the very first, you—James Tiptree Jr.—were for me an *il* and not an *elle*. Of course. Obviously. Goes without saying. Not even the smallest inkling of the possibility of a doubt. Especially since the two other authors who had immediately come to my mind when seeing those titles were men. And since most SF writers were still men in the '70s despite the women's surge from the sixties on—well, they *still* are, although not by as wide a margin as way back then. Said surge was not especially felt in France as our image of (English-speaking) SF has always depended on publishers' translation choices. In fact there were not many women, if any, translated into French. I had begun reading in English, fortunately, as I couldn't get my SF fix anymore in the French productions or translations. But even so. I was beginning to get bored with SF. Fed up. Disappointed. I didn't know how to express what I was feeling, but I know now: I was suffering from a testosterone overdose. Too many cowboys in space, that kind of thing. Even my cherished ones—Sturgeon, Simack, Zelazny, Dick et al. were not enough anymore. And then Ursula Le Guin happened to me. I was holding on to *The Left Hand of Darkness* for dear life—literally: *that* was what I felt SF could and should be. *That* was what I wanted to read—and write. Or your stories—although I didn't see myself as a short story writer, at the time. Even though you were a man, you were one I could always read with wonder and delight. The man to redeem them all—or at least most of them. The poetry of the titles, the depth of thought and feeling, the poignant characters … even the darkness, it all rang *truer*, somehow.

It's hard to remember exactly after more than forty years. But I did love James Tiptree Jr. *He* was the one I rabidly begged to translate (*Up the Walls of the World*) when working for a French publisher in 1977. *He* was the one I peddled tirelessly to the SF community I found at last in Quebec (in France, except perhaps during the two last years, '72-73, I was the Only Weirdo Who Loved SF In The World, like every one of us).

But I do remember very vividly when I learned that you were a woman. And that you were also Raccoona Sheldon, a young and promising SF writer I had pegged as a soul sister, another James Tiptree Jr. afficionado, hey—with that title, y' know, "Your Faces, O My Sisters! Your Faces Filled of Light!"

Although I now lived in the New World, the Americas, the *real* SF world, I knew very little of what was happening in the US community—the declarations of this or that author about "the man to beat", or the various rumours... I knew nothing of all that. It came out like thunder from the proverbial blue sky—well, blue is the color of little boys, isn't it?

A woman was James Tiptree Junior.

It was 1978 by then; I had become a fervent Sfeminist. And I'd just spent several months translating you—*him* (with endless joy, it was not *work*, you see...). Jaw-dropped, I rounded up all my James Tiptree Jr. stories, mostly in English by then, and re-read them. And of *course* it was written by a *woman*. It was *obvious*. Those *titles*. "The Women Men Don't See"??? OMG.

Not so. It had *not* been obvious. I hadn't seen it *at all*.

So why did I see it so clearly now?

I could pretend that a part of me knew, suspected, surmised. And perhaps it is even true—a part of me may have, so subconsciously as to be unconscious! But honestly I didn't think so at the time. I had bought it hook, line and sinker. I didn't feel angry at you or anything like that. Just stupefied. At the assumptions I suddenly discovered I had. At the fact that a mere *name* could orient the reading of a fiction that much... Well, all that jazz, which is so familiar to (most of) us now, but wasn't then.

I always say I have become a feminist through reading (and thinking) science fiction and not the feminist canon, which I read afterwards, hence "Sfeminist". Yes. And the final nail *out* of the potential coffin of certitudes was The James Tiptree Jr. Incident. Before that, I was beginning to think I had *answers*. James Tiptree Jr. rescued me from that slippery slope. Alice, Raccoona, you rescued me. What is a woman, a man, what is it to be a woman or a man—a human being? *Question.* Women's and men's writing, is there any difference? *Question.* And so on. And so forth.

Well, it was Sturgeon who said to always ask the next question. Bless him for being the voice of Science Fiction itself, for it is what first drew me to SF: the never-ending need to ask questions and invent answers (plural, and always biodegradable). But it is you, Raccoona, Alice, James, who really taught me how deeply vital it is, how liberating, and how truly human. You were who you were, you had your own life, your own painful questions that you answered as you deemed fit. But nothing you did, and perhaps even nothing you wrote, could equal what discovering *a woman was James Tiptree Jr.* did for me, and for many of us young women and men of your time. I can only hope that a similar illumination happens to the young ones in ours, as those questions you forced us to ask ourselves have not been answered yet—and may never be. May asking them never stop.

With everlasting gratitude and love
Élisabeth

Ahead of her time, and lost in time:
On Gender, Feminism, and Bisexuality.

Dear Tip,

Wish you were here.

I try to imagine how we would have communicated if circumstances had been different, if our generations had intersected, if I had been older or you younger. I imagine you coming to grips with email, the long letter chains we might have passed back and forth, whom we might have brought into the conversation.

That is, if you deemed me to be an okay gal.

If only you could have seen what you helped construct. The conversation about gender in science fiction continues, has morphed, bisected, bifurcated, merged, broken, and been pieced back together again since you left us, all with a strong thread back to you. You are one of the best examples, layer after beautiful gendered layer. Women can't write science fiction? Tell James Tiptree Jr. that.

I wonder, with your troubled history with gender essentialism, how you would parse that.

I can't call you a mother or a father of modern science fiction—you were both and neither. You rejected and embraced women, in life and in science fiction. You wrote our stories with such quiet ferocity. You portrayed toxic masculinity with such finesse, yet struggled with your own masculine and feminine traits.

You loved women, but you found it difficult to like them. Through strong currents of enforced femininity, socialised lack of ambition, and problematic aspects of the feminism of the time, you were taught not to like, or even love, much about yourself. You diverged from preconceptions of femininity, and through the bigotry you faced in the military, your workplace, the literary and academic worlds, and your personal spaces, you were told your performances of masculinity AND femininity were wrong. There was no firm ground to be found for you.

I am devastated at your pain of being the Exceptional Woman, the depression you struggled with over gender identity, body dysmorphia, socialisation versus biology, the structures and constrictions you faced. It is heartbreaking and maddening at the same time. You loved women, and yet were so critical and mean about them. I love you, and I am angry at you, and for you, too.

But anger from a woman was always so hard for you to understand. You found it quite ugly. We could have shown you how much strength there is in righteous anger. You feinted at it, allowed yourself some of it as Tiptree. I wish you could have owned that anger, but it turned inwards on you, gutted you out. Eventually, that anger and pain became so toxic, there was no way around it for you.

If only you could have talked it out—if not with me, then someone else. If only you could have seen the other side, the changes feminism has gone through, and is still going through. How the chains are slipping off, how the binary is being broken, how it *was* always broken, the spectrum was there but you were only shown glimpses of it. You never saw the whole.

You were genderqueering science fiction, and it was glorious, but, as for many, it came at a price. But now we have a community. We're not alone anymore. I wish you were here to see it, that you had known you were not alone.

But would you reject it out of hand because of your fierce dedication to aloofness? Your distrust of feminism?

It's painful seeing your rejection of feminism, how you internalised some of the most toxic ideas about it when Tiptree upheld some of the most feminist ideals in science fiction at the time. It must have been a terrible catch-22, loving being a man, but hating that a man was taken more seriously when espousing women's stories and experiences as bold, fierce truth. The Exceptional Woman tripped you up again—you wanted change, but found it hard to imagine it beyond your self, your socialisation, what it would mean to break the binary of gender, both physically and mentally. You were angry, frustrated, and afraid for women when they didn't measure up to your impossible standards.

We could have shown you that there was such great love to be taken hold of, spiritually, emotionally, in literature, and physically.

It's hard to know whether you had a name, or even wanted one, for your sexuality. You wrote fondly (and harshly) of your fantasies. Your body dysmorphia, and lack of connection to, and support from, the wider community shows in your descriptions of physical closeness to women, in your personal papers, and science fiction work. Though you are intimate with the minds of men and women, the true physicality of your writing shows in your non-human creations. Your most human creations are the ones that are not—spindly, fragile, many legged things, the imagination of their touch causing shivers. Their sexual relations and reproduction, the all-female worlds, are monstrous.

We know that you had sexual relations with women, but to you they were not real. It hurts to know the wilful Alli was afraid, and that she was afraid to show this vulnerability. Your love affairs were intellectually based, a good way to keep that distance and not be eventually let down by the failings of another's femininity.

This is also evident in your correspondence as Tiptree. You had the distance, emotionally and physically—a distance you would have tried to resolve as "only" masculine—to be wonderfully flirtatious and charming. You had incredible intellectual discourse with female science fiction authors of the time. Oh, if only I could read your full correspondence with Joanna Russ!

You came up in a time when femininity and feminism was devalued, and you wanted to help reset the scales. It was a struggle you took on valiantly, in life and in literature. But eventually the struggle became too much. While there was a world and communities out there, you were too embedded in the pain and expectations, and the loneliness you required from this.

If only you had known you weren't alone. There were many others who struggled with gender and sexual identity in your time, and still do today. Your fiction is part of the conversation that gives them a voice.

I know you weren't speaking just for women. Though you might not have had the language for it, you spoke for All Of Them, in your harsh, spidery, prickly, fiercely intelligent way.

I miss you Tip. I wish we could have talked it out.

The fondest of regards,
A.J. Fitzwater

Oy/Alice Or The Kikuyu, The Kleins, And The Cohens

Dear Ms. Tiptree,

It feels right to address you as "Ms. Tiptree" rather than as "Ms. Sheldon." Whenever I mention you in my scholarly writing, I call you "James Tiptree, Jr." (I always place "Alice Sheldon" in parentheses.) What does not feel right is publishing a letter addressed to someone who died in 1987. Perhaps, then, it is best to begin with juxtapositions between feminist science fiction and the absurd.

In her afterword to *Ammonite*, Nicola Griffith says she is tired of "women-only worlds where all the characters are wise, kind, beautiful, stern seven-foot-tall vegetarian Amazons … [and] aliens who are really women, or women who are really aliens."[1] In this vein, Joanna Russ, in "The Clichés from Outer Space," a satirical story I included in my guest-edited issue of *Women's Studies International Forum*, offered this sentence: "Four ravaging, man-hating, vicious, hulking, Lesbian, sadistic, fetishistic Women's Libbers motorcycled down the highway to where George was hiding behind a bush."[2]

---

1   Griffith, Nicola. "Nicola Griffith Talks about Writing *Ammonite*." *Ammonite*. 1992. New York: Del Rey, 2002. 375-376.

2   Russ, Joanna. "The Clichés From Outer Space." Ed. Marleen S. Barr. "Oh Well, Orwell: Big Sister Is Watching Herself: Feminist Science Fiction in 1984." *Women's Studies International Forum*, vol. 7 no. 2 (1984), 121-124.

I have spent my professional life writing about seven-foot-tall vegetarian Amazons, extraterrestrials who are really women, women who are really extraterrestrials—and the over the top perturbed leather clad libbers in hot pursuit of George hiding behind a bush. (Russ's "George" was not *that* George Bush; despite her brilliance, even Russ could not be that prescient.) In light of my attention to giant meat- eschewing woman warriors and feminist incredible hulks, I suppose it could be business as usual to write a letter to a deceased person. There is a literary precedent to an epistle of this ilk. In Alice Walker's *The Color Purple*, Celie writes letters to God.

But I digress.

It is hard to come to the point. I have something painful to say to you, something which I have not articulated for twenty-eight years. I have, in contrast, described a similarly difficult circumstance which relates to Octavia E. Butler. I will digress further by, before saying what I want to say to you, mentioning the Butler circumstance.

Butler gave me permission to publish one of her stories in *Afrofuture Females: Black Writers Chart Science Fiction's Newest New-Wave Trajectory.* When I asked her about remuneration, she generously said that she merely wished to receive a copy of the book. I promised that I would honor this request. I could not keep my promise. Butler died before *Afrofuture Females* was published. I wrote about this in a piece, published in *Callaloo,* called "Oy/ Octavia Or Keeping My Promise to Ms. Butler."[3]

I have never mentioned the impact your death had upon me in

---

3 "Oy/Octavia: Or Keeping My Promise to Ms. Butler," *Callaloo,* 32(Fall 2009), 1312-1314.

relation to my first full-length book *Alien to Femininity: Speculative Fiction and Feminist Theory*. This letter, then, functions as a companion piece to "Oy Octavia." I am giving the letter a less euphonious title: "Oy/Alice"—which, I think, sounds better than "Oy/James."

It is not easy to break a twenty-eight-year-long silence. I am nervous. I can be brave; no one will motorcycle down the highway to where Marleen is hiding behind a bush.

Alien to Femininity contains a chapter completely devoted to you. I wrote a letter to you to tell you about the Tiptree chapter. I have never before or since written a fan letter to any writer. The book includes many feminist science fiction writers. Why did I write only to you? Because you were my favorite feminist science fiction writer; I thought that you were the best; I loved your work—and I loved you. I still love your work. I still love you.

And, lo, you answered my letter. You sent a postcard which I still have and cherish. You said that you wanted to read the Tiptree chapter. Young scholar thirty-four-year-old me desired to make a good impression. I wanted to send the published chapter, not the manuscript copy. I waited for *Alien to Femininity* to be published. It appeared in 1987. I waited too long. Like everyone, I was shocked by the news of your death and the cause of your death. Unlike everyone, my bereavement included the fact that I could not ever, ever send the Tiptree chapter to you. I have never gotten over this disappointment. I learned from my mistake. Whenever I subsequently needed to send someone a manuscript version text, I did so immediately.

It is 2015. I am sixty-two. I am ten years younger than you were when you died in 1987. Does this mean something? I am not sure. Perhaps someone up there (Celie's "Dear God?") wants me to use the rest of this letter to try to articulate exactly why you meant—and mean—so much to me. This text is after all a letter, not a scholarly essay. I do not have to adhere to one topic.

I can digress.

My first publication appeared in a fanzine called *The Witch and The Chameleon* edited by Amanda Bankier. I recall receiving that green covered typewritten stapled volume. I perused the contents and noticed two contributions from "Raccoona Sheldon." I remember seeing the double "c's" and the two "o's" and wondering how the hell anyone could name their kid "Raccoona." I thought that "Raccoona" was an appropriate name for a ravaging vegetarian Amazon. Who knew that "Raccoona" was you? Not me. It took me a few years to make the connection. I remain proud that my fledgling foray into feminist science fiction criticism appeared in a venue which includes your work.

Your influence pervades my scholarship. I have referred to the phrase "the women men don't see" innumerable times. I think that I have spent my life checking the title "Houston, Houston, Do You Read?" to make sure that the commas are in the correct place. (I just this minute checked again.) And your wonderful titles: *Warm Worlds and Otherwise*, *Star Songs of An Old Primate*, and *Ten Thousand Light-Years From Home*, for example. The number of "Works Cited" lists I compiled containing your titles are passing before my eyes.

Your work impacted upon my real life as well as my professional endeavors. When I was facing the horror-fictionesque events involved with purchasing a Manhattan apartment (which of course entails trying not to be screwed by real estate professionals), I thought of your extraterrestrial real estate agents in "The Screwfly Solution." I am a Fulbright scholar who loves the fact that protagonists in "The Women Men Don't See" are extraterrestrial Fulbright scholars.

Despite the affinity I feel toward you, there are great differences between us. It strikes me that you share something in common with Margaret Atwood, Ursula Le Guin, and Doris Lessing: these writers' parents took them to exotic places during their childhoods. Atwood's parents made it possible for her to live in the Canadian woods; Le Guin spent summers at a Napa Valley estate surrounded by anthropologists; Lessing is out of Africa. Your parents took you to Africa. The "James Tiptree, Jr." *Wikipedia* entry includes a photo whose caption reads "Alice Sheldon with the Kikuyu people, 1920s." (If you would like, I can define "*Wikipedia*" under separate cover.) You are surrounded by beaded necklace-wearing half naked men carrying spears. You, like several of your stellar feminist science fiction writer colleagues, experienced during childhood a real version of what Elaine Showalter calls the "wild zone."[4]

I had no such childhood adventures. A caption to a picture of young me would read "Marleen Barr with the Jewish people, 1950s." I would be surrounded by thick gold chain wearing,

4   Showalter, Elaine. "Feminist Criticism In the Wilderness." *Critical Inquiry*. Vol. 8 no. 2 (1981), 179-206.

polyester leisure suit-clad men carrying golf clubs. Marge Piercy shares more in common with me than you do. Like me, she is an urban Jew who attended the University of Michigan. The green world wilds of the Ann Arbor Arboretum was our "wild zone." Oy—unlike Marge and me—Alice, Doris, Margaret, and Ursula are not Jewish. Your work celebrates difference. You help me to value my own life. I grew up with the Kleins and the Cohens—not the Kikuyu. But I hail from Forest Hills, Queens which is the home of none other than Hugo Gernsback and Spiderman. Feminist science fiction in general—and your work in particular—proclaim that despite differences, the lives of all women matter.

I ultimately became a little more like you. I had adventures. I lived in Africa (as a Visiting Professor at the University of Cape Town.) I belatedly published two novels. (They both have "oy" in their titles: *Oy Pioneer!* and *Oy Feminist Planets: A Fake Memoir.*) James Tiptree, Jr. probably never said "oy" in her life. No matter. My second "oy" novel is currently on the "Recommended Works for the 2015 James Tiptree, Jr. Award" list. The James Tiptree, Jr. Award celebrates both you and future feminist science fiction writers.

Your influence will never die.

Love,

Marleen

PS Dear Goddess, please, when the time comes, introduce me to Alice Sheldon. I want to show her my Tiptree chapter. And, last but not least, please, for all eternity, keep me far far away from motorcycles and Bushes.

My dear compatriot

I call you that, rather than saying Alice, or James Jr., or Raccoona. I'm not sure where you sited your identity—I suspect somewhere in Alice, but who knows? But you are my compatriot, another woman writing speculative fiction, and a foremother too. Your stories amaze me. I use the beginning of "Your Faces, O My Sisters! Your Faces Filled of Light!" in one of my classes and show how subtly the narrator's unreliability is shaded into the story from the first moment of the title.

Shall we lay aside thoughts of hubris and speak frankly among ourselves, two women who know how false modesty is relentlessly imposed on us from day one? The fact of it is, I've reached the point where I can say of some writers, "Okay, I'm as good as them," but there are so many others who have gone so much farther, deeper, more perfectly and in ways I am still stumbling towards. You. Carol Emshwiller. Samuel R. Delany. Nicola Griffith and Kelley Eskridge, whom I always feel compelled to mention in one breath, lest either think I hold the other in lesser esteem. And farther back, others: Woolf. Eliot. Joyce. Austen. Shakespeare. Chaucer. And then the deepest layers of anonymity, where many women have been lost, layers built of folktales and fables.

How did you do it? Was splitting your consciousness part of that? Because I can understand Tiptree, the male impersonation in a field still soaked in sexism and double standards, where all the weapons detailed in Joanna Russ's *How to Suppress Women's*

Writing (a text we must fight to preserve, which we must pass along to the feminists following after us, lest they lose that useful and instructive tool) are employed. But Raccoona? Was that beating them at their own game, saying "Look, I am that damn good, I can do it on my own terms"? But then—why Raccoona rather than Alice? Was that to shelter Tiptree? How did you feel when their stories battled each other on the ballot? And oh my sweet goddess, how did you keep the secret so long? I so desperately wish our conversation was not one-sided.

That's one reason writing is such a lonely profession. So many of the people we want to talk to the most are dead.

Here's the shameful thing. If you were here, and you happened to be looking at the calendar year, you would be surprised not by how far we've come, but how little. You know the day when an all-woman ballot would be as unremarkable as an all-male one, just a statistical accident? Yeah, that's still pretty far out.

In fact, that all-woman ballot happened but it's been used as a rallying cry for the men who'd like to see us stop writing, stop working, stop teaching, stop influencing, stop making a change for the better in the world. This year—well, if you were here, I'd hide the Hugo ballot from you, if I could, lest it hurt you as it has me, and Connie Willis, and George R.R. Martin, and so many others whose only crime was loving science fiction and fantasy enough to open our hearts enough to allow that savage blow.

Yeah, you're right. That's hyperbolic. But returning to my point—the situation's still bad. There's a lot of bright points, but they are fewer and farther between than you'd think.

I do wonder what you'd think of the Internet. I know you'd see the potential, the excitement of having college educations available online to anyone with a net connection. Would you have been able to pull off your multiple identities in the face of that for so long though? You were smart enough that I think you might have.

And when that inevitable failure did happen, what effect would that revelation have? I use "revelation" because I think it would have had the same mystical effect, an almost supernatural heartening for every female writer who hit that, an internal *attagirl* that rallied us. Strengthened us. Maybe you came at the point in time when you did because you were needed. I do notice some of the other female authors of your time getting mentioned less in a way that doesn't happen to you, probably half because of the award, half because of the story of Alice B., who knocked it out of the ballpark no matter what team's uniform she was wearing. So let's mention a few, so readers of this essay have some breadcrumbs to lead them into the thickets of neglect and copyright issues which are growing over their works: Joan Aiken, Vera Chapman, Suzette Haden Elgin, Carol Emshwiller, Zenna Henderson, C.L. Moore. That should get you started. And one more—Grace Paley, who did not write F&SF but was the most wonderful short story writer in the world and to whom I once had the honor of serving dinner capped with homemade sweet potato pie.

Alice/Raccoona/James, I would feed you too. Out of gratitude and love and an entirely selfish desire for your friendship. I would love to bring all the women writers together, a potluck's worth, and sit around telling stories and sharing experiences. Networking too, you bet, and all the leaning in you might like but it's the storytelling that preserves our history. The world is the lesser for not having you telling yours in it so when that imaginary and wonderful party is taking place inside the narrow confines of my skull, you are there, and I finally get a chance to ask you questions.

I want to know, for instance, what lay behind "The Screwfly Solution." For me the uncertainty caused by your authorial identity is one of the things that makes it so brilliant. For those readers unfamiliar with the story, go read it, and come back. There. Now you will understand what I mean when I say the story reads differently when the context is a female author than when it is a male one. (And the gender of the reader and their experience also splinters the possibilities.)

Is the story an attempt to say something about women's experience or a constructed experiment in what would be received well at the time or something that was meant to be read with the understanding that it changes according to the author's gender? That's my question—is the Tiptree identity adaptation to the additional hurdles the field presented (still present, to a differing degree), a survival strategy, or is it itself a rhetorical device?

Goddamn it, Alice B. I want to know what lay behind that story. Surely a news article, but what experiences was it colliding with in your psyche to come up with that brilliant, brutal story? So many of the Tiptree stories change depending on the light you're seeing them in. I marvel that anyone could read "Houston, Houston, Do You Read?" and not say the author was female, but I probably would have been as gulled as the others.

I'm glad I got the chance to write this essay, to start this conversation. I know it'll prompt me to dig out all my anthologies of your work and reread them, a barrage of amazing that will humble and instruct me. It's why I come back to you (and the others) over and over again. Someone has borrowed my copy of your biography, Julie Phillips' *James Tiptree Jr: The Double Life of Alice B. Sheldon* and I want to read it again, but that story's ending breaks my heart, Alice B., every time.

You are lost, and gone forever, or rather I can see you retreating from the present day as your work falls away into the dark tunnel of time. It's up to us to keep pulling you back into visibility, keep asking the same questions, keep using your example to illuminate our path. Which is not to say that we should all write under male names—no! —but that we know you pulled it off either way. And this means we've all got that same choice to take or not. It doesn't really matter which as long as we are writing as ourselves, with all our talent and passions, and trying to make things that talk back to you, and to future readers, and the whole long and weirdly configured conversation that is human history.

Goodbye, my compatriot. Goodbye, my sister. I'll honor your memory and perpetuate it as best I can.

Cat

Dear Alli,

That is the name that you prefer, right? At least, that's what Julie Phillips says, and she seems to have got to know you quite well. Of course she never actually met you, so she could be wrong, especially about someone as private as you. I know a little bit about being private, about having things you don't want anyone to know about you.

I never met you either, but I like to think that we might have had things to talk about, you and I. We both love science fiction, obviously. Also we are both fascinated by gender, and the way that society constricts us to follow gender roles. The difference is that I was able to do something about mine; gender, that is.

I guess you know what I'm talking about. No one can manage to hide from the news media these days. Did you look on, puzzled, when Christine Jorgensen arrived back in New York in 1953 to face the press?[1] Did you wonder why anyone in their right mind would *want* to be a woman, given how society treats them?

It is a question that psychiatrists love to ask. Over the years they have invented all sorts of strange and bizarre "conditions" with which to label people like Ms. Jorgensen; people like me. They seem to have an unnatural obsession with diagnosing sexual perversions in others. Someone should get them to see a psychiatrist about it, don't you think?

---

1   https://en.wikipedia.org/wiki/Christine_Jorgensen

Of course back then circumstances conspired to make it all seem true. Trans men were practically invisible. Trans women survived any way they could, and that generally meant show biz or working the street. I don't expect you to have thought much of Andy Warhol, or the Velvet Underground. I liked the Velvets, but I was a teenager; it came with the territory.

Lou Reed did that song, remember? "A Walk on the Wild Side", singing about Holly Woodlawn, Candy Darling and others like them.[2] They were glamorous, but in a very seedy sort of way. They weren't exactly good role models. My parents would have been horrified, had I said I wanted to be like those women. My parents were your age, and I could see that they were quite relaxed about social issues compared to their parents. Goodness only knows what *your* parents would have thought of such things.

So I kept quiet; private. No matter how much I hated my life, I didn't tell anyone how I felt. I didn't want to end up in an asylum being poked with electrodes, after all. It would not have been fun. Locking it all inside seemed far less painful, but it isn't pain free, is it?

Of course in your case there were friends to worry about too. I'll bet Joanna Russ was all righteously angry about Warhol's friends. Radical feminism of the time hated trans people. It is easy to see why. If you want to form separate societies based on gender, the last thing you need is someone who wants to move from one to the

---

2   https://en.wikipedia.org/wiki/Candy_Darling & https://en.wikipedia.org/wiki/Holly_Woodlawn

other, or thinks they belong to both, or neither. And there was all that stuff about gender being *solely* a social construct; something you were taught as a child. People used to believe that. If you can access Google wherever you are, look up David Reimer.[3] That will show you just how deadly such ideas can be.

The thing is though, that I'm not sure that Joanna believed it all. Sure she wrote that book,[4] and I'll bet she had a few things to say back then as well. In later life, however, she changed her mind. She was Guest of Honor at a convention called Wiscon some years back. I'm sure you know what that is; they do that award named after you. She was too ill by then to attend in person, but she did a video interview followed by a Q&A. A trans girl I'd met there, someone far braver than me, stuck her hand up and asked Joanna what she thought about trans people these days. There, in front of everyone, Joanna apologised. She said that she'd got some things wrong in her youth. I still get chills thinking about that moment.

What I keep wondering about, however, is what Joanna actually believed back then. There's this passage in *The Female Man* than I can't explain, and I was hoping you could throw some light on it. It goes like this:

> *There must be a secret feminine underground that teaches them how to behave; in the face of their comrades' derision and savage contempt, in the face of the prospect of gang rape if they're found alone on the streets after curfew, in the face of the legal necessity to belong—every one of them—to a*

---

3   https://en.wikipedia.org/wiki/David_Reimer

4   Joanna Russ, *The Female Man* (Beacon Press: Boston, 1986).

real-man, somehow they still learn the classic shiver, the slow blink, the knuckle-to-lip pathos. These too, I think, must be in the blood. But whose? My three friends and I pale beside such magnificence! Four lumpy parcels, of no interest to anyone at all, at all.[5]

She's talking about The Changed there, and while they might be characters in the book they are surely based on actual trans women. That's certainly how we were all expected to behave back then. She may even have met some trans folk. Or perhaps she had talked to Chip. I know he had met some. Joanna, I'm pretty sure, must have wondered why anyone would want to become a woman. She will have wondered how people like Jorgensen, Woodlawn and Darling managed to learn all that femininity without the benefit of social conditioning. Any why no amount of social conditioning seemed to have made any difference to her and her friends. Did she talk to you or Ursula about it? I'd love to know.

Maybe it is all in the blood, or at least partially in the body somewhere. Biologists are busy delving into the mysteries of how our bodies and minds work. One day maybe they'll come up with a reason why people like me are the way we are. In the meantime, empirical evidence is telling us that gender is way more complicated than anyone thought.

In some ways, society progresses in generational leaps. Your parents will doubtless have had all sorts of hangovers from the nineteenth century. My parents, your generation, loosened those social strictures, but by no means as much as was necessary for

---

5   Russ, *The Female Man*, p171.

me to take the great leap into the unknown. It wasn't that easy for me. I had to go through a lot of self-doubt and heartache before taking the plunge. And back then there were expectations. We had to see psychiatrists to prove that we were worthy to be women (or men), and boy did we have to conform to stereotypes.

It was crazy. Old men—doctors—telling us how to be women. You would have laughed. Joanna would have burst a few blood vessels. Floaty cotton dresses; skirts, twinsets and pearls; pumps with heels; we had to perform the code. Outside the doctors' offices, we'd go back to wearing jeans, but we didn't feel any less female because of it. That was, after all, how most of our female friends dressed.

Gender: it's not just about clothes and performance, it's not just about your role in society, it is also who you are. We are beginning to understand those things now. Out of that, something new is emerging. There are boxes. They are called "male" and "female". The old doctors tried to fit everyone into them. If you didn't like the one you had been assigned at birth, well you should go and sit in the other one instead. Woe betide anyone who didn't fit in either.

But the generation after me is doing something very interesting. They are taking those boxes and ripping them apart. They call themselves "non-binary", because they don't want to have to choose between two restrictive stereotypes. People of my generation mostly scratch their heads and think this is all really weird, but I don't. I can see where they are coming from. No one is wholly male or female. I'm pretty girly as such things go. I enjoy clothes and make-up and all that stuff. But I was also raised to love watching sport. My mum loved it too, so I never thought it was something that girls shouldn't do. As it is, I fit fairly comfortably into the gender binary; but having spent decades of my life pretending to be male, I can quite understand how some people might be far less happy with such restrictions, and might chafe against them.

That's the world we are building here today. Not just a world in which women can have full legal rights alongside men; not just a world in which women are, at least in theory, able to take any job they want; but a world in which the whole idea of "men" and "women" is slowly being eroded.

And that's what I wanted to talk to you about. It is pretty clear that you were not very happy being Alice. I don't know how committed you were to being James. Was he you? Or was he just a persona that you adopted because you felt that you couldn't do what you wanted to do in life without performing maleness?

These days it doesn't matter. If you want to be James, we can make it so. The doctors have got very good at it. But if you don't want to be James, and don't want to be Alice, you can just be Alli. That's a choice you get to make, and nothing you do in life should be constrained by that choice. None of this has to be shameful; none of it has to be kept private. The important thing is that you should be happy being you. And that, having read Phillips' book, is something I very much wish you could have had.

Best wishes,
Cheryl

Dear Tiptree,

You are an enduring inspiration! Your independence, your zest for life, your craziness and your sanity! Your arc across the twentieth century burns an imprint like a comet on feminist science fiction. As a writer, you have touched me deeply with your ability to combine the cosmic with the commonplace, you have taken me to brutal places I needed to go to in my wanderings around feminism, and you taught me how layered and finessed gendered genre writing can be. Tiptree, I love your writing and I am a hopeless and devoted lifelong fan!

As a fan I would like to say thank you. Firstly for the sheer pleasure of your prose and all of the interesting (and often instructive) predicaments that populate your stories. Even people outside the genre are familiar with stories like 'The Girl Who Was Plugged In" and "The Women Men Don't See", but I want to say a special thank you for your two full-length novels, which are largely unappreciated masterpieces. I say this with almost as much tongue in cheek as I'm convinced you had when writing them! What fantastic, fun and intelligent books! Yoga poses in print, they stretch the medium to its maximum capacity, crammed with heroic humans, aliens, plots, technologies, interstellar bodies, time and civilisations, and they make the reader stretch too. Good yoga presents a challenge (almost a pain?) to the uninitiated, but after an intense stretch we surface feeling stronger and much more aware!

It is not surprising that both *Up the Walls of the World and Brightness Falls From the Air* have a central fascination with time, because the way you have written these stories is an exercise in balance across an entire century, a century that has seen unprecedented change technologically and politically. These novels capture the very essence and innocence of space opera as we have understood it from its inception, yet they also take us to the core of the complex issues of a postcolonial and postfeminist world where national security and the protection of the vulnerable are becoming center-stage in our concerns. For me, your big stories about little people are a sort of Buzz Lightyear finds *Heart of Darkness*, so the pleasures of reading and rereading your books are strangely mixed and deeply affecting. Within the pages of these novels lies an invitation to escape and have fun with the space cadets, the opportunity to rethink every cliché unintentionally absorbed about women, children and aliens, and the dull thud of meeting human inertia and history eyeball to eyeball. The more we change, the more we need to change and the less we want to change. Time is sticky, tricky stuff and obviously to be played with in pretty much the same way that you play with everything from the CIA to the Enlightenment. *Don't like it?* Blow it up, run it backwards, redirect it, reinvent it. Use a pulsar as a clock for lost ones in love with their days and hours, murder a star to create time flurries as narrative windows for plot change. Seamlessly stitch an afternoon experiment on earth with the drawn out agonies of an expiring species enduring the endless doom of a planet. Kill and resurrect at will. Do anything and everything you want with whatever aeon, moment or empire you choose. Tiptree, inside the pages of your novels you are god!

That requires narrative bravery of a special order. To mess with the meager social realities of a few people in a novel is one thing—but to mess with the very stuff of the universe! To reorganize dimensions and really imagine that *anything* is possible is taking the invitation of science fiction very seriously. Speaking through the prematurely aged Cory at the end of *Brightness Falls from the Air* you express your mild contempt for the simple mirroring of banality: "As though reality needs encouragement ... *reality doesn't need friends.*" You know that reality has the endorsement of the whole establishment and you prefer to show it unzipped, exposed and embarrassed. For you, imagination equals courage and adventure, and our stories should be spectacular! And the wit that is loaded into your prose! Even the fact that Cory is saying this to someone called 'Pace' sounds like a literary joke! A pun about the very construction of your book! Haha! The whole novel is a dilemma-solution-dilemma-solution roller coaster of the barely ridiculous travelling unstoppably and breathlessly atop a modern tragedy. If extreme writing were an athletic event you would have won gold, Tip! And as for *Up the Walls of the World*? Literary parkour, no less!

But the other thing I love about you? Your warmth. Not intimidated one iota by the grandeur of the universe you determinedly colonise the deepest, coldest reaches of space. Not with the all too familiar tropes of technology, militarism or even an expansionist capitalism (though they are there too!), but with human love, compassion and wisdom. And in your particular colonisations you pay attention to each traveller, lightly bringing the arrogant and vicious undone while raising up the poor and sad. Bless you for making Margaret Omali the pilot of everything—the divine director of the omnipotent cloud! The violent trauma of her genital mutilation sits at the very centre of a big, big story that reaches out to understand the powers of the universe—to understand what should be important to us as human beings. Forget riches, social status, and political power, the story instructs. These are only illusions and not the genuine metaphysical fabric of life. The thing that makes or breaks our humanity is our response to a little girl, violently assaulted and permanently damaged. Until that little girl sits in the centre of our hearts, and drives our decision-making we are not saved. You have my vote for queen of the universe, Tiptree! You'd organise the place decently! Your authorial kindness makes the smallest among your cast of thousands shine, but those who are destructive and cruel simply can't prosper.

And finally, I have to tell you, I believe your secret heart lies with your doctors. Balthazar Baramji and Daniel Dann are among your most redeeming creations. Despite their own imperfections and hopeless love stories, these are good men whose desire is to help and to heal. They recognize the ill, the old, the young, the infirm, and the heedless and treat them with a beautiful equalising candour. They nurse their own deep wounds but they have not squandered their intellectual and emotional potential—they educate themselves and contribute to the emotional capital of their group with their empathy, their intelligence and their determination to follow an oath to do good. No closet neo-Darwinists these men of science, rather good right-hand helpers for the women who sacrifice to create the path forward. Margaret Omali and Cory Korso change the future and pay a heavy price for change, but the good doctors support them in knowing and loving ways to a bitter and complicated end, and then some.

Tiptree, your voice is unique among women, among science fiction writers, among writers. I know your personal story and the stories you wrote will not be forgotten, but I just needed to let you know about my particular attachment to your big books. They sit on a small pile of rereads that will go with me wherever I may travel. They remind me to think big. They remind me that I am not wrong when I see a world of love and horror. They remind me I am not alone in my ironic views and odd perspectives. And they remind me I will grow old in my body but I surely never have to in my heart.

With the deepest admiration and greatest affection
Dr Tess Williams

Dear James Tiptree Jr.,

I wish I had known you earlier.

I only met you as a teenager, when I started voraciously reading science fiction and fantasy—devouring stories like candy and never quite remembering the names of those who had written them. I read "The Women Men don't See", but I didn't remember your name. I remembered the story, though—that powerful statement on how women, no matter how invisible and mousey, could still have their own stories; could still yearn for the stars.

I wish you had been there when I grew up; when I became aware that for all our talk of an equal society, women are still the inferior of men; that there would be people who didn't listen to me merely because of my gender; that there would be moments where I would have to bite my tongue and be gentle—twice as gentle as a man, because men are decisive and ambitious, whereas everyone else is shrill and neglectful of their families. I wish you had been there when I realised that I would have to be twice as good and twice as persistent as a man to make it in life. I wish you had been there, because I am sure you would have understood.

Later, much later, after I became an adult—when I was pregnant with my own child—I finally read your stories; and I felt as though you blew away my mind. You spoke of anger and of desire and of the yearning to be free—of the cruelty and thoughtlessness of power—of the inevitability of death and the impossibility to cheat it; but also of the frenzied beauty of life; of the effort that we expend into flowering before we fade away. It was not always a happy message, but it spoke truths to me; because sometimes what we need is not happily-ever-after, but simply the knowledge that we do what we can with what we have.

The one story I remember very clearly is "Your Faces, O My Sisters! Your Faces Filled of Light" (it was listed as a James Tiptree Jr. story and I only found out later it was written by Raccoona Sheldon)—there is something in that slow, heartbreaking tragedy of a woman running away that keeps calling to me. I knew, even as I was reading the story, that it could not end well, that it was never going to end well; that the blind, childish trust the nameless narrator has in every woman cannot possibly sustain her in the modern world—and yet; and yet, isn't her world more beautiful, more hopeful than the dark one she's running away from?

I think this is a major part of what appeals to me in your work: this dichotomy. On the one hand, that full knowledge that the world is dark, and cruel, and dangerous; that men kill women; that people kill each other and tear each other apart given a chance; that utopias are so often built on the pain and suffering of others, on the servitude of millions. And yet, there is happiness; there is camaraderie; and even in the throes of death there is bliss. Even in the face of despair, and the meaninglessness of life, your characters struggle; trudge on towards the heights of the mountains, or back to their own times; make their last reports to Earth, fall in love in the shadow of transcendence. It is not because we are doomed that we are helpless, or because we are oppressed that we lie weak and inactive. It is a powerful message, and one that comes across in your stories with the intensity of a gut punch.

Intensity. That is the other thing I love about your stories—that they are never timid or halfway there. They are fully inhabited by anger, by bitterness; by bliss, by passion and obsession. They make the reader rage for what could have been, or rail at the stupidity and shallowness of characters such as Paul in "The Girl Who Was Plugged In". They pan out, lyrical and painful and yet full of tenderness, such as at the end of "The Man Who Walked Home"; always with that same boundless energy in the prose, that same river of vitality running through characters—to me, the epitome of "raging against the dying of the light"; of being alive and screaming.

Your stories are never dull, never leave the reader indifferent; they always challenge, always push at the boundaries inside the reader's mind; always ask questions about the value and meaning of life, of sex, of death. This is something I want to emulate, as a writer: both the lyrical prose and the gut-punch liveliness of them: I want to elicit a reaction with passionate writing, rather than a sinking into indifference with mere competence.

You did not shy away from sex. It's unusual in science fiction, and even more in your time—you were frank, unwilling to pull a veil over this fundamental human drive. It is sex entwined with death, such as in "A Momentary Taste of Being" or "Love is the Plan the Plan is Death"; it is futile, sterile sex in "And I Awoke and Found Me Here on the Cold Hill's Side"; and yet it is beautiful. It is the bliss that, thrown against death, brings life into sharp contrast. It is the thing that tears us apart, that brings us together; and I am thankful to you for not eliding its importance in your stories.

Finally, there is your choice of a male pseudonym—because this is an integral part of what you did, and it would be churlish of me to write a letter to you and never even allude to this.

As a woman in the field, I return, always, to gendered writing; or rather, to gendered perception of writing, as if all women were concerning themselves with domestic things and all men were forever doomed to write about war and violence. You proved, brilliantly, that there was no such thing as female writing; and carved a trail that I and others do our best to follow—that being male or female or non-binary should not be a limitation on what we choose to write, on what subjects we're qualified to tackle.

I know it was not an easy road for you; and that life was not kind to you. It feels too little, and too late, to be telling you how you touched my life, and how much you meant to me even though it took me time to discover you properly. But I hope this belated letter reaches you, wherever you are; and proves to you that you are still a wonderful, invigorating inspiration to so many of us.

With my very best regards,
Aliette

Dear Alli,

(may I call you Alli? I feel it's how I have come to know you, rather than Alice, and certainly not James or Tip or Raccoona),

It wasn't very long ago that I didn't know who you were. It's only been a few years since I heard about "The Tiptree Award", and then I came to learn more about science fiction history, about the woman who fooled the rest of the field by writing so splendidly under a man's name. It was only this month, though, that I came to really make your acquaintance, exploring extracts of your journals, letters and private thoughts in a jigsaw pieced together by the patient and thorough hand of your biographer Julie Phillips. From there I was compelled to read the stories she examined and unpacked in their entirety, and I found myself so immersed in this chronicle of your life that it was difficult to return to the present. One hundred years since you came into this world, nearly thirty since you left it; almost five decades since you became a presence in science fiction. Such a long expanse of time, with so many changes, and yet, so much resonates as the same. As I read about your life, I couldn't help but highlight excerpts from your story that particularly struck me. Points like:

...his male ego demanded victory...[1]

Man, she concluded, 'had never forgiven woman for existing'...[2]

1 Phillips, J. (2007). *James Tiptree Jr.: The double life of Alice B. Sheldon*. Picador. p. 94
2 *Ibid*, p. 131

*There is a faint feeling that a roaring adventure story by a
women isn't quite as, well, interesting as if it was by a man...*[3]

*Maybe more important was that no editors had come
forward offering to befriend Raccoona in the same way they
had Tiptree. Alli came to feel that Raccoona wasn't taken
seriously because she was a woman...*[4]

What does it say about our society that every one of these could
have been written today? Perhaps the despair apparent in so
many of your stories had more prescience than anyone might
have wished. It is beyond frustrating, bordering on devastating,
to consider how much things have remained the same.

With that in mind, I cannot help but wonder at the person you
may have been had you been born sixty years later than you were, in
my year of birth, 1975. Your childhood adventures would certainly
have been different. The privilege of your family would have meant
different things for your upbringing, given the movement of the
times and cultural mores. But allowing for different freedoms,
different understandings, about sexuality, mental health, relationships... Would you still have found your voice? Would you have
felt you needed to? Would you have been able to write as Tiptree
wrote, but as Alice? Or would the walls you sidestepped by being a
man writing science fiction, walls still standing strong today, have
stayed your hand? Would you have despaired of these barriers, or
railed against them? Would Tiptree have needed to spring to life?

---

3 *Ibid*, p. 260

4 *Ibid*, p. 331

Could he have even done so? Without Tiptree as a mantle, what work would we, could we, have had from you?

There are those, even today, who keep their true identity in shadow, acclaimed as author but never seen. In the online world we inhabit, I wonder how many of us truly present a real face? Or what that even means?

I don't know if you could have become who you were in any other circumstances but those in which you existed. I don't know if my heart breaks for you and what your life gave you or if I rejoice for the same. Because it seems that while you struggled and despaired, you also soared. Your stories (and indeed, your story) persevere; they resonate and endure. As you endured and changed and grew. That your life became what it was because of both prerogative and tribulation says to me that life, any life, requires each. Perhaps we cannot become the best we can be without tempering from hard and soft, hot and cold, pain and pleasure.

And your legacy also endures. In the words of your biographer, I take one final, more hopeful message from your story:

"...Alli's act of claiming science fiction has made other women bolder in taking liberties with the field."[5]

Thank you, Alli, for giving us that star to guide us.

Fondest regards,
Tehani Wessely

---

5 Ibid, p. 459

Dear James/Alice,

I still remember the first time I ever heard of you. I was eighteen years old, in my second year of university, desperate to become a professional writer but far too shy and insecure to tell other people about my dreams. I was a music student twenty-three hours of every day and a writer for that one last cherished hour, typing up fantasy stories and pieces of novels that I didn't show to anyone. Even as a music student, though, I still got to take some English classes, so I signed up for a class in post-apocalyptic fiction. Of course, that meant reading a lot of science fiction, which I loved— and one morning, while a group of us waited with our professor for our classroom to be free, she told us your story.

…Or rather, she told us an abridged form of your story, and it was exactly what I needed to hear. "…That was back when people were still saying women couldn't write science fiction," she said, with a sniff. "One very famous male writer even held up James Tiptree, Jr. as an example, saying that no woman would ever be able to write like that … but guess what?" She grinned. "James Tiptree, Jr. was actually Alice Sheldon. And when the news came out, that showed *everyone!*"

Well. I'm thirty-eight now, not eighteen any longer, and I know that the true story was much more complicated than that. For one thing, I've read your biography, by Julie Phillips, where all the complexity and pain of that public revelation were exposed. You didn't choose for that news to come out, to teach the science fiction field a lesson. You were outed involuntarily, and I hate that that happened to you. I still have to thank you, though, as guilty as that makes me feel, now that I know what that experience was like for you. But for a shy eighteen-year-old girl years later, that story of victory—victory for our whole gender!—resonated through me like the ringing of a bell.

It's kept on resonating for me over the years. It resonated for me recently when I was part of a conversation of professional women fantasy writers all talking about whether it would be smarter to write and publish under a male pen name. There are good reasons why that *would* be smart, to be honest, based on sales numbers and reader biases. But I felt an aversion to the idea that was so intense, I felt sick. And yet again, I found myself remembering your story.

We already proved this, I thought. *Remember James Tiptree? We shouldn't have to do this anymore.*

It was smart of you to publish the way you did, and it was the right thing for you at that point. But somehow, in my eighteen-year-old brain, in 1996, it became firmly settled with the hearing of your story that women *didn't* have to do that anymore, because you had already proved our point for us (…at great cost to yourself, I'm aware). I know you never set out to prove that point, or to *show everyone* what a woman could really do. But still, that's the message that's resonated in me every time I've seen the same old ridiculous debate popping up again in the f/sf field. Are women as good at science fiction and fantasy as men? Is it worth picking up a novel by a female writer, if you're a man?

Come on. Remember Tiptree? We already proved this point. Move on!

Of course, hearing your story didn't change everything for me. I may have felt validated, but that didn't turn me confident. That summer, I got a job as the Assistant to the Director of the Clarion East Science Fiction & Fantasy Writing Workshop, working for the same professor who had told me your story in the first place. As an aspiring f/sf writer myself, I was so excited by the opportunity. So many of my writing idols were going to be teachers there! I'd be living the dream!

...But I wasn't. Unsurprisingly, there's a big difference between being an actual part of the workshop and helping the workshop run smoothly. I still feel incredibly lucky to have had that job at nineteen, to have met writers like Maureen McHugh, Elizabeth Hand and Judith Tarr in person. I was surrounded by people doing exactly what I dreamed of doing myself. But the truth was, I felt even more personally silenced than ever about my own writing as the workshop went on, through nobody else's fault but my own.

Every day at work, I was surrounded by "real" writers, both the beginning writers who were good enough to get into the workshop, and the experienced professional writers who were teaching there. Who was I to call myself a writer by comparison, even in the privacy of my own head? I was friendly with all the writers there, many of whom were fantastic people ... but I felt like I was playing a part the whole time, because I was intentionally hiding my deepest self, my deepest desires and my true feelings, so that I could pretend to be a chirpy, bright, enthusiastic reader who had no interest in writing herself. That was who I thought I was supposed to be.

I think you knew a lot about that kind of role-playing. After all, "James Tiptree, Jr." wasn't only a name attached to the manuscripts you submitted. You carried on whole friendships—real, intense, and very personal friendships—conducted by letter with other writers, from Ursula Le Guin to Robert Silverberg, Joanna Russ and Harlan Ellison, and you approached them all specifically *as* a man, playing out a role that set you free. When you wrote later about the public revelation of your real identity, you said, "My secret world had been invaded, and the attractive figure of Tiptree—he *did* strike several people as being attractive – was revealed as nothing but an old lady from Virginia."[1]

Playing a role gave you the freedom to be the person you wanted to be. Playing a role myself made me feel as if I were being squashed and suffocated. But I kept on playing that role by choice, for years, as I progressed through my university career, pretending to be a passionate academic who most wanted to advance in my field. Really, most desperately, I wanted to be someone else entirely: a novelist. But I rarely even admitted to my classmates and friends that I loved reading f/sf, much less that I was secretly writing it at night. I wanted to fit in. I wanted to be normal. I wanted, at

---

1 As quoted in Julie Phillips, *James Tiptree, Jr.: The Double Life of Alice B. Sheldon*, Picador, NY, 2007, p4.

the base of it, for people to like me—and (much like you) I didn't think that could ever happen if they knew the real me.

After I went as a student to the Clarion West workshop, at twenty-four, I finally started telling people—people I trusted, at least—the truth. A year later, I started writing my first online blog, where I wrote not about Stephanie, the enthusiastic and ambitious academic, but about Steph, the real person, the writer. Like you, I found some of my most important friendships through my writing, and I finally got to let out my secret self. Writing my blog and connecting with other writers through the blogosphere, as well as publishing my short stories and my first three novels, I finally stopped trying to fit the "normal" mould that I'd been trying to crush myself into, my whole life. I started letting all of my quirks and my passions show, instead. It felt vulnerable. It felt scary. It also felt deeply right.

When I got married, a few years later, I changed my legal name, adding my husband's surname to my own, but I never changed my writing name. "Stephanie Burgis" was the name I was born with, the name I'd blogged under, showing my private self to the world, and the name I'd started publishing with. It felt (and still feels) like the name of my true, original self, and I didn't want to change it. It's the name that will be mine all through my life, no matter what.

Last Christmas, I sold my first fantasy novel for adults. The first thing my agent asked me, after he told me that we'd sold it, was: "Do you want to use a pen name?"

Well, the truth is, I've toyed with that idea at various low points in my career. And there were a lot of sensible reasons why it might have been a good idea to do just that. After all, my new book, *Masks and Shadows,* is in a different genre from my first three books, which could potentially cause confusion to both readers and booksellers. In publishing, it's rarely a bad idea to start fresh. And of course, although my agent, who is wonderful, would never have suggested this to me, it hadn't been long since I'd been part of that practical conversation about pen names with other women writers ... and the truth is, statistically speaking, it really is still smart in terms of sales numbers, when publishing in adult f/sf, to use a gender-neutral name, if you don't use a male one outright.

But the idea of a pen name—any new name, whether it was male or female, making me once again split my identity and hide who I really was from the world—honestly made me feel as if I was suffocating.

I remembered your story. *We already proved this.*

"No," I told my agent. "I want to keep my name."

I want to be myself.

Thank you so much for helping me to do it.

All my best,
Steph

"how can I escape it"

Tiptree's story is one that loves to be told: a writer of award-winning stories, remarkable feminist stories, a man, *certainly* a man, revealed to be a woman. Easy narratives are comfortable: know a person in a sentence, know a situation in a paragraph. Bam! James Tiptree Jr. is actually Alice Sheldon. Bam! All it takes is a name—a pair of names—to demonstrate that innate differences in gender do not exist in the context of writing fiction. It is yet more evidence that innate differences do not exist at all. It is so *satisfying*: look! It is so *necessary* to our ongoing discussions about men and women writing science fiction. Look at this story. Too easy. "Oh god pity me I am born damned they say it is ego in me I know it is man all I want is man's life," Alice Sheldon wrote. "... my damned oh my damned body how can I escape it I play woman woman I cannot live or breathe I cannot even make things I am going crazy, thank god for liquor."[1] What does it mean for the story of Tiptree—of gender in science fiction—if Alice Sheldon was a man? Too easy. Alice Sheldon is dead. Alice Sheldon, James Tiptree Jr., Raccoona Sheldon—they never said it straight. They never used easy words. Yet we do. What does it mean if Alice Sheldon was not our easy narrative?

Alex Dally MacFarlane

---

1   Quoted in Julie Phillips, *James Tiptree Jr. The Double Life of Alice B. Sheldon* (Picador: 2006). The book argues that "her life does have a pattern, the pattern of a woman writer."

Letter to Tiptree, Letter to Alice (Plus Notes)

Dear James Tiptree, Jr.,

I first met you in "The Women Men Don't See". I thought it a strange story for a man to have written, and could not understand why I had heard so many people call you an iconic feminist science fiction writer. As a young woman in my early twenties, I was interested in reading feminist stories by feminist women, who certainly, I thought, did not write science fiction anyways. So after our first brief encounter, James, I'm sorry to say I avoided you. I hadn't yet discovered my love of science fiction, and I didn't know the story of your life. We would not meet again until many years later.

In graduate school I finally realized that "James Tiptree, Jr." was a pen name, and that you were, in fact, a woman. I reread "The Women Men Don't See", and this time I was able to appreciate how brilliantly you capture the subversive capability of feminism in reframing gendered relationships, of giving voice to the alien among us. Since I was researching feminist cyberpunk for my dissertation, "The Girl Who Was Plugged In" was the natural next choice on my reading list. How sharp the tragedy of the poor, suffering P. Burke, whom I so badly wanted you to save but you didn't.

As I left the academy and my scholarship progressed, I became interested in disability studies, and again I found myself returning to your work. It was then I fell in literary love with your writing. I wasn't drawn to the gentler and more popular narratives like "Houston, Houston, Do You Read?" but to the ones you set in visceral and fevered worlds with their startling and awful characters. "With Delicate Mad Hands", "She Waits For All Men Born", and "Your Faces, O My Sisters! Your Faces Filled of Light!" kept me awake at night when I first read them. Your stories are never lullabies. I knew then that I wanted to get to know you better. I needed to figure out how someone can write so beautifully about such horrible things.

Your work is rich in cutting social critique, and to me it is worth countless of pages of academic analysis. As the inaugural Le Guin Feminist Science Fiction fellow, I have had the honour of spending time with the archives of Ursula Le Guin and Joanna Russ, both of whom had extensive correspondences with you (and I admit that I was initially most excited to be reading these exchanges above all others). There is such candor in your letters, from your opinions on the politics of the day to your personal motivations for writing science fiction, that I have definitely grown as both a scholar and a feminist. Both your stories and your letters have taught me that feminism is a continuous process of rethinking who we are and figuring out, not what we want to be, but *how* we want to be in the world.

Whenever someone asks me which science fiction writer they should be reading, I always make sure to mention you. I don't tell them that they will undoubtedly find your stories challenging or that they might not even enjoy reading them. I know, however, for the careful reader, your words will linger with them long after they have put their book down. Thank you so much for your stories that sting.

Sincerely,
Kathryn Allan, PhD

Daily Reflection Notes on Archival Research

(University of Oregon, May 2015)

May 28: I guess that while I was originally feeling that this day was the least productive so far, I am actually mistaken. I gained a lot of insight into a few writers in a relatively short period of time. I think part of the issue for me is that there aren't any documents that say "here is your answer". That's just not going to happen. I must sift through and gather the bits of data that jump out at me and, at a later time, when there is distance from this research process, figure out exactly what it is I have learned. At the moment, I can think of a few directions in which to take my research, but none of them feel right. The personal nature of these letters worries me. I am used to working with writing that is removed from the writer as a person (in that their stories are meant for a public audience); I am unsure as to what I can do with personal correspondence.

May 29: The morning went by quickly without a lot of "hits", but the afternoon was possibly one of the more difficult ones to date. Reading Tiptree's letters to Le Guin was unexpectedly troubling. I will discover in my next stage with the Joanna Russ archive how Tiptree wrote to other people, but her letters to Le Guin are heartbreaking. I was brought to tears several times and even had to leave the room at one point to blow my nose. I never expected to read suicidal thoughts—and really, that's what these letters from Tiptree are like. They are unfettered depression written in a powerful, beautiful voice. I can't entirely imagine what Le Guin would have felt at the time of reading these letters, but she must have reacted strongly because her responses are just as impressive. Tiptree and Le Guin's letters are so rich that I think I took pictures (or have ordered scans) of all but one.

May 30: This was a very long day; not only was my energy just low, but the content of the material I was looking at—mainly Tiptree's letters to Joanna Russ—was emotionally exhausting to get through. I honestly don't have much to say because it's kind of a blur. In one letter to Russ, Tiptree writes, "there are so many ways of being human"[1]. And so many of them are messy. I took a lot of pictures though, which I will fully reference once I get home. I guess I instinctively took the approach of taking pictures of stuff that will be useful (instead of closely reading and trying

---

1   "There are so many ways of being human," Tiptree to Russ, 22 October 1974, copyright © 2015 by Jeffrey D. Smith. James Tiptree, Jr correspondence, Coll. 261, Box 10, Folder 28, Special Collections and University Archives, University of Oregon Libraries, Eugene, Oregon.

to comprehend everything now). Things that I focused on: pain/healing, suffering, health issues, strategies of writing.

May 31: Having been able to get rest last night, I was able to make better (or at least, more coherent) progress today. Still working with the Russ archive but I have finished the Tiptree letters. Tiptree's correspondence ends in a very depressing way: a Peanuts comic with a simple handwritten note alongside, "PAIN LOVE TIP."[2] *I wept.*

Dear Alice,

I thought I knew what it meant to be a feminist until I met you and your feminist science fiction sisters in the private thoughtful space of your letters. Your published short stories are grim and disturbing, and I have found your personal correspondence, while engaging, full of admirable wit and all of the best stuff of life, nonetheless disturbing as well. I have been a fly on the wall and I feel too small to be writing to you.

Decades removed, I have witnessed you in your intimate anger and weariness. It is always risky to pull back the curtain and glimpse the master behind it, and I have been changed by what I have found there. When people ask me about my experience in the archive, one of the things that I tell them is that I had the rare

---

2   "PAIN LOVE TIP," Tiptree to Russ, 20 April 1985, copyright © 2015 by Jeffrey D. Smith. James Tiptree, Jr correspondence, Coll 261, Box 10, Folder 40, Special Collections and University Archives, University of Oregon Libraries, Eugene, Oregon.

opportunity to get to know more about you. I clumsily try to explain that in learning about you, I have ended up learning about myself. You make me want to write. You have given me permission to express my anger and despair out loud. You have told me that we need to put these thorny, unlady-like feelings somewhere solid. And if we can put them on to the page, then perhaps we can carry their weight together. We cannot move such burdens alone. Your stories are places where we don't need to smile or shape our mouths in practiced ease.

I meet you so many times now. In memory, in sorrow. Your words have stopped me from doing my research because tears cloud my vision. When people ask me about my experience in the archive, one of the things that I never tell them is that I am haunted by you. I read your last words to Ursula. I read your last words to Joanna. I cried over your letters in the open, sunny reading room of the library where they are safely kept. I am sorry if these were intrusions too far into your privacy, which had already been ripped open and exposed when you simply wanted to sit quietly and write. I was not prepared to encounter you at your end.

Allie, forgive me for my familiarity, but you have come to mean a great deal to me. Your writing was a light in this world, but not like a guiding glimmer at the end of the tunnel or the warm glow of a kitchen calling in the tired to rest. No. Those are lights that comfort and they are not what draw me to you. Yours is the fire that burns off the shadows of social politeness and shows us all that there are still dark places where we must go. Allie, you revealed to me the deep painful truth of what we can and cannot bear. You wrote about the breaking points, the edges of madness. This is a difficult gift.

I have needed to sit with your words in mind for a year now. How can I rush to an understanding of everything I have learned? When I start to write about what I discovered, I am going to focus on the safe facts first: the letters to agents, the conversations about literary conventions, and the state of feminist politics as you saw them. One day in the future though, I am going to have another long visit with you. This time we will meet in my home. I will invite you into my private space, and I hope that we will talk as friends do.

In solidarity,
Kathryn

Dear Alice James Raccoona Tiptree Sheldon, Jr.,

I stole that naming from Ursula Le Guin's introduction to your 1978 Del Rey paperback collection, *Star Songs of an Old Primate*. I'm glad I found it, since the question of what to call you has been my biggest hurdle in composing this. It's funny the things that will stop a person from writing sometimes, the little things that result in a letter being stuffed into a drawer or discarded. Names are important, and I didn't want to use the wrong one. I'll use them all, just to be safe.

I considered "Dear Mr. Tiptree" because Tiptree is the name on the stories I adore most. At the same time, I wondered if in using that name at this late date I would fail to acknowledge the woman behind it. Perhaps you would appreciate that. Perhaps there was a thrill in using his name, in your coded correspondence, in reading the knowing essays about your ineluctable maleness.

If I wrote "Dear Ms. Sheldon" it might have addressed Alli or Raccoona. Would that be a presumption in itself? Was there a further freedom you gained in Raccoona's creation, another splitting of yourself? I'm not sure I have the right to address one for a story attributed to another.

Years ago, I wrote concert reviews under a pen name. I chose the first name of a favorite musician, and a surname from my wife's family, ethnically and culturally thousands of miles from my own identity. I found it both freeing and dissociative. And yet, when I began my own music career, I never once considered using a stage name. I did have to become a different person in order to get on stage in front of ten thousand people. I had to become a person who wore clothes that ordinary me wouldn't wear, whose body language was bolder than my own. I had to inhabit a space that was larger than myself. She and I have moved closer to each other over the years; I've become more of her and she's become more of me. Do we have that in common?

I'll start again.

Dear Alice James Raccoona Tiptree Sheldon, Jr.,

That Le Guin introduction says a lot of things I wish I could say, and some I'm in no position to say. She speaks so beautifully about the person who is both Tiptree and Sheldon that I know I shouldn't bother taking that approach. She knows both of you, all of you. I can't presume to know you, and I'm no academic, so this is a fan letter. Still, I'll borrow that multiple naming, so that I can speak to all of you at once.

I know what I want to tell you, about what your stories have meant to me, about the electric pulse of them. About the ways I've tried to carry those rhythms, to adapt those energies to my own style, even if I could never approach your brilliance. About the darkness of your vision, and the way that darkness somehow nonetheless hides a seed of hope, or if not hope, at least beauty; about how even your story titles make me weep at their power and perfection. The weight they carry, those titles.

I'm sitting at my kitchen table with three paperback collections: the aforementioned *Star Songs of an Old Primate*, *Out of the*

Everywhere, and *Warm Worlds and Otherwise*, with its oft-quoted Silverberg introduction. Also a hardcover first edition of *Up the Walls of the World*. I stole all four off my parents' shelves years ago. I don't remember when I read them first, or when I read them last. I have always read them. I have never not read them. There may have been some sort of osmosis involved.

Stories are like rivers; you never enter the same one twice. The words are locked in, the structures, the characters, but the reader approaches as a different person every time. I don't remember what I got from yours in my teenage years. I blame the electricity. Your stories fried my circuits. Reboot. Start again.

There are themes the younger me couldn't have grasped. She marveled at those most alien of aliens in "Love is the Plan the Plan is Death," but I don't know that she recognized the more mundane alien-ness at play in "The Women Men Don't See." I don't think she saw the weariness or the darkness that underpins so many of your stories.

For a while, in later reads, the darkness was overwhelming. There were stories to which I swore I would never return. Your vision of humanity, as presented in your stories, is not mine. I think I'm glad of that. You present characters who struggle and rage against inevitabilities that I hope are not inevitable, who claim such small victories and are grateful for any victory at all. CP's doomed romance in "With Delicate Mad Hands," the transformations in "A Momentary Taste of Being." Then I read them again, and find something cathartic in that same darkness. I read them again and find whole new layers.

Your titles. Those lyrical, unforgettable titles. They sparkle, they spark, they stand steady under the weight of the stories resting upon their frames. I may not remember when I first read any particular story, but the second I see each title, I know exactly which one it is, and I'm excited all over again.

I had planned to write a calm and collected letter, writer to writer, about how impressive I find your stories. I would find some other common ground. A mutual love of ____ or ____ , something external to our writing that nonetheless informs it.

Unfortunately, as you may have noticed, I will not be able to complete that letter as planned. The thing is, I have to gush. If you can't gush about your favorite writers, what can you gush about? Sure, gushing AT said writer is not exactly smiled upon. It's an awkward position to put somebody in. I've learned to talk drinks or weather or anything else but the matter at hand, which is simply: I love your stories.

I love your stories. I come back to them again and again because I am not the same for having read them, and the new me can read them again and be transformed into someone else entirely. If one of these me-people, one of these days, could write a story half as brilliant as any of yours, I think I can safely speak for all of the me-people in saying that would make me very happy. In the meantime, I'll simply say thank you.

Sincerely,
Your fan(s?),
Sarah Pinsker

Dear Zora,

Don't be scared. I can imagine how a letter, appearing out of nowhere on a desk of a high school teacher, might be strange and unsettling. Please believe me, you are not going mad, you are not in danger, and this is not somebody's wicked idea of a practical joke.

I want to make you the Bulgarian James Tiptree Jr. Actually, her real name is Alice Sheldon, but first I have to explain myself. I am from the future, and I just managed to get hold of a time machine. I have it for a short while, and I have to hurry, but I have written this letter in my mind many times before. I really have to put words on paper, because my machine is not like the one of Herbert Wells, that travels back and forth. This one can only send things back in time.

The idea to write to you came up many years ago, when somebody organized an essay competition about Tiptree. They asked us to write a letter to her. She was famous, she had become an icon because she was a woman who wrote speculative fiction. At the time she wrote, this was almost exclusively a men's field, and she was a woman, so she took a man's pen name. Tiptree wrote a lot about gender, sometimes subtly, other times directly. Sometimes she was locked into the gender pigeonhole, but I think she was much more than that, a philosopher writer, with a great range of ideas.

All this happened ... for you it will happen in 1967. In a way, *he* was born in 1967, although Sheldon at the time was in her fifties. I realize that this is the same year you published... again, you *will* publish your novel *The Treasure of the Planet Earth*. You see, old science fiction books are a hobby of mine. I write a series of retro reviews, called *Resurrected Books*. And I noticed *The Treasure* because it was the first novel in the Bulgarian speculative fiction genre written by a woman.

Don't get discouraged, please! I started reading it because of your gender, but your book was interesting. It is just that about two decades later the political system in Eastern Europe collapsed, and the books based on the communist idea became unpopular. It is not your fault you were born when you were born. Besides, the novel was a valuable document of the epoch. I read it, and I enjoyed it, and this is what matters. The thing I liked most about it was the positive outlook to the future. Books nowadays are somewhat darker than in your age, and the futures are usually dystopian, that is, the opposite of utopian, but this is because these settings tend to generate more suspense, I think. I like to think.

Stripped of the details, the plot of the novel you will write sounds like this: emissaries from a doomed alien civilization arrive on Earth in search of a better place to make a life, but at first they contact the wrong people, who hurt them trying to extort wealth and technological secrets. Eventually, the good Earthlings save the extraterrestrials and help them to revitalize their civilization. The advanced alien technology opens deep space to humanity. The story would sound familiar to my contemporaries; many modern day space operas... let's say, space adventures, have re-told it, or various aspects of it. The moral dilemma was whether to help or not to help the aliens, who would eventually grow to compete with humanity for the resources of Earth and the entire Milky Way, for that matter. Some characters chose to walk the altruistic path, and all humanity was rewarded at the end.

Your story was told ... it will be told ... oh, forget it ... it was told in a key that essentially rehearsed the East-versus-West conflict. I know, this was a major concern in the sixties, when the Cold War could turn hot at any moment, and the nuclear threat was at its peak, but this was not the only topic to write about. In 1967, the Hugo (a prestigious award in the genre) for best novel went to Robert Heinlein's *The Moon is a Harsh Mistress*—a story of a revolution against a corrupted world government. Runner ups were *Babel-17*, a novel by Samuel R. Delany about a weaponized language that could control people's behavior, and *Flowers for Algernon* by Daniel Keyes—a novel about evolution, neurodiversity, the nature of intelligencec, finding and losing love.

I do appreciate your effort. Unfortunately, it was lost, because you entrenched the novel in the present-day problems and realities that surrounded you. Tiptree looked beyond these, or rather, she turned to the deep biological drives, that moved the individuals, people or aliens. He has a story about a world, where the aliens underwent a strange life cycle. They were intelligent beings during the Summers, but lost their intelligence and become animals during the harsh Winters. I am sure you would be protesting—it should be another way around, the intelligence would be needed to survive the harder times. This is Tiptree's provocation—to make us wonder what is the primary mode of survival—reasonable collaboration or wild competition. I am also sure, given the moral choice that the characters in your novel must face, that you have something to say on the subject. Go and say it.

Sheldon was born in 1915; you were just five years older than her. You both have seen revolutions, you both have taken part in World War II. You both know personal loss. At any given moment you are at least as experienced, wise and world-weary as her, probably more. Of course, being born in a small country in the East, you won't have access to many works of speculative fiction that we now consider classics, and there won't be much of an organized fandom in Bulgaria for years to come. Still, there are some people you could check your literary watch with: the works of Svetoslav Minkov from the 1920s are still around, and the new books of Strugatsky and Efremov will soon break the monotony of the Easter speculative fiction landscape.

The conflict that brought down the alien civilization in your novel was internal—one tribe (I suppose, this was an euphemism for a country), more violent then the rest, got hold of weapons of mass destruction and ruined the planet with them. Another echo from the Cold War, but a valuable seed that could have germinated into a great story. Tiptree also took the realities of the Cold War, and turned them into a story of a disillusioned bioweapons expert who travels around to carry a murderous virus, designed to completely obliterate humanity. What set him on this killing path? The desire to punish humanity or to free the planet? Later, Tiptree reversed the idea into a tragic love story of a planet and a woman. Who betrays whom, and who punishes whom for this betrayal? Offering alternatives like these is what sets apart the great writer from a merely good one. I see in your book the possibilities to take this road, and I wish you could have used them.

You wrote about interstellar space travel. It is often used to bring vastly different cultures into contact. But your aliens are essentially troubled copies of the humans, and the only significant difference they have from us is their advanced space travel. What if they were radically different? The differences don't have to be physical. Tiptree used the time dilation of space travel to transport three near-future men to a far-future female-only society. Some resources, including water, oil, and gender, or even such intangible thing as imagination, are often exhausted or killed off in the speculative fiction of my times; it provides a powerful plot device). Unlike many others, he refrained from a violent exploitation of this premise, preferring instead to reveal slowly the enormity of the differences between the societies from which the men and the women originated. Or another of his stories comes to mind, in which the alien tourists came to visit Earth, to remain surprised at not finding any living gods walking amidst humans.

The first landing of the aliens in *The Treasure* takes them to the West, into a country tellingly named Dollarland. You proceed to criticize Western consumerism, the corruption of their politicians, and the power of the big corporations. Tiptree wrote a novella about a girl, locked in an ugly body, who is offered the social role of what thirty years later would be called a reality TV star. Like yours, it is a work that criticizes the mass obsession of beauty products and appearances, of the reality where merciless corporate competition rules the day. But a great writer like Tiptree could turn this otherwise one-dimensional arrow of a storyline into a debate of the nature of the personal I. Who is the protagonist—the deformed woman or the picture perfect fifteen years old starlet? Is the artificial body, powered by an external brain, an object or a subject? Is she a victim of the society, forced to live a virtualized life, or a collaborator, inflicting on the mass mind the idea of pseudo-perfection at all costs? The character didn't rebel against the system, and fell victim to misguided love, punished for the discord between mind and body that was not her fault.

I know I am harsh on you and your writing. I apologize. I tried to be kind, but there is a lot I have to tell you, and there is only so much I can include in a short letter. I think you deserved a better future, and I hope this piece of paper inspires you to reach for it. It seems pathetic to hope to change somebody's life with a couple of thousand words, but then greater ideas have been written on pieces of paper, smaller than this one, and with far fewer words.

Sheldon was a powerful and atypical writer. Only a handful of others can be compared with her: Philip K. Dick, Samuel R. Delany, a few others. I am offering you a great challenge, and I am asking you to take a long and difficult path.

Good luck,
a fan
Valentin

PS A fan in my time is called an admirer of somebody's work.

Jun 4-7, 2015

Garching bei Munich

Germany

Dear James,

I am finding it very hard to express myself. So please forgive me for my stutters, my mistakes and words that might sound strange to you.

I hope this letter doesn't come across as fangirling. Oh yes, fangirling. A new word. That means "in total awe of idol so much so that person is in total joy". So. Ahem. Here I go.

You are an enigma. You are also an inspiration. You are what we should aspire to. It would be your forty-eighth birthday. It would be your one hundredth too, if you take Alice Sheldon into account. You would have lived a long and rich life. But in so many ways, you still do.

I think I first 'saw' you fifteen years ago. Your story sank into me when I read a book about Wiscon and feminist science fiction, gifted to me by the late Philippa Madden on my MA graduation night. Here you are: Alice, Raccoona, James—one and the same person. I was gobsmacked. How could one person be three persons at the same time?

Back then I was a baby writer. Of course, I started writing when I was a teenager. But I only started to take myself seriously when I was in my mid-twenties. I dipped my toes in fanfiction. I wrote dribs and drabs for university magazines and the LBTQ version of the *Prosh* paper at UWA (The University of Western Australia). I had my first rejection letter (it stung) and I had my first open-mic experience. I used many pseudonyms, especially for my fanfiction.

With my pseudonyms, I was able to hide in plain sight and write what was not acceptable in the eyes of the mainstream. I was an Asian writing slash.

You did something like that too, right? Hiding in plain sight. You wrote and drew, in an environment that was unfriendly to women writers and gosh, to creativity itself. You created. And when I heard about you, you made me go "wow" and sit up. I wasn't alone. I am not alone. I am never alone. Even now, when I write under my real name and a pseudonym (because urban fantasy by women is apparently girl cooties!), I know that I am not alone in this. This hiding from plain sight. Publishing hasn't been a level playing field.

You also made me question gender and names and how fluid they are. Gender is fluid. Alice to James to Raccoona. Names are not fixed. We are not confined by who and what we are.

Or are we?

Where I am from, my name defines who I am. A direct translation means Dawn Flower/Rose. That's my Chinese name, by the way. Joyce was a later add-on, when Christian/English names became the norm/craze in Singapore. So I am Joyous and Dawn Rose. But when I started submitting fiction, my name pigeonholed me to the realm of the Cultural Revolution, bound feet and angst, even though I wasn't born in China. My paternal grandparents were. They fled their village. China, at that time, was facing famine and civil war. Nanyang was their promised land, a place where they could find safety and work. I am a second/third generation

Chinese, born in Singapore. My knowledge of China is at best second-hand, restricted to stories and touristy experiences.

Even now, even with the push for diversity in the United States (the rest of the world is already diverse, mind you), people still expect a certain something from Asian writers. Yet, nothing is more ironic when we write something Asian and are branded as "too Asian". So, what does the world expect me to do?

I will still write and speak my own voice, my own truth.

My name is mine. You have encouraged me to be brave with it. Experiment with it. Play with it. Be comfortable with it, because ultimately, we are who we are. Our names do not limit us. They might mark and identify our writing at that particular time, because writing matures and evolves like a person or a good wine.

Our names do not limit us.

Our names should not limit us.

Our names will not limit us.

I apologize, James, I have to stop writing for a while. I am trembling a bit from those words of mine to you. They thunder to you through the ether.

Did you tremble when you wrote? Did you tremble, because you were afraid? Did you?

Your life gave me hope. Your life inspires me so much. Even when I tremble and feel my voice stifled and choked in my throat, I remember you and I write on. Even when I suffer a bad case of imposter syndrome, I write on. I have to tell myself that my writing means more than just this, that I am more than just a name.

My voice is needed.

My voice is valuable.

My voice is brave, unsilenced, loud.

This letter is a letter of gratitude, to you and to your work.

Thank you, thank you, thank you.

Yours most sincerely,

Joyce Dawn Flower Chng

Dear Alice,

The short version of this letter is really, really short. It reads: Thank you. The longer version goes like this…

You said once, in an interview with *Isaac Asimov's Science Fiction Magazine*, that you'd had too many experiences being the first woman in some damned occupation. As a woman who grew up to reap the benefits of your pioneering—and the pioneering of your peers, those intrepid women who refused to remain shackled, diminished and dismissed by social expectations and pressures—I can only imagine the battles you fought, the scars they left on your soul. How weary you must have felt, so often, as you ran the gauntlet of male derision, challenged society's presumptions and its attempts to define or silence you. Carving out a place for yourself in domains traditionally occupied by men; in particular the world of literature. Your courage humbles me. Where would I be today without it?

I shudder to think.

A century has passed since the year you were born. *One hundred years*. I am amazed when I think of it. So much has changed in our world since the day you entered it. Right now, I'm re-reading a favourite novel: *Gaudy Night*, by Dorothy L Sayers. One of its themes is the place of women in the world, the struggle to be taken seriously, to be recognised by men as intellectual equals. To be seen as people first, gender second, so that talent and contributions and achievements are judged on merit, without bias. The book was written in, and is set in, the mid-1930s. The struggles it dramatises are the struggles you faced, growing up. Reading that book while thinking about composing this letter, somehow it's helped me get closer to you.

I've also been reading discussions on the internet about the current portrayal of women in popular culture, in fiction. Right now, as I pen this letter, there's a loud outcry from certain quarters because Charlize Theron's character Furiosa, in *Mad Max: Fury Road*, is prominently figured in the story—as an individual, with her own narrative, her own authority and agency, instead of being simply the appendage of a male heroic character. There's also a loud outcry over the use of women's rape as a storytelling device in the dramatised version of *A Game of Thrones*.

It's so strange. On the one hand, it grieves me beyond words that we are still being confronted by this kind of gender nonsense. But on the other hand, I am heartened by the responses I'm reading. The men who are threatened by a strong female character, Furiosa, are remarkable because they are being seen by the online community— which reflects the real world community—as increasingly out of touch and backward-thinking. No longer the silent, complacent majority, no longer the default position in our society, instead they are increasingly dismissed as anachronisms—by men as well as women. The day you were born, Alice, the world was at war. And while there were indeed heroic women in that terrible conflict, they were largely rendered invisible by the men who recorded that era. One hundred years later, a heroic woman is being celebrated. True,

Furiosa is a fictional character—but we know the power of stories. We know that the tales we tell ourselves often come true in real life. That so often real life changes *because* of the stories we tell.

The reactions to the use of rape in *A Game of Thrones* is also heartening. There is a longstanding tradition in fiction of all genres, in which women exist only to propel the men on their narrative journey. The women are murdered or raped or otherwise conveniently misused or sidelined so that the story can then focus on the men's needs. The women in these stories are catalysts, nothing more. Of course, you know all about that. You wrote, with sorrow, anger and eloquence, about the invisibility of women. I can't tell you how much I wish this tired trope was long since done with. Sadly, I can't. But what I *can* tell you is that more and more men and women are rejecting it, loudly. There are real conversations happening, passionate and informed and persuasive and *immediate*, about violence perpetrated upon female characters in order to further a male character's journey—or simply to be 'shocking' or 'adult'. There's also vigorous discussion about the use of female nudity and sexuality, the oppressive and omnipresent use of the 'male gaze', where women are reduced to sexual objects for male gratification.

That remains a problem, I can't deny it. And yet—there's *Spartacus*. Where male nudity is prevalent, the male body uncovered, displayed, in the way women's bodies have been displayed forever. One hundred years ago—hell, *ten* years ago—that was unthinkable. But the groundswell of change continues.

The world at large today, a century after you were born, remains hostile to many, many women. But in the world of science fiction and fantasy, a new reality burns bright. Women's voices are heard everywhere. Women write books. We direct and produce film and television and we write the scripts. Women star in the films and the TV shows. Women publish. Women edit. Women win awards.

Speaking of which, I was honoured to have two books short-listed for the 2007 James Tiptree Jr. Award. But you know what's amazing? When I wrote those books, the idea that I might be doing something unusual or award-worthy, that I might be challenging the status quo or gender stereotyping, that never occurred to me. I was telling a story, that's all. A story about two women fighting to control their own lives, create their own destinies. Sure, I had a bunch of male characters too, but just like in *Mad Max: Fury Road*, their journeys weren't the only journeys, or the most important. In my stories, the women stood side by side with the men. They mattered as much, they achieved as much, they succeeded and failed, as much as the men.

Not once, not *once*, while I was writing those books, did I think I was doing anything remarkable. Why would I? I had the example of so many astonishing female novelists to follow: Lois McMaster Bujold, Octavia Butler, Ursula Le Guin, CJ Cherryh, Mercedes Lackey, Kate Elliott, Katherine Kerr, Melanie Rawn, Katherine Kurtz, Anne McCaffrey, Jennifer Roberson, JV Jones, Kage Baker, Sara Douglass, Diana Wynne Jones, Connie Willis, Janny Wurtz...

With their voices—and many, many more—singing so sweetly, so proudly, how could I think I wouldn't be heard?

Without your example, without your courage and your willingness to write about women, the things that matter to women, the way society looks at and uses and abuses and discards and dismisses women, the power and strength and truths of women, the pitfalls of being human, the ecstasy and agony of life ... without your woman's voice speaking up in a time when women were expected to remain silent, to remain circumspect, to accept a permanent subordinate position in the human race ... then perhaps the women who inspired me would have instead done what was expected of them. Perhaps I'd have done the same.

Honestly, I think it's shameful that you needed to adopt a male pseudonym for your work. Even now, women sometimes do the same, and for the same reasons. Things might be changing, but change is hard and it's too damned slow. There's a part of me that mourns the fact that for so long you let the world think you were a man. But I get it. The bitter truth is that there was no other way for your work to be judged on its merits alone. Without all the baggage that goes along with being one of the first, of being a woman playing a man's game.

And let's face it. The delicious glee when the truth was finally revealed ... and all the praise of your work could not be unsaid and unwritten ... that was sweet.

You're right. It's a thankless task, going first. Being a pioneer. Breaking the rough, rough ground so that those who follow you might travel more easily. Of course, the ground is still rough in too many places, and we who follow in your footsteps must work hard to make sure we finish what you started and ensure the path is tended, to fight the regressive thinking that wants to take us back to the bad old days. We owe you that. But more, we owe you today.

Thanks, Alice. Your life wasn't easy but it was inspirational. Wherever you are, I hope you know the difference you made. I hope you're proud. I hope you're happy.

Peace,

Karen Miller

Dear Alice/James/Raccoona,

(Why choose? You didn't.)

I hope you'll be pleased to know that your work is still easily found in print, and often read, discussed, and taught in university courses. I picked up a collection of some of your best stories from my local public library. There's also an annual award given in your name for excellence in SFF that explores or expands gender (I've chaired one of the juries). An excellent biography of you by Julie Phillips came out a few years back.

Your legacy seems to be doing fine, in case you were worried.

I've been an editor in SFF for about seven years now. Amusingly, my fiction editing career began on the south side of Chicago, five blocks away from your childhood home in Hyde Park. At Harold's Chicken Shack (built long after your time there), Tiptree Award-winner Catherynne M. Valente suggested that I take over as the new editor of *Apex Magazine* when she stepped down from that position. I ended up doing so, and after a couple of years, moved on to found a new market, *Uncanny Magazine*, in partnership with my husband.

Given how often your name has come up over the course of my editorial career, I was glad for the opportunity to spend some quality time with your work through the call for contributions to *Letters to Tiptree*.

Damn. Even given that this particular collection, *Her Smoke Rose Up Forever*, is considered to have gathered the absolute best of your work, I can easily see why an award got named for you.

Here are some things that completely impress me about your work.

Your explorations of gender, and gender roles, how we inhabit and perform them, and how they can change, shape—and, in some cases, completely *warp*—ourselves and our individual psyches, and the societies we construct and in which we function, is astonishing. In story after story, the theme that jumps out at me is that our insistence upon shoving ourselves into specific, binary boxes of what men "should do/be" and women "should do/be" is detrimental to *everyone*, no matter how well we do or do not fit into those rather specific boxes. You demonstrate how easily we turn our anger upon each other, instead of at the boxes.

Your work would likely resonate strongly with later gender theorists like Judith Butler, whose foundational book *Gender Trouble* describes gender as a performance. In your stories, characters struggle mightily with that performance, even when they "succeed" at it. You explore, in story after story, how the boxes keep us making the same mistakes: they inform and enforce our relationships with power or a lack thereof. And everything seems to grow out of that.

"The Girl Who Was Plugged In" explores the existence of P. Burke, a young woman from the bottom of the economic scale who accepts an offer to have her personality projected into a newly generated, undamaged body, that she controls from an immersion tank. P. Burke's new flesh avatar, Delphi, is held up as an ideal image of young womanhood, and used for product placements in reality television. Burke falls in love with Isham, who falls in love with Delphi, not realizing the existence of Burke. The story works out about as well as a reader may expect, exploring the tensions between the existences of Burke and Delphi, who share a brain and personality, but radically different physical experiences.

CP in "With Delicate Mad Hands" spends the entire first half of the story attempting desperately to be invisible to protect herself. The verbal and physical abuse heaped upon her merely for daring to exist while unattractive is jarring in its familiarity. Her invisibility handily lends itself to her plan to escape Earth society all together, after murdering the colleagues that tormented her so viciously. In the second half of the story, she finally experiences happiness and actual kindness and affection just before she dies of radiation poisoning on another planet. Humans, and the ways we treat each other simply based upon our perception of what one "should" do or be based upon physical or social markers of gender and sex, are the real monsters.

In "The Women Men Don't See," Mrs. Parsons and her daughter are stranded, along with Don Fenton, in the Yucatan. The interactions between Fenton and Parsons when they go off and search for water alone illuminate the continuously challenging social navigation required of both parties to function adequately as a team. Mrs. Parsons ultimately, in this story, seeks escape from society by leaving the planet, much like CP above, but without resorting to murder.

"Houston, Houston, Do You Read?" plays with the notion of how gender roles change as time goes by and societies change. In this case, in our near future, a reproductive sterilization virus on Earth leads to clones—mostly female-gendered—trying to keep society going. A previously lost space capsule from Earth, full of men who retain their socially sanctioned 1960s attitudes towards women (from anti-sex zealot to self-styled lotharios) is picked up by spacefaring future Earth clones. The tensions and clashes resulting from differing ideas of gender roles and identity cause massive problems for *everyone* involved.

I must admit, I'm a bit disturbed at the dim view you seem to take of humanity. Of course, lovely, happy people don't always make the most interesting stories. Yet every character in these stories makes choices that make *perfect sense* for them in the frames you've constructed or reflected back at us. Your stories show humans replicating the same struggles over and over again, from planet to planet, from interaction to interaction, stuck in an endless loop of shame, self hatred, and outward-facing anger at anything that doesn't *fit*. We are, on our best day, toddlers who smash things—and people—when they don't work as expected. We smash a lot in your stories.

Perhaps your framing for "the human condition" is that we rarely feel as though we fit somewhere. Or anywhere. While that's distressing, it's hard to categorically state that you're totally wrong, no matter how much I would prefer to be less cynical.

Your work embraces a lack of easy answers.

Your stories have two endings. The initial ending, where the logical conclusion arrives tidily, and I get a sense of satisfaction that the ending was earned. And the second ending, which comes about ten minutes later, when my back brain has a chance to finish parsing what you just pulled off in terms of emotion, character, framing, plot, and worldbuilding. "Your Faces, O My Sisters, Your Faces Filled of Light" is disturbing, and brilliant, because there is no easy answer to whether the protagonist is better off in her delusions, where she is completely trusting, and happy, or in the "real world," which seems to be in a police state in which she has already been institutionalized.

That is a lot to accomplish with such elegance in short form. You were, given my difficulty in adequately addressing this topic, way better at it than I am. It was a challenge to wrap my brain around some of the things that you accomplish in your stories, while still articulating them to both myself and the readers of this letter.

Perhaps that's as it should be. I suspect I could spend a lot of time re-reading your work and attempting to parse it. It's perhaps more valuable to encourage people who haven't read you before to get their hands on your work as soon as possible, to see for themselves what I've struggled here to convey.

They won't be sorry. And neither will I.

Fondly,
Lynne M. Thomas

~~Dear Alice, James, Raccoona,~~

If I may…

~~Dear Alli~~

Too familiar

~~Dear Tip~~

Possibly ditto

~~Dear Alli-Tip-Raccoona~~

Too ponderous.

Protocols exist in letter-writing, which survive even when the actual physical pen and paper have vanished into the virtual world of email. How to address a beloved ghost, a stranger but eerily familiar? The task is made even more difficult by the emotions summoned in memory of another ghost, familiar and family, one Marian Sussex.

She was my mother, a contemporary of Tiptree, one year younger. Both lived through many of the same struggles, as creative women of strong personality and feminist sympathies, doomed to live in the twentieth century. At the end of Marian's long life she had no interest in the new internet, but she had always written letters, articulate and rather too empathic. After her death, I told a fellow art-student of hers, recently bereaved, that somewhere/somehow Marian was writing a letter of condolence. I do not believe in any particular afterlife, but people leave traces of themselves, like footprints in time. In some cases they are powerful, persistent.

As yours are, dear Tiptree.

To: James Tiptree Jr
Tip@Tiptree.com
From: lsussex@writer.com.au

I sit writing these words, the day after Mother's Day, on a beach in Sabah, North-Eastern Malay Borneo. You sailed through the South China seas once, with your powerful, intelligent mother, seeking the matrilineal societies of the Minangkabau, Sumatra. I was in Borneo for a wedding, of a New Zealand couple, the bride as Anglo as I am, my niece Julia, the groom Iqbal, half Sikh, half Dusan (indigenous Borneo). It was a conjunction hardly to be envisaged when you ventured across these seas. After the wedding, a civil ceremony held on a resort beach, we travelled inland to attend a village party of 700 souls. There I had conversations about Indigenous peoples, Australian refugee policy, and how Sabah had been Paradise until it had been taken over by monkeys—and they were not talking about orangutans.

All such matter is grist to a writer's mill, and particularly for you, dear Tiptree, with your first-hand experience of empires rising and falling, colonialism at work. It was something you witnessed as a child, a little girl in white frock and pith helmet, a white-faced doll on display, among a cabinet of exotica, *Alice in Elephant-* and *Jungleland*, the raw material of your mother Mary Bradley's books.

Mothers make daughters, for better and worse. I give thanks to Marian for rearing me as a feminist, in the wake of first-wave feminism, the vote for women gained, in New Zealand in 1893, followed by the Austral colonies. Thirty thousand signed a petition for female suffrage in the colony of Victoria in 1891. Various female relatives of mine signed it, but only one direct ancestor, a paternal great-grandmother, Temperance activist Nancy Wardman Sussex.

For whatever reason, the matrilineal line did not sign the petition. And here is the rub, the moment that created a feminist, the child Marian hearing the open regrets that she had not been a boy. Thus a difficult, passionate, impressionable girl internalised the need for the missing son, and set out to over-compensate. It took various forms, agonising twistings and turnings, most of which you experienced too, dear Tiptree, with the same level of white-hot intensity. As you said in your male persona: "women are human beings who have been drastically oppressed, deprived, and warped out of shape by our male-dominated and largely lunatic culture."[1] Mid-century, unhappy women were legally drugged into

1   James Tiptree Jr, "With Tiptree Through the Great Sex Muddle", *Khatru* 3-4 (Nov. 1975) 17.

silence. You sought meaning, purpose, in art studies, debutante marriage, enlistment in WWII, your PhD in psychology … until along came the stories, out of the blue, a late blooming of talent, and all the more powerful for it.

You had the chance to study art, but abandoned it: "I was just good enough to understand the difference between my talent and that rare thing, REAL ability."[2] Marian did not doubt her talent, but had to wait through years of dutiful marriage and motherhood, travelling the world from France to England to the tropics, before being able to explore it.

I am drawing similarities, dear Tiptree, and here is the direct link. My family was living in tropical Australia, in the heat and humidity which I experience here in Borneo. It brings back the memories hard and fast from a dark time of life. I read a lot of science fiction, obsessively. The end of the world, not the post-war apocalypses, but the entropy of J. G. Ballard's "The Voices of Time" and other works, seemed a most attractive idea. You wrote of your teenage years, how the feeling of being "one dot of life among billions of brief lives on an insignificant planet" was personally liberating. "My life, my death—Sirius was utterly indifferent. And that was so comforting, the cold indifference of those stars."[3]

At the time Marian was emerging from her own vortex of despair, and trying to connect with a surly teenager, her youngest

2   James Tiptree Jr, "Everything but the Signature is Me, " *Khatru* 7, (Feb. 1978) 9.

3   Quoted in Julie Phillips, *James Tiptree Jr: the Double Life of Alice B. Sheldon* (New York: St Martins, 2006) 66.

child. She picked up my library copies of Le Guin and instantly admired them. For Tiptree she had a different, visceral reaction: a "Wow!" Dear Tiptree, you took no prisoners, neither in style nor subject matter. After I got more into the fanzine culture, and read Tiptree's non-fiction, the shared experience of the two women born in the WWI years, though living thousands of miles apart, became apparent. Trying to please everyone, whilst being profoundly untrue to themselves, with appalling damage to the psyche. And then, in middle age, kicking off the shackles, in an incredible burst of creativity.

These late but formidable bloomings came some ten years apart. The Tiptree persona began in the late sixties, early seventies. Marian had her chance at serious art work a decade later, with a fine art degree completed in her sixties. She was thus in full artistic bloom when Alice Sheldon died. I heard the news while attending the 1987 SF World Convention in Brighton. It came as a profound but not wholly unexpected shock. "Mother's ghost [did] Tiptree in", you wrote, words that remain genuinely chilling.[4] James Tiptree Jr got de-bagged, and the writer was never quite the same, nor the person. Tiptree died a long time before Alice, but the themes—of sex, death, annihilation—had been visible in your work almost from the beginning.

The story I liked most of the late works was "Slow Music", with its elegiac end, the boy following the girl following the milch-deer into "the closing mists of infinity". Marian didn't like that ending;

---

4   James Tiptree Jr, "Everything but the Signature is Me," *Khatru* 7, (Feb. 1978) 16.

she wanted human life to survive. It was a profound difference between mother and daughter, but it was the conclusion you chose.

I wrote to Jeff Smith in the weeks following Alice Sheldon's death, wanting to write a biography. He never replied, and when we finally met, we agreed it would have been a difficult project to write from Australia. In any case my head was full of another beloved ghost, roused from researching the nineteenth-century crime writer Mary Fortune, a personality so strong I experienced a near-haunting. For the sake of my sanity, I did not really want so close an engagement with the dead again. It was too disturbing.

I raised funds for the Tiptree award, even judged it, and from going to Wiscon gained a World Fantasy shortlisting for *She's Fantastical*, co-edited with Judith Buckrich. When Julie Phillips' biography was published in 2006, I reviewed it and lent my prized hardback of the book to Marian, in the last year of her life. While she never ceased her art, she was debilitated by the after-effects of cancer treatment. Marian was suffering her own slow decline—early on she had read my stories and commented on them, even edited them, saying she had grown more appreciative of how writing was done as a result. Now her intellect had lost its edge, her motor control was shaky. When I got my copy of the biography back, I was angry that it was splattered with food scraps and stains, something of which she seemed unaware.

Did you, Tiptree, watch the similar decline of your beloved Ting? Is that why you loaded the gun, to create an end for two lovers that was, to borrow from Silverberg, "ineluctably masculine"?

Raging against entropy, driven by an empathy too powerful to be endured? I had to make the decision not to prolong my mother's life unnecessarily. "You decide, dear," she said, but the alternative was cruel. It was not really a choice; and she knew it.

After her death I found she had marked a passage of Le Guin's, which I read at the funeral. It might easily have been one of yours, dear Tiptree. Because, as surely as you informed my writing of sf, your example also informed Marian's late blooming, her studies and graduation from art school in her sixties, at an age when your male persona had done his brilliant dash. She became an exhibited artist, as a printmaker internationally.

I walk on the beach in Borneo, in the pre-monsoonal heat, the clouds rising high above me. Soon the crabs and migratory seabirds will dance over my footprints, in the slow natural process of erasure. Back at the wedding marquee, another marriage will be celebrated with white bougainvillea and orchids. Traces in the sands of time, a small stand against entropy, the end of the universe and all our words and deeds.

Goodbye, good wishes, my beloved ghosts
Lucy

PS There is a curious aftermath to this piece. After the wedding, we toured for three days in North Borneo, ending in Sandakhan, a city with a current travel advisory warning. It is disputed territory, close to the Sulu archipelago, Muslim Philippines. On this coast a group affiliated with the foul ISIL, the Abu-Sayyef, have been kidnapping mainly Chinese nationals for ransom ("because they pay up"). I was informed that the beaches, alone, at night, were to be avoided. We ate dinner at the Ocean King, a seafood restaurant extending over pylons into the sea. That was on the Tuesday. Two nights later, on Thursday, the terrorists arrived unobserved in a small boat and at gunpoint abducted two Malay citizens, the female restaurant manager and a male patron. The two have not been seen since.

Before leaving on my trip I had joked that I was going to Borneo for a family wedding and, I hoped, story ideas. I was not expecting a violent tale of post-colonialism and patriarchy—perfect Tiptree material.

Dear Tip,

It's late, up here on the mountain, and dark and cold. Not an auspicious evening for confessions. I've poured the wine and cleared the desk, but it's hard to make the words come, knowing you will never reply.

A little over a year ago I travelled to Wisconsin, and stood in a ballroom where a thousand people were gathered in your name. I knew you'd been to Wisconsin at least once. There was that story Peter Sheldon had told about you letting him drive your old Buick, when he was just a boy. How he'd almost killed you both, but you'd never betrayed him. You'd kept his secret right up till the day you died.

You had your own secrets. Those you kept. Those you gave away. Those that were taken from you. I've no wish to uncover any more of them. The secrets that need revealing are not about you, but about ourselves. I suspect that some of them are about why we need you. What you gave us, what you left for us. A secret debt we may never adequately repay.

It's something to imagine you in the passenger seat of that big old car as it slewed out of control across an unpaved road. As you felt your life lurch within you, almost loosen. Not for the first time, and certainly not for the last time, either, your life was in the hands of a man who had no control of the vehicle. As is mine. As are all our lives. It should have been you in the driver's seat.

It should have been you in that ballroom, too.

I'll tell you a story, shall I? Since you were always fond of a grand and audacious lie. Of the force with which a story can reveal everything by concealing the things that matter in its bones.

There's a library in the town where I grew up that had closed down before I was born. The doors were locked against the weather, but you could see through gaps in the boards across the windows that there were still books housed in that place. Books we weren't allowed to read. Books that had never been written, and would never be read.

To the left of the locked doors there was a chute into which long-dead borrowers had once tipped the books they were returning. If you went to the library at night and bent down and told your wishes to the library, they were supposed to come true. Nobody believes in wishes anymore. Or prayers or anything like that, but I was a child back then, so I made a wish.

I wished for a saviour. For an angel. For inspiration. And though you never spoke to me, though we never met, you arrived.

Did you know that in the old iconography angels were not women or men? They were absurd, impossible, monstrous things. Aliens without bodies. St Thomas Aquinas writes in the *Summa Theologica* that:

> *since the angels are not bodies, nor have they bodies naturally united with them, as is clear from what has been said, it follows that they sometimes assume bodies.*

It was cunning of you—old angel, old alien—to assume the body of a man. A body of work, that is: a body of air and ink and paper. And it was cunning, too, to lodge yourself on the shelves of a dead library, in a town at the edge of the known world, in a world at war.

Later in the *Summa*, Aquinas writes that angels form bodies out of the air. That they are air condensed by Divine power. Which seems about right. The air in that library (there is always a way to get in to where the books they keep from you are held. A lock that can be picked; a broken window you can climb through) was the stuff of angels. You could breathe it in. You could feel the words moving through you like dust.

We sat in the dank, unembarrassed ruins of the library together. You told me stories about the things between the worlds, in the gaps and chinks and narrows. You lied all the time, which was part of your charm, part of your beauty. About a woman's body held in a bunker beneath an illuminated city while the other part of herself rises up into numb beauty, about a femicidal plague, about a future without men in it. Of aliens longing for women; women longing for aliens. And men lost, rudderless, in worlds upon worlds here their sense of themselves was inverted, upended, confused.

I had known you for twenty years before I discovered that you both were, and were not, a man.

There's a story you didn't write about a boy living in a war-zone who wishes for an angel to be his friend. And the angel arrives, only he isn't 'much of a friend'.[1] When I wished for you, when I screamed into the returns chute at the shuttered library, I must

---

1 The story is Etgar Keret's 'Hole in the Wall'.

have already known that wishes never quite come true. That the magic of fairytales, and the technology of science fiction, may make things more strange, and sometimes more beautiful, but they don't make things any easier.

This is something I think you always knew. That the wishes we grant ourselves in stories reveal both our desires and our fears. Our ambition—our hope—and our despair. That women may become visible, only to disappear. That men may disappear, only to be found necessary. That we may finally escape our bodies, only to find that without them, we are lost.

In 'The Screwfly Solution' you imagined an alien race whose solution to the problem of a pre-populated earth was to infect the inhabitants with a femicidal plague.

But the truth is that here, in your future, as in my past, we are already our own mortal enemies. We hold the blade against our own throats, and those of our sisters and sons. We lay bombs in our own beds, and curl around them in our sleep. Crooning lullabies to the instruments of our impending death.

We are all, still, living in a war zone, and yours is the name of the angel I invoke to save us. An avenging, wounded angel, sword in hand, rising up from the ashes of the patriarchal ruin.

I still pray for inspiration. For the flaming swords of a thousand queer angels to show us the dark limits of our misbegotten dreams. A thousand more to illuminate the worlds we have forgotten, and the worlds we are still too timid to imagine. Worlds without wars, worlds without pain.

In a story nobody has yet written, a human and an angel-without-a-body sit on a ledge overlooking the city. The angel's body (your body) is a body made of words, made of clouds compressed by the Divine power of story. The words sink and rise along the streets, are breathed in and out by the citizens, are pressed like bombs into the hands of the children, and thrown against the walls of the city. And the walls of the world tremble and shudder. And the walls of the world fall down.

With love and admiration,
Nike

The Women You Didn't See

Dear Alice Sheldon,

YOU WERE BRILLIANT, I think, but consumed by the inevitability of the abattoir. In your fiction all the gates are closed; characters are funneled down a chute to flashing knives. In your best fiction, the characters know what is happening, but the knowledge makes no difference; there's no way out.

You didn't believe in the possibility of escape. Assuming the *nom de plume* and persona of *James Tiptree, Jr.* meant at least you could step outside the chute and be the one wielding the knife. As *Raccoona Sheldon*, on the other hand, you were bound—as were we—inside the doomed and running cows; then you sometimes tantalized your victims with a vision of a better reality before tearing it to shreds before our eyes ("Your Faces, O My Sisters! Your Faces Filled of Light!"), and sometimes you focused unwaveringly on the stark machinery of death ("The Screwfly Solution"). But for you there was no way out.

When you were little, you saw filth, death, deprivation, and suffering in India and Africa. So too, of course, did the hundreds of millions who lived there. Unlike many, you were not, as far as I know, physically brutalized. But you were alone: a pretty, pampered, privileged little girl plunged unprepared into violent contradiction—then exposed by your writer mother just before puberty to the hot breath of public scrutiny. You had no herd protection, no people just like you, nowhere to turn for comfort or take shelter. Did it warp you in the chrysalis? Or were you exactly as you were born to be?

We'll never know. And it doesn't matter. But it is why, if I had to guess, you hid all your life. Why you picked up professions and dropped them as soon as you got good, and why, when you found writing as an adult, you took pseudonyms: the best way to stay safe was not to be known. You could rotate a facet of yourself before a curtain with a single slit. No one ever got to see the whole, not even you.

We never met in person. I didn't smell your skin or feel the vibration of your voice. I can't call up a memory of how you moved or the way you responded to particular sounds. But I heard your written voice; I read your fiction. Now that you're beyond hurt, I admit: I did not admire your novels or most of your later short fiction. For this reader, you produced your best work when you were behind the curtain.

One of the things we don't know about that person, the one who hid, is whether choosing to write as a man meant you also wanted to be, or felt as though you were, a man.

You wrote a letter in response to Joanna Russ in which you said, "I am a Lesbian."[1] If this is true, you identified as a woman

---

1   A letter Tiptree sent to Russ. "Oh, had 65 years been different! I like some men a lot, but from

who loved women—or tried—rather than as a man in the wrong body. Weighed against this is the youthful (I think, and, according to your biographer, probably drunken) *cri de coeur* scribbled in a sketch pad. "[I long to] ram myself into a crazy soft woman and come, come, spend, come, make her pregnant Jesus to be a man … I love women I will never be happy…"[2] We don't know, we can't know. Given the (possible) youth and (probable) drinking this might be a melodrama of immaturity. It could be a test, an exploration of the kind teenagers indulge in, donning and doffing identities and attitudes to see what suits the emerging self. You emerged many times, of course, most spectacularly in middle age.[3] I suspect that if wanting to be a man was a thing of the body rather than the spirit, if you wanted physically to have been born a man—as opposed to yearning to be treated with the respect usually reserved to men—being among women would not have made you feel free or proud. But that's exactly how you felt when you joined the WAC: "the first time I ever felt free enough to be proud."[4]

---

the start, before I knew anything, it was always girls and women who lit me up." https://www.sfsite.com/fsf/2006/eh0610.htm

2   https://www.sfsite.com/fsf/2006/eh0610.htm

3   "How many times in one's life does a door open to total escape, utter newness? I was so profoundly dispirited, alienated [....] And suddenly I was in the middle of a different light, a new me, first having a good joke of being someone else, and then as the stories went on and out, having started genuine friendships among delightful people whose native language—crude, childish, humorous—rational—was mine…" http://jamestiptreejr.com/asawriter.htm

4   "… in the rain, under the flag, the sound of the band, far-off, close, then away again; the immortal fanny of our guide, leading on the right, moved and moving to the music—the flag again—first time I ever felt free enough to be proud of it; the band, our band, playing reveille that morning, with me on KP since 0430 hours, coming to the mess-hall porch to see it pass

So I will take you at your word: you were a lesbian, a woman who loves women.

There are two words—both with the same root in *covert*, the past participle of *covrir*, Old French for to cover—that I suspect you understood in your bones: covert and coverture. I have no doubt that working for the CIA you were deeply and consciously familiar with the denotation, connotations, and consequence of the former. The latter is a legal doctrine, probably introduced to English common law by the Normans, by which a wife's legal identity is covered and subsumed by her husband's. As Wikipedia puts it, in a marriage there is only one person, and that person is the husband. Some aspects of coverture survived into the second half of the twentieth century—fifty years and more after you were born.

This doctrine influenced the relative status, behavior, and regard (including self-regard) of women and men. Men were real people, judged as such. Women were not. And it's my belief that "James Tiptree, Jr.", three words, gave you cover, a way to be free in the world without risking a particular scrutiny. A man, even a clearly pseudonymous one, is judged as a person, not for the myriad ways she is a not-quite-person. Given your experience, you believed Tiptree could be a writer. Alice Sheldon could only have been a female not-quite-person who wrote.

---

in the cold streets, under that flaming middle-western dawn; KP itself, and the conviction that one is going to die; the wild ducks flying over that day going to PT after a fifteen-mile drill, and me so moved I saluted them [...]" http://jamestiptreejr.com/army.htm

You became Tiptree because as a man you could write what you thought and how you felt, be respected and liked. You deserved to live in a place of respect, a place we all deserve, a place we all belong: recognized as real people without having constantly to fight to be a human being. Nobody knew who James Tiptree, Jr., was. You liked that.

So why did you—ex-CIA—let slip a vital piece of information about the death of your mother that led to your unmasking?[5] Did you want, on some level, to be revealed? Or did grief fuck with your head? Grief does that; it can make you crazy.

And so you were grieving far more than your mother when your first novel came out under the Tiptree byline, but was understood to be written by Alice Sheldon. You were mourning the cover and camouflage that kept you secret, kept you safe. You had lost the hidden place that felt like home. Once again, you were exposed to the world.

I'm a woman. A dyke. Foreign (even in the UK, where now I'm often thought to be Canadian). A cripple. In today's parlance I suffer a lot of intersectional micro-aggression: the constant insult, mostly unintentional but damaging nonetheless, the unthinking words and attitudes scraping along my hull below the waterline. Most of us in oppressed groups tend to seek out our own kind as a matter of survival; people like us offer us a mirror, a place to belong and be understood. Shelter from the cold.

---

5 James Tiptree, Jr., let his fans know that his mother had died, that her name was Mary Hastings
  Bradley. The obituaries made it clear—Bradley had only one child, a daughter, Alice Sheldon

I'm the only expat lesbian cripple I know. It gets lonely.

Being out my whole life—even when I was four I knew I would not marry a man; actually falling in love with a woman when I was fifteen was just a detail—meant I never had anywhere to hide. Queer was the only minority I knew without grants, government departments or liaisons, laws, schools, or families of origin who understood how hard it is, and whose mission was your encouragement and support. I felt isolated, alone. I've no doubt you did, too. Many of us do.

So I understand why you might not have wanted to be out in the early twentieth century. Being out was hard. It cost a lot.

Of your major works, "The Women Men Don't See" is singular. Two women charter a plane and fly into the Mexican jungle with a man they meet and their pilot. It turns out they hope to be taken by aliens. They don't know what they're heading towards, exactly, don't know whether they are jumping from the frying pan into the fire. They know only that they are burning and must get out. They do. The men are left, bewildered.

Two things about this story interest me particularly. First, we are left with hope for the women, that an alien world will be better for them. It's only a sliver of hope, true, and sharp with irony, but it's there. Second, neither of the women has—as far as we know—suffered physical violence. They are damaged, yes—as are all of us who, day in and day out, navigate cold and hostile waters, scraped and battered and weighed down by that ice—but not broken, not essentially breached. They will live. They are making a choice.

It's a forced choice, but a choice. We are shown some of their circumstances but not all; we have to make assumptions. We can't know for sure whether what they're doing is a good idea.

Similarly, we can never know a writer's reasons. We can make assumptions—about why, say, for one woman gender-neutral initials will be enough to provide cover to write; why another keeps an obviously female name but clears her path by hosing everything with rage, why yet a third takes a male name—but we can never know. They all grow in different microclimates, under different gravities.

Living under a higher gravity than those around us levies a weight penalty: we have to use more energy, more strength, more attention to run the same distance and hurdle the same obstacles.

I listened the other day to a panel of women talk about diversity in fiction. They talked about how difficult it was to grow up as immigrants to another culture, how they were pressured by family to succeed in a profession—engineering, medicine, law—rather than art. Some of their experience resonated but in another way it did not. I could not imagine growing up in a world where my family and wider society assumed I was capable of a profession, where I would be welcome in a profession, where I could survive in a profession.

I can't know anyone's struggles. I do know that they and you and I labored under different burdens; our eras, places, classes, and cultures were different. But for the women on that panel access to a profession was a given. We may as well have been born on different planets.[6]

Today, women and quiltbag folk still live under a greater gravity than others, but that is changing every day. Hopefully, by the time others read this the gravity will have dropped a notch: same-sex marriage will be the law of the land. I've written elsewhere about how, in my opinion, this will change gender equality on a fundamental level.[7] It will take time, of course; it always does. But already, today, there are women growing up who will not labor under any weight penalty.

Girls losing their milk teeth today will become women who won't have the faintest idea what coverture means unless they become historians. These women will be able to put their strength, attention and brilliance into forging new paths, making new connections, dreaming of new possibilities rather than carrying extra weight or keeping themselves safe.

These are the women you didn't see. They will own the world.

Rising...
Nicola Griffith

---

6   This makes me glad — though every now and again my gladness is bittersweet. This is something anyone from any traditionally downtrodden minority understands: the new generation has no clue how hard it was. We are happy for that. Mostly.

7   "Wife," June 23, 2014, http://nicolagriffith.com/2014/06/23/wife/

Dear Alice,

The women men don't see
are sometimes seen
but our gossamer bodies
can vanish any moment.

With delicate, mad hands
we write, imagining
a momentary taste of being
equal and unfettered.

We who stole these dreams
from the ether of tomorrow
have not yet breached command
to pilot our own starships.

Alice, Alice, do you read?
We search for you by lost ways
across cold hills' sides
following your smoke, forever rising.

Your sisters! Our faces,
Our faces filled of light!
The trail you began blazes
beneath our future-bound feet.

The plan is not death.
No last flights, no screwfly solutions,
no weary souls drifting
like slow music.

Love is the plan:
One last hillside afternoon,
necks craned to watch the dream
finally launch into orbit.

We will explore nebulae,
raise children, write poems,
map alien genomes, tame singularities,
and so on, and so on.

By then, I will be with you.
In dark, in nothing, in between.
We will wait for all women born.
We will walk home together.

Rachel Swirsky

About the Authors

Kathryn Allan, PhD. is an independent scholar of feminist SF, cyberpunk, and disability studies. She is co-editor (with Djibril al-Ayad) of *Accessing the Future*, an anthology of disability-themed intersectional SF short stories (from Futurefire.net Publishing), and associate editor and reader of the speculative fiction zine, *The Future Fire*. She is editor of the interdisciplinary collection, *Disability in Science Fiction: Representations of Technology as Cure* (2013, Palgrave MacMillan), and the inaugural Le Guin Feminist Science Fiction fellow (2014). Her writing appears in both academic and creative publications, such as *The WisCon Chronicles Vol. 7* (2013, Ed. JoSelle Vanderhooft, Aqueduct Press), *Outlaw Bodies* (2012, Eds. Lori Selke and Djibril al-Ayad, futurefire.net), *SF 101: A Guide to Teaching and Studying Science Fiction* (2014, Eds. Ritch Calvin, Doug Davis, Karen Hellekson, and Craig Jacobsen, SFRA), *and Techno-Orientalism: Imagining Asia in Speculative Fiction, History, and Media* (2015, Eds. David Roh, Besty Huang, and Greta Niu, Rutgers University Press).

Kathryn's archival research focuses on the collections of Ursula Le Guin, Joanna Russ, Sally Miller Gearhart, and Suzette Haden Elgin, and was made possible thanks to the Le Guin Feminist Science Fiction Fellowship and its sponsors (Center for the Study of Women in Society, Robert D. Clark Honors College, and University of Oregon Libraries Special Collections and University Archives). She is currently writing a book exploring the intersection of disability studies theory and science fiction, which will include a chapter on the transformative potential of feminist SF.

She lives in Hamilton, Ontario with her partner Andrew J. Holden and one really unphotogenic cat, Olive. You can find her blogging and tweeting as Bleeding Chrome.

Marleen S. Barr is known for her pioneering work in feminist science fiction and teaches English at the City University of New York. She has won the Science Fiction Research Association Pilgrim Award for lifetime achievement in science fiction criticism. Barr is the author of *Alien to Femininity: Speculative Fiction and Feminist Theory*, *Lost in Space: Probing Feminist Science Fiction and Beyond*, *Feminist Fabulation: Space/Postmodern Fiction*, and *Genre Fission: A New Discourse Practice for Cultural Studies*. Barr has edited many anthologies and co-edited the science fiction issue of PMLA. She is the author of the novels *Oy Pioneer!* and *Oy Feminist Planets: A Fake Memoir*.

Aliette de Bodard lives and works in Paris where she works as a System Engineer. In her spare time, she moonlights as a speculative fiction writer. She was on the Tiptree Award Honor List for 2013, and has garnered two Nebulas, a Locus Award and a British Science Fiction Association Award. Her novel *The House of Shattered Wings*, set in a devastated and decadent Paris peopled with Fallen angels, Vietnamese immortals, witches and alchemists, was released by Roc/Gollancz in August 2015. Visit www.aliettedebodard for free fiction, book geekery and Franco-Vietnamese recipes.

Stephanie Burgis grew up in a university town in Michigan, USA, and now lives in a small market town in Wales, surrounded by castles and coffee shops. In-between, she studied music history in Vienna as a Fulbright scholar, worked for an opera company in northern England, and read as many novels as humanly possible. The first book in her Regency fantasy trilogy for kids (known as the *Kat, Incorrigible* trilogy in the US and *The Unladylike Adventures of Kat Stephenson* in the UK) won the Waverton Good Read Children's Award for Best Début Children's Novel by a British Writer. Her first fantasy novel for adults, *Masks and Shadows*, will be published by Pyr Books in 2016. She has also published over thirty short stories for adults and teens in various magazines and anthologies. To find out more, visit her website: www.stephanieburgis.com

Born in Singapore but a global citizen, **Joyce Chng** writes mainly science fiction and YA. She likes steampunk and tales of transformation/transfiguration. Her fiction has appeared in *Crossed Genres, the Apex Book of World SF II, We See A Different Frontier, Cranky Ladies of History*, and *Accessing The Future*. Her YA science fiction trilogy is published by Singapore publisher, Math Paper Press. She can be found at A Wolf's Tale (awolfstale.wordpress.com)

L. **Timmel Duchamp** is the author of two collections of short fiction (*Love's Body, Dancing in Time* and *Never at Home*), a collection of essays (*The Grand Conversation*), and six novels (The five-volume Marq'ssan Cycle and *The Red Rose Rages [Bleeding]*). She has been a finalist for the Nebula and Sturgeon awards, short-listed for the Tiptree Award several times, and awarded a Special Honor for the Marq'ssan Cycle by the 2009 Tiptree jury. She is also the founder and publisher of Aqueduct Press and has edited several anthologies. A selection of her essays and fiction can be found at ltimmelduchamp.com.

AJ Fitzwater resides between the cracks of Christchurch, New Zealand. A graduate of the Clarion class of 2014, they were awarded the Sir Julius Vogel Award 2015 for Best New Talent. Their work has appeared in *Beneath Ceaseless Skies, Crossed Genres Magazine, Scigentasy*, Lethe Press' *Heiresses of Russ 2014* and other venues of repute. A dragon-wrangler of regard, they hope to have a stellar dinner party one day with James Tiptree Jr., Joanna Russ, and Anne McCaffrey.

Lisa Goldstein has won the Mythopoeic Award, the American Book Award for Best Paperback, and the Sidewise Award. Her latest novel, *Weighing Shadows*, will be coming out this November. Her stories have appeared in *Ms., Asimov's Science Fiction, The Magazine of Fantasy and Science Fiction*, and *The Year's Best Fantasy*, among other places, and her novels and short stories have been finalists for the Hugo, Nebula, and World Fantasy awards. She lives with her husband and their irrepressible Labrador retriever, Bonnie, in Oakland, California. Her website is www.brazenhussies.net/goldstein.

Theodora Goss's publications include the short story collection *In the Forest of Forgetting* (2006); *Interfictions* (2007), a short story anthology co-edited with Delia Sherman; *Voices from Fairyland* (2008), a poetry anthology with critical essays and a selection of her own poems; *The Thorn and the Blossom* (2012), a novella in a two-sided accordion format; and the poetry collection *Songs for Ophelia* (2014). Her work has been translated into ten languages, including French, Japanese, and Turkish. She has been a finalist for the Nebula, Crawford, Locus, Seiun, and Mythopoeic Awards, and on the Tiptree Award Honor List. Her short story "Singing of Mount Abora" (2007) won the World Fantasy Award. She teaches literature and writing at Boston University and in the Stonecoast MFA Program.

Nicola Griffith is a native of Yorkshire, England, where she earned her beer money teaching women's self-defence, fronting a band, and arm-wrestling in bars, before discovering writing and moving to the US. Her immigration case was a fight and ended up making new law: the State Department declared it to be "in the National Interest" for her to live and work in the country. This didn't thrill the more conservative powerbrokers, and she ended up on the front page of the *Wall Street Journal*, where her case was used as an example of the country's declining moral standards.

In 1993, a diagnosis of multiple sclerosis slowed her down a bit, and she concentrated on writing. Her novels are *Ammonite* (1993), *Slow River* (1995), *The Blue Place* (1998), *Stay* (2002), *Always* (2007) and *Hild* (2013). She is the co-editor of the *Bending the Landscape* series of original short fiction. Her multi-media memoir, *And Now We Are Going to Have a Party: Liner Notes to a Writer's Early Life*, is a limited collector's edition. *With Her Body* (2004) collects two stories and a novella. Her essays and short fiction appear in an assortment of academic texts and a variety of journals, including *Nature*, *New Scientist*, and the *Los Angeles Review of Books*. Many of these essays and most of her short fiction have been reprinted in various anthologies. She's won the Washington State Book Award, the Tiptree, Nebula, and World Fantasy Awards, the Premio Italia, Lambda Literary Award (six times), and others. She used to review but these days prefers to comment on the work of dead writers. Every now and again she gets exasperated enough to write something about how bias works, particularly in publishing.

Nicola, now a dual US/UK citizen, is married to writer Kelley Eskridge. They met at the Clarion Writers Workshop at Michigan State University in 1988 and now live in Seattle. Nicola is currently lost in the seventh century, emerging occasionally to drink just the right amount of beer and take enormous delight in everything. You can find her at nicolagriffith.com, @nicolaz, and facebook.com/nicolagriffith.

Valentin D. Ivanov is a professional astronomer and an amateur Speculative Fiction writer. He was born in Bulgaria in 1967. He is married, with three children. Valentin received his M.S. in Physics with a specialization in Astronomy from the University of Sofia in 1992, Ph.D. in Astronomy from the University of Arizona in 2001, and has been working for the European Southern Observatory ever since. His research interests range from extrasolar planets to obscured Milky Way clusters, and has published more than one hundred refereed papers in scientific journals. Valentin began to write science fiction and fantasy in high school. He has published in his native country about forty genre stories, reviews and essays in a variety of magazines and anthologies. A collection of fantasy stories based on Bulgarian folklore, written in collaboration with Kiril Dobrev, appeared in 2006. Valentin has a special interest in promoting Bulgarian Speculative Fiction abroad, and often used Science Fiction as an educational tool to popularize science. He has published non-fiction reviews and essays in English in *New Horizons, SFF Portal* and *Europa SF*. His story "How I Saved the World", appeared in the educational anthology *Diamonds in the Sky*, edited by M. Brotheron; his story "Job Interview" appeared in the international science fiction magazine *InterNova*.

Gwyneth Jones was born in Manchester, England, educated by the long-suffering nuns of the Sacred Heart, Blackley and at Notre Dame Grammar School Cheetham Hill. She took an undergraduate degree at the University of Sussex, in History of Ideas (with Latin), specialising in seventeenth century Europe, which gave her a taste for studying the structure of scientific revolutions, and societies (scientific and otherwise) in phase transition; a background that still resonates in her work. In the seventies, she embarked on a career in the UK Civil Service, but dropped out to spend three years in South East Asia, where she found work as a freelance journalist and (briefly) a columnist for the Singapore magazine *Her World*. In the eighties, she spent two lucrative years writing scripts for a sci-fi tv cartoon series called *The Telebugs*, (giving her a curious cult status with currently thirty-something UK *Telebug* fans). Since then, she's been not so lucratively employed writing (and occasionally teaching creative writing) full time. She's written more than twenty novels for teenagers, mostly using the pseudonym Ann Halam, and several highly regarded science fiction novels for adults, notably the Aleutian Trilogy: *White Queen* (co-winner of the James Tiptree Memorial Award); *North Wind* and *Phoenix Café*; and *Life*, the fictional biography of a woman scientist of genius, and a study of the fluidity of human sexual 'gender'; winner of the P.K. Dick award. *Bold As Love*, the first novel of a series based on alternative cultures, revolution and rock music in the darkening world of the near future, won the Arthur C. Clarke award. She self-published the sixth book of the series (so far) *The Grasshopper's Child* in 2015. *The Fearman* (1995) won the Dracula Society's Children of the Night Award. Her short story collection *Seven Tales And A Fable* won two World Fantasy Awards in 1996. In 2008, she was awarded the Pilgrim lifetime achievement award for sf criticism by the SFRA. Collections of her critical writings and essays *Deconstructing The Starships* and *Imagination/Space* appeared in 1999 and 2011 respectively. She has also published short story collections, *The Universe Of Things* and *The Buonarotti Quartet* (USA), and *Gravegoods* (UK). Several stories and essays are available free on line at www.gwynethjones.uk. She practices yoga, has done some extreme tourism in her time, likes old movies, and enjoys playing with her websites. Email her at: gwyneth.jones@ntlworld.com or visit her websites: www.boldaslove.co.uk and www.gwynethjones.uk.

Sylvia Kelso lives in North Queensland, Australia. She mostly writes fantasy and SF set in analogue or alternate Australian settings, and likes to tinker with moral swords-and-sorcery and elements of mythology. She has published eight fantasy novels, including *Amberlight* and *The Moving Water*, which were finalists for best fantasy novel in the Australian Aurealis genre fiction awards. Her short stories have appeared in Australia and the US, including anthologies from DAW and Twelfth Planet Press, and the online e-zines *Luna Station Quarterly* and *Eternal Haunted Summer*. Her novella *Spring in Geneva*, a riff on Frankenstein, appeared in October 2013 with Aqueduct Press. Her most recent publication was the short story "Due Care and Attention" in the Australian anthology *Cranky Ladies of History*, in March 2015.

Rose Lemberg is a queer, bigender immigrant from Eastern Europe. Her work has appeared in *Strange Horizons, Beneath Ceaseless Skies, Lightspeed*'s special issues *Queers Destroy SF* and *Queers Destroy Horror, Interfictions, Uncanny, Sisters of the Revolution: A Feminist Speculative Fiction Anthology*, and other venues. Rose co-edits *Stone Telling*, a magazine of boundary-crossing poetry, with Shweta Narayan. She has edited *Here, We Cross*, an anthology of queer and genderfluid speculative poetry from *Stone Telling* (Stone Bird Press), and *The Moment of Change*, an anthology of feminist speculative poetry (Aqueduct Press). She is currently editing a new fiction anthology, *An Alphabet of Embers*. You can find Rose at http://roselemberg.net and @roselemberg, and support her work on Patreon at patreon.com/roselemberg

Sandra McDonald's first collection of fiction, *Diana Comet and Other Improbable Stories*, was a *Booklist* Editor's Choice, an American Library Association Over the Rainbow Book, and winner of a Lambda Literary Award. She writes adult and young adult books with gay, transgender and asexual characters, including the collection *Drag Queen Astronaut*, the thriller *City of Soldiers* (as Sam Burke) and the award-winning *Fisher Key Adventures* (as Sam Cameron). Her short fiction has appeared in *Asimov's Science Fiction*, the *Magazine of Fantasy & Science Fiction, Lightspeed, Clarkesworld, Strange Horizons*, and many other magazines and anthologies. Four of her stories have been noted on the Tiptree Award Honor List. After serving in the U.S. Navy she earned an

MFA in Creative Writing from the University of Southern Maine and currently teaches college writing in Florida. Visit her at www.sandramcdonald.com and @sandramcdonald.

Alex Dally MacFarlane is a writer, editor and historian. When not translating from Classical Armenian or researching narrative maps in the legendary traditions of Alexander III of Macedon, Alex writes stories, found in *Clarkesworld Magazine, Phantasm Japan, Solaris Rising 3, Gigantic Worlds* and *The Year's Best Science Fiction & Fantasy: 2014*. Alex is the editor of *Aliens: Recent Encounters* (2013) and *The Mammoth Book of SF Stories by Women* (2014) and in 2015 joined Sofia Samatar as co-editor of non-fiction and poetry for *Interfictions Online*. Questions of gender are vital to Alex in science fiction and history, particularly the relationship of both with each other and the present. Alex has written about post-binary gender in SF for *Tor.com* and in some fiction. Follow @foxvertebrae on Twitter for more.

Brit Mandelo is a writer, critic, and editor whose primary fields of interest are speculative fiction and queer literature, especially when the two coincide. She has two books out, *Beyond Binary: Genderqueer and Sexually Fluid Speculative Fiction* and *We Wuz Pushed: On Joanna Russ and Radical Truth-telling*, and in the past has edited for publications like *Strange Horizons Magazine*. Her other work has been featured in magazines such as *Stone Telling, Clarkesworld, Apex*, and *Ideomancer*. She also writes regularly for *Tor.com* and has several long-running column series there, including Queering SFF, a mix of criticism, editorials, and reviews on *QUILTBAG* speculative fiction.

Seanan McGuire is an American author of urban fantasy, science fiction, and biomedical horror, with a strong fascination for the sort of horrible diseases that will probably kill us all one day. She is not a comforting dinner table companion. Seanan won the John W. Campbell Award for Best New Writer in 2010. She currently lives in California with her two abnormally large blue cats, in a crumbling farmhouse filled with horror movies, comics, and of course, books. When not writing (she releases an average of four books a year), she can be found in swamps, corn fields, and Disney theme parks. No one's quite sure where that last one came from, but it keeps her happy. You can find her online at www.seananmcguire. com, which has convenient links to all the other places she hangs out. She is also Mira Grant, and doesn't seem to sleep very much.

Seanan regularly claims to be the vanguard of an invading race of alien plant people who will one day devour our world. She hasn't really done anything to make that seem unlikely.

Karen Miller was born in Vancouver, Canada, and raised in Australia where she lives today. Before she realised her dream of becoming a professional writer, she studied for and was awarded a Bachelor of Arts (Communications) degree and a Master of Arts in Children's Literature, and worked in a wide variety of jobs, including: horse groom, college lecturer, PR officer in local government, publishing assistant, and owned a specialist science fiction, fantasy and mystery book shop. She has been writing professionally since 2005, and since the publication of her first fantasy novel *The Innocent Mage* has written nineteen novels. They cover epic historical fantasy, media tie-in work for *Star Wars* and *Stargate SG-1*, and the Rogue Agent fantasy series under her pen name K. E. Mills. Her work has been shortlisted for the James Tiptree Jr award and the Aurealis Award. When she's not busy at the computer, Karen enjoys acting and directing at her local theatre company. Find her at www.karenmiller.net

Judith Moffett was born in Louisville in 1942 and grew up in Cincinnati. She is an English professor, a poet, a Swedish translator, and the author of twelve books in six genres. These include two volumes of poetry, two of Swedish poetry in formal translation, four science-fiction novels plus a collection of stories, a volume of creative nonfiction, and a critical study of James Merrill's poetry; she has also written an unpublished memoir of her long friendship with Merrill. Her work in poetry, translation, and science fiction has earned numerous awards and award nominations, including an NEA Creative Writing Fellowship in Poetry, an NEH Translation Grant, the Swedish Academy's Tolkningspris (Translation Prize), and in science fiction the John W. Campbell Award for Best New Writer and the Theodore Sturgeon Award for the year's best short story. Two of her novels were *New York Times* Notable Books.

Moffett earned a doctorate in American Civilization from the University of Pennsylvania, with a thesis on Stephen Vincent Benét's narrative poetry, directed by Daniel Hoffman. She taught American literature and creative writing at several colleges and universities, including the Iowa Writers' Workshop, the University of Kentucky, and for fifteen years the University of Pennsylvania. She has lived for extended periods in England (Cambridge) and Sweden (Lund and Stockholm), as well as around the US, living/ teaching/ writing in Kentucky, Ohio, Indiana, Colorado, Wisconsin, Iowa, Pennsylvania, and Utah. In 1983, she married Medievalist Edward B. Irving, Jr., her colleague at Penn. Widowed in 1998, Judy now divides her year between Oxford OH and her hundred-acre recovering farm near Lawrenceburg KY, sharing both homes with her standard poodles, Corbie and Lexi. Her website is at www.judithmoffett.com.

Cheryl Morgan was the first openly trans person to win a Hugo Award. She has been a book reviewer, an editor (including for *Clarkesworld*) and a publisher. Very occasionally she writes fiction. Currently she is responsible for Wizard's Tower Press (wizardstowerpress.com), and blogs regularly at *Cheryl's Mewsings* (www.cheryl-morgan.com). In her copious spare time (ha!) she co-presents the *Women's Outlook* show on Ujima Radio (www.ujimaradio.com) in Bristol, and writes a column on feminist issues for *Bristol 24/7* (www.bristol247.com). You can follow her on Twitter as @CherylMorgan.

Pat Murphy has won numerous awards for her thoughtful, literary science fiction and fantasy writing, including two Nebula Awards, the Philip K. Dick Award, the World Fantasy Award, the Seiun Award, and the Theodore Sturgeon Memorial Award. She has published seven novels and many short stories for adults, including *Rachel in Love*, *The Falling Woman*, *The City Not Long After*, *Nadya*, and *Adventures in Time and Space* with Max Merriwell, a novel that *Publisher's Weekly* called the "cerebral equivalent of a roller-coaster ride".

In 1991, with writer Karen Fowler, Pat co-founded the James Tiptree, Jr. Award, an annual literary prize for science fiction or fantasy that expands or explores our understanding of gender roles. This award is funded by grassroots efforts that include auctions and bake sales, harnessing the power of chocolate chip cookies in an on-going effort to change the world.

Sarah Pinsker is the author of the novelette "In Joy, Knowing the Abyss Behind," the 2014 Sturgeon Award winner and a 2013 Nebula finalist. Her story "A Stretch of Highway Two Lanes Wide" was a 2014 Nebula finalist, and another story, "No Lonely Seafarer," made the 2014 Tiptree Award longlist. Her fiction has been published in magazines including *Asimov's*, *Strange Horizons*, *Lightspeed* (including the *Women Destroy Science Fiction* and *Queers Destroy Science Fiction* special issues), *Fantasy & Science Fiction*, *Uncanny*, *Daily Science Fiction*, *the Journal of Unlikely Cartography*, and *Fireside*, and in anthologies including *Accessing the Future: A Disability Themed Anthology of Speculative Fiction, How to Live On Other Planets: A Handbook for Aspiring Aliens, Long Hidden, Fierce Family,* and *The Future Embodied.*

She co-hosts the Baltimore Science Fiction Society's *Dangerous Voices Variety Hour,* a reading series/quiz show. She is also a singer/songwriter with three albums on various independent labels (*Charmed,* disappear records; *Wingspan,* Reinventing Records; *This is Your Signal,* The Beechfields, with the Stalking Horses) and a fourth forthcoming. She lives with her wife and dog in Baltimore, Maryland and she can be found online at sarahpinsker.com and twitter.com/sarahpinsker.

John Barth described **Cat Rambo**'s writings as "works of urban mythopoeia"—her stories take place in a universe where chickens aid the lovelorn, Death is just another face on the train, and Bigfoot gives interviews to the media on a daily basis. She has worked as a programmer-writer for Microsoft and a Tarot card reader, professions which, she claims, both involve a certain combination of technical knowledge and willingness to go with the flow.

In 2005, she attended the Clarion West Writers' Workshop and began publishing F&SF stories. Among the places in which her work has appeared are *Asimov's, Weird Tales, Clarkesworld,* and *Strange Horizons,* and her work has consistently garnered mentions and appearances in year's best of anthologies. Her collection, *Eyes Like Sky and Coal and Moonlight* was an Endeavour Award finalist in 2010 and followed her collaboration with Jeff VanderMeer, *The Surgeon's Tale and Other Stories*. Her most recent collection is *Near + Far*, from Hydra House Books, which contains Nebula-nominated "Five Ways to Fall in Love on Planet Porcelain", with a follow-up, *Neither Here Nor There*, to be released in late 2015. Her most recent novel is *Beasts of Tabat*, first volume of a fantasy quartet, and her most recent nonfiction is *Ad Astra: The SFWA 50TH Anniversary Cookbook*, co-edited with Fran Wilde.

Rambo has edited multiple anthologies, including *Lightspeed Magazine's Women Destroy Fantasy* special issue, as well as the online award-winning, critically-acclaimed *Fantasy Magazine*. Her work with *Fantasy Magazine* earned her a nomination for a World Fantasy Award in 2012. She teaches a series of online classes as well as for Clarion West, the King County Library System, and Fields End. A long-time volunteer with the Science Fiction and Fantasy Writers of America (SFWA), she served as its Vice President from 2014-2015 and currently is its President. For more about her, as well as links to her fiction, see http://www.kittywumpus.net

Tansy Rayner Roberts is an author of science fiction, fantasy and crime fiction (the latter under the pen name of Livia Day). She runs a small business from her home in Tasmania, co-parents two daughters, and is an active commentator on SFF media and the publishing scene via Twitter, blog essays, and podcasting. She is the co-host of two popular all-female podcasts: *Galactic Suburbia* and the *Verity!* Podcast.

Tansy has a PhD in Classics, which she used shamelessly with her short story suite, *Love and Romanpunk*, as part of the Twelve Planets series (Twelfth Planet Press). Her other books under her own name include *Splashdance Silver*, the Creature Court trilogy (*Power and Majesty, The Shattered City, Reign of Beasts*) and *Musketeer Space*. Her most recent short story, "Fake Geek Girl", appeared at the *Australian Review of Fiction*. Livia Day's crime titles include *A Trifle Dead*, and *Drowned Vanilla*.

Tansy has won a variety of Australian and international awards, including the Hugo for Best Fan Writer in 2013, the Aurealis Award for Best Fantasy Novel in 2011, the Washington SF Association Small Press Award (twice) and various Ditmars. She is particularly proud of winning the William Atheling Award for Criticism and Review five times, including that one year she tied with herself.

Justina Robson was born in Yorkshire, England in 1968 where some time later she dropped out of Art College, then studied Philosophy and Linguistics at York University. She sold her first novel in 1999.

Since then, she has won the 2000 *amazon.co.uk* Writers' Bursary Award. Her books have been variously shortlisted for The British Science Fiction Best Novel Award, the Arthur C. Clarke Award, the Philip K. Dick Award and the John W. Campbell Award. An anthology of her short fiction, *Heliotrope*, was published in 2012. In 2004, Justina was a judge for the Arthur C. Clarke Award on behalf of *The Science Fiction Foundation*. Her novels and stories range widely over SF and Fantasy, often in combination and often featuring AIs and machines who aren't exactly what they seem. Her latest novel is *Glorious Angels*, a story set within a matriarchal world in which technology is mined out of the ground and cities are an entirely moveable feast.

She still lives in t'North with her partner, three children, a cat and a dog.

Nisi Shawl's story collection *Filter House* co-won the James Tiptree, Jr. Award in 2009. *Filter House* and one of the collection's stories, "Good Boy," were nominated for the World Fantasy Award. Ursula K. Le Guin has called her writing "brilliant." Recently, her stories have appeared in the *Strange Horizons* and in the critically acclaimed anthologies *Cranky Ladies of History* and *Steampunk World*.

With Cynthia Ward, Shawl coauthored *Writing the Other: A Practical Approach*, recipient of a Tiptree Honorable Mention in 2006. She edited *WisCon Chronicles 5: Writing and Racial Identity*, and *Bloodchildren: Stories by the Octavia E. Butler Scholars*. She also writes reviews for *The Seattle Times*, and writes and edits reviews for the feminist literary quarterly *Cascadia Subduction Zone*.

In 2014, Shawl coedited *Strange Matings: Science Fiction, Feminism, African American Voices, and Octavia E. Butler* with Dr. Rebecca Holden. In 2015, she coedited *Stories for Chip: A Tribute to Samuel R. Delany* with Bill Campbell. Her Belgian Congo steampunk novel *Everfair* is forthcoming from Tor in 2016. She serves on the boards of the Clarion West Writers Workshop and the Carl Brandon Society, a nonprofit dedicated to improving minority representation in fantastic fiction. She's fairly active on Twitter and Facebook, and promises to update her homepage soon.

Nike Sulway is an Australian writer, who lives and works in Toowoomba. She is the author of several novels, including *Rupetta*, which—in 2014—was the first work by an Australian writer to win the James Tiptree, Jr. Award. Her next novel, *Dying in the First Person*, will be published by Transit Lounge in 2016.

Lucy Sussex is a New Zealand-born writer living in Australia, though she has also resided in France and England. Her award-winning work covers many genres, from true crime writing to horror. She began in science fiction, from her teens, and attended a Writers' Workshop with Terry Carr and George Turner. Later she taught at Clarion West. Though always keeping in touch with the speculative community and its authors, she has also written in many areas. Her bibliography includes books for younger readers and the novel, *The Scarlet Rider* (1996, St Martins; reissued Ticonderoga 2015). She has published five short story collections, *My Lady Tongue*, *A Tour Guide in Utopia*, *Absolute Uncertainty*, *Matilda Told Such Dreadful Lies* (a best of), and *Thief of Lives*. *Matilda* received a starred review in *Publisher's Weekly*. She has also edited anthologies of fiction for younger readers; and the World Fantasy award shortlisted anthology *She's Fantastical* (with Judith Raphael Buckrich).

She has been an academic (La Trobe University), researcher, editor and weekly review columnist for newspapers including *The Age* and *Sydney Morning Herald*. Her literary archaeology (unearthing forgotten writers) work includes *Women Writers and Detectives in C19th Crime Fiction: the mothers of the mystery genre* (Palgrave). She has also edited pioneer crime-writer Mary Fortune's work and an anthology of Victorian travel writing, *Saltwater in the Ink* (ASP). Her current project is a book about Fergus Hume and his 1886 *The Mystery of a Hansom Cab*, the biggest selling detective novel of the 1800s. It has been released by Text publishing as *Blockbuster!* (2015), to be followed by a new e-edition of Ellen Davitt's *Force and Fraud* (1865) the first Australian murder mystery novel, by Clan Destine Press. She maintains an interest in women's writing, Victoriana, Australian and New Zealandiana, and genre fiction. In her free time she is deconstructing the Victorian novel *The Notting Hill Mystery* into a tale of shape-shifters and quantum physics.

Rachel Swirsky has an MFA in fiction from the Iowa Writers Workshop and graduated from Clarion West in 2005. Her short fiction has been published in numerous magazines and anthologies and reprinted in year's best anthologies by Horton, Dozois, Strahan, VanderMeer and others. Her work has also been nominated for awards including the Locus, the World Fantasy, the Sturgeon and the Hugo, and twice won the Nebula Award. Her second collection, *How The World Became Quiet: Myths of The Past, Present and*

Future, was published by Subterranean Press. Her favorite Tiptree stories are probably "Love is the Plan; the Plan is Death" and "Screwfly Solution," but there's so much to choose from.

Bogi Takács is a neutrally gendered Hungarian Jewish person who's recently moved to the US. E has had speculative fiction and poetry published in a variety of venues like *Strange Horizons, Clarkesworld, Lightspeed—Queers Destroy SF,* and *Apex Magazine,* among others. Last year e won the *Strange Horizons* Readers' Poll in Poetry category with eir animated poem "You Are Here / Was: Blue Line to Memorial Park". E posts SFF story and poem recommendations on Twitter on a semi-daily basis under #diversestories and #diversepoems. You can follow Bogi at @bogiperson or visit eir website at www.prezzey.net.

Three-time Hugo Award winner **Lynne M. Thomas** is the Co-Editor-in-Chief and Publisher of *Uncanny Magazine* with her husband Michael Damian Thomas. The former Editor-in-Chief of *Apex Magazine* (2011-2013), she co-edited the Hugo Award-winning *Chicks Dig Time Lords,* as well as *Whedonistas* and *Chicks Dig Comics.* She moderates the Hugo-Award winning *SF Squeecast* SF/F podcast, and contributes to the *Verity!* Podcast. In her day job, she is the Head of Special Collections and Curator of Rare Books and Special Collections at Northern Illinois University, where she is responsible for the papers of over seventy-five SF/F authors. You can learn more about her shenanigans at lynnemthomas.com.

Jo **Walton** comes from Wales but since 2002 she has lived in Montreal, where the food and books are much better. She writes science fiction and fantasy, reads a lot, talks about books, and eats great food. She has published twelve novels, three poetry collections and an essay collection. Her books have been translated into more than a dozen languages.

She won the John W. Campbell Award for Best New Writer in 2002, probably for her first three novels, *The King's Peace* (2000), *The King's Name* (2001) and *The Prize in the Game* (2002) which are all historical fantasy. She won the World Fantasy Award in 2004 for *Tooth and Claw*, a sentimental Victorian novel in which all the characters are dragons who eat each other. This was followed by the Small Change series, *Farthing* (2006) *Ha'Penny* (2007), and *Half a Crown* (2008), all alternate-history mysteries. *Lifelode* (2009), a high magic domestic fantasy, won the Mythopoeic Award. *Among Others* (2011) a bibliophilic fantasy novel, won the Hugo, Nebula and the British Fantasy Awards. *My Real Children* (2014) won the Tiptree Award, the Romantic Times Reviewer's Choice Award, and was an American Librarian Association RUSA Top Pick. Her most recent novels are *The Just City* and *The Philosopher Kings* (2015) are the first two of the Thessaly trilogy, about Greek gods and time travellers setting up Plato's Republic. The third and final book in this sequence, *Necessity*, is complete but undergoing revision, and should be published sometime in 2016.

She blogs about older books on *Tor.com*, and a collection of her posts has been published as *What Makes This Book So*

Great (2014). It won the Locus Award as Best Non-Fiction in 2015.

Her poetry has appeared in *Asimov's*, *Goblin Fruit*, *Strange Horizons*, *Mythic Delirium*, and numerous other places. Some of it is available as chapbooks from NESFA and Aqueduct, and all of it is on her website, www.jowaltonbooks.com. She plans to live to be ninety-nine and write a book every year.

Catherynne M. Valente is a *New York Times* Bestselling author of fantasy and science fiction novels, short stories, and poetry. She lives on a small island off the coast of Maine with her husband, two dogs, one enormous friendly cat and one less enormous, less friendly one, six chickens, a red accordion, an uncompleted master's degree, a roomful of yarn, a spinning wheel with ulterior motives, a cupboard of jam and pickles, a bookshelf full of folktales, an industrial torch, an *Oxford English Dictionary*, and a DSL connection.

She has written over a dozen volumes of fiction and poetry since her first novel, *The Labyrinth*, was published in 2004. Her full-length novels include (chronologically) *Yume no Hon: The Book of Dreams*, *The Grass-Cutting Sword*, *The Orphan's Tales* (a duology consisting of *In the Night Garden* and *Cities of Coin and Spice*), *Palimpsest*, *The Habitation of the Blessed*, *Deathless*, and *The Girl Who Circumnavigated Fairyland in a Ship of Her Own Making*.

She is also the author of two novellas, *Under In the Mere* and *The Ice Puzzle* as well as several collections of poetry, including

Apocrypha and Oracles (2005), *The Descent of Inanna* (2006) and *A Guide to Folktales in Fragile Dialects* (2008). Her first collection of short stories, *Ventriloquism*, came out in the winter of 2010.

Her poetry and short fiction can be found online and in print in such journals as *Clarkesworld Magazine*, *Tor.com*, *Fantasy Magazine*, *Electric Velocipede*, *Lightspeed Magazine*, *Subterranean Online*, and *Weird Tales*, as well as in anthologies such as *Interfictions*, *Salon Fantastique*, *Welcome to Bordertown*, *Teeth*, *Paper Cities*, *Steampunk Reloaded*, *Haunted Legends* and featured in numerous Year's Best collections.

She has been nominated for the Hugo (2010), Locus (2010 & 2011) and World Fantasy Awards (2007 & 2009). *In the Night Garden* won the James Tiptree Jr. Award for expanding gender and sexuality in SFF (2007), and the series as a whole won the Mythopoeic Award for Adults (2008). *Palimpsest* won the Lambda Award for LGBT fiction (2010). Her story "Urchins, While Swimming", received the Million Writers Award for best online short fiction in 2006 and her poem *The Seven Devils of Central California* won the Rhysling Award in 2008.

In 2010, *The Girl Who Circumnavigated Fairyland in a Ship of Her Own Making* became the first self-published work to win a major literary award, winning the Andre Norton Award for YA literature before it saw print in 2011, going on to become a national bestseller.

In 2012, she received the Locus Award for Best Novella (*Silently and Very Fast*), Best Novelette (*White Lines On A Green Field*) and Best YA Novel (*The Girl Who Circumnavigated Fairyland in a Ship of Her Own Making*).

As part of the SF Squeecast, she won the Hugo for Best Fancast in 2012. She was nominated for the Hugo and Nebula awards for her dystopian novelette *Fade to White* in 2013.

She keeps a popular blog at Rules for Anchorites.

Élisabeth Vonarburg was born to life in 1947 (France), and to science fiction in 1964. She taught French Literature and Creative Writing on and off at various universities in Quebec (since immigration, in 1973). She has been a "fulltime writer" since 1990, (despite a PhD. in Creative Writing, 1987), i.e. singer-songwriter, translator, SF convention organizer, literary editor (*Solaris* magazine), essayist. She has still managed to publish some fiction, among which are fifteen SF novels, some translated into English (*The Silent City, The Maerlande Chronicles* (Philip K. Dick Special Jury Award), *Reluctant Voyagers, Tyranaël*, Books I and II); six SF short story collections in French, and two in English (*Slow Engine of Time, Blood Out of A Stone*); three poetry collections (not SF) and four fantasy books for children and young adults. She has won more than thirty awards in France, Canada, Quebec and the United States. Her most recent series, *Reine de Mémoire* (2005-2007, five books), received four major awards in Quebec, while her most recent novel, *Hotel Olympia*, won the 2015 French Aurora Award.

Tehani Wessely was a founding member of *Andromeda Spaceways Inflight Magazine* in 2001 and started her own boutique publishing house, FableCroft Publishing, in 2010. Now firmly entrenched in Australian speculative fiction and independent press, she has judged for several national literary awards and reads far more in one genre than is healthy.

Tehani has twice co-won the William Atheling Jr. Award for Criticism and Review, sharing the honours first with Alexandra Pierce for their Vorkosigan Saga review series, and then as part of a *Doctor Who* conversational reviewer team with Tansy Rayner Roberts and David McDonald. Her most recent publication is an essay examining the character of Tegan from *Doctor Who*, in the Mad Norwegian Press publication *Companion Piece*.

In her spare moments, she works as Head of Library in a Canberra boys' school and enjoys spending time with her husband and four children. You can find Tehani on Twitter @editormum75.

Tess Williams is an author and academic. Her first novel was *Map of Power* (Random House, 1996), and her second was *Sea as Mirror* (Harper Collins, 2000). Both were shortlisted for the Aurealis Award and *Sea as Mirror* was also shortlisted for the James Tiptree Jr .Award in that year. She has also contributed short stories to various Australian anthologies and publications, including *Eidolon, Borderlands*, the Sybylla Press collection *She's Fantastical* and the World Fantasy Award winning anthology, *Dreaming Downunder*. The latter story was nominated by Ellen Datlow in the ten best horror stories of the year. Williams also co-edited the benchmark feminist science fiction collection *Women of Other Worlds* with Dr Helen Merrick, a collection that was awarded the William Atheling Jr. Award for contributions to Australian Science Fiction. Her creative writing was significantly interrupted by a commitment to a PhD on evolution and feminist science fiction, and by health problems requiring a kidney transplant. Having survived via attachment to a machine and an organ transplant she has a particularly ironic appreciation that life and the art of science fiction writing are intimately related, and the themes in her writing are closely connected to feminism, science, technology and nature. Currently, she is working on publishing material from her PhD and completing her third novel, *All the Wild Children*.

I Never
Wrote You
Anything
But
The Exact Truth

Ursula my dear,

Could I ask you to keep a secret for a shortish while?

The thing is, a Baltimore fan has winkled out my quotes real life identity—I had no idea Chicago obituaries would be splashed around Baltimore, and he wrote me with Proof A through zed. Luckily it was Jeff Smith, whom I'd always promised would be the first to know if there was a secret to Unveil. So of course I said yes he was right and please hold it for awhile (letting Ballantine fumble around with this silly novel, etc.) (and also sparing me an avalanche for which I'm ill-prepared, loss of friends, etc.). Two parentheses in one sentence being enough, let me take a breath and start in again.

The thing is, I want you, alone, to know first from me because of our special relation. I write this feeling a great & true friendship is wavering on the balance, about to slide away forever to the dark. But—this is important—I never wrote you anything but the exact truth, there was no calculation or intent to deceive, other than the signature which over 8 years became just another nickname; everything else is just plain me.

The thing is, I am a 61-year old woman named Alice Sheldon—nickname Alli—solitary by nature but married for 37 years to a very nice man considerably older, who doesn't read my stuff but is glad I like writing it.

(I told you, or somebody, it would be the anticlimax of the year.)

All the rest is true, the Army, business, government, academe—I'm the kind of doctor who doesn't do anybody any good, as someone said—and recently retirement as I got sick and Mother's condition required constant trips to Chicago with briefcases full of exams to grade by her bedside in the intensive care ward. The depression is partly from retirement partly from glands and partly because my dear man may be going blind. (Retinal blood-vessel growth in the macula.) His name is Ting, short for Huntington D.

Maybe you would prefer to know what I look like. Five ft 8, blond-brown hair going greystreak, thin, vague remains of a young woman who grinned a lot and was said to be good-looking vaguely visible under the 61 years of skinniness and wrinkles, like all depressed people like to laugh a lot; active in convulsive spurts. Wear mostly pale blue or tan cords, shirts or turtle-necks, sawed-off nails, flat feet, passion for gardening. (Now weakening under the stress of Other Things.) …When I get dressed up to Go Out I prance a little, like a plush horse. Slather self with Chanel 19 or Joy or Diorissima. (Smells, important.) Smoke—lately like the proverbial chimney. Handy with a screwdriver. Get crushes on people whose work or souls I admire.

So now you know….. But the funny thing, I swear Tiptree has a funny reality of his own. The name came from seeing a marmalade jar in the Giant's imported food section. Maybe he was waiting there for incarnation, anyway sometimes believe me this sort of voice speaks from somewhere behind my pancreas. He insisted on

"Tip", by the way; he wouldn't be "Jim." Also he dictates stories, or worse, the starts of ones I have to finish.... I was looking for a forgettable name, consternation when it all sold.

Ursula, Ursula, I am petrified. All the friends, the sf world—will they take it as "deception?" Will I have any friends left? Will the women who mean so much to me see it all as an evil put-on? I never <u>felt</u> evil. And I was able to help, there are anthologists who got sharp queries from Tiptree about Why no women writers.... Also you can see why I withdrew that WOMEN MEN DON'T SEE thing – I was afraid too many women would vote for it to regard a man being so insightful. False pretenses.

Well dear Starbear an old age is dead and time to begin a new. But I think I'm finished. I had been planning to gradually shift over to that other pen-name, Raccoona Sheldon, and phase Tip out that way. (Funny thing; editors who are screaming for Tiptree stuff send back Raccoona's mss with beer-can mARKS ON THEM—WELL, NOT ACTUALLY THAT bad—scuse typer—but almost.)

If there's anything I forgot to mention I should have, just ask.

Tip says goodbye to a very dear friend and all that is hers.

Let me know what you think if you're still speaking to

Tip / Alli

Dearest TREE,

oh strange, most strange, most wonderful, beautiful, improbable—
Wie geht's, Schwesterlein? sorella mia, sistersoul! How do you do,
Gideanna? (please see enclosed or accompanying shortstory for
footnote on that)

Do you know what? I don't think I have ever been <u>surprised</u>
before. Things have happened but when they happen one thinks
Oh, of course, this had to Be, etc., deep in my prophetic soul I
Knew, etc. —but not this time, by God! And it is absolutely a
delight, a joy, for some reason, to be truly absolutely flatfootedly
surprised—it's like a Christmas present! don't ask me why, I don't
know. —I will now proceed to tell you one thing that has made
me slightly unhappy in our peculiar & extremely precious-to-me
relationship: I had thought, I wonder if Tiptree is not a homo, and
unable to talk about it, having been hurt too often, or because I
am so blatantly hetero-wife-mother-etc etc, but that would explain
why he sounds very alone, and also why he has this marvellous
insight into women just like E.M. Forster or Angus Wilson, and
oh hell why can't I <u>ask</u> him, but I can't, and so there will always
be this sort of vast lacuna or gap in our Meeting of Minds… I am
a coward not to ask, but one cannot pry into what might be an
area of great pain & privacy, etc…. So, there was a little knot of
sexual unhappiness & reticence, which always bothered me, and

which you have now BLOWN INTO SMITHEREENS and I want to laugh, also slightly to cry, because the whole thing now is on this huge and unexpected scale and real and total reversal—only what does reversal mean? Explain to me, my Gethenian Friend. No, don't, you got enough worries! —I know something I will miss: in writing you, the slight edge of flirtation… I do like to flirt, to bat the eyes just a trifle, I like the little edge of sexual tension between men & women that there is there even in letters, I enjoy that & will miss it between us, who knows, maybe Tip will it too? because you needn't pretend, you know, that there isn't any Tip & never was nor never will be; I know my Tree <u>that</u> well, & to hell with gender. But Tip is also Alli & I can't flirt with Alli, never could flirt with women, the tension just isn't there for me; which is why, of course, my few dearest friends have been women, Jean who died, Jane & Natalie. If I want to flirt I will just have to flirt with Charles, which is always the best, or passing idiots like the Welsh Professor of Economics whom I really flirted up a storm with the other night, it was lovely because he was <u>such</u> an idiot but eminently flirtable and I knew that after 1 hour I would never see him again. I was wearing Je Reviens that night, but had no intention whatever of <u>doing</u> so! I have never tried Joy, they make such an issue of its being the most expensive perfume in the world. Forgive me, I wander. I wonder as I wander. Forgive me also for sending the Tiptree's Marmalade label! You responded so guardedly that I thought, oh dear, I <u>have</u> got onto the right family by mistake, shut up you silly cow, Tip has a right to his privacy. Snort. Little did I know. Oh, why it such a joy to be cut down to one's proper size? ANSWER: Because joy lies in just proportion. —I don't know about people's reactions, I suppose there are some who resent being put on, but it would take an extraordinarily small soul to resent so immense, so funny, so effective & fantastic & ETHICAL a [mistake], that says put-0n, once more into the breach dear friends: put-on. There, I typed it. ANYHOW, why should anybody mind? Why shouldn't they be delighted? I can't imagine, honestly. If any women ever put you down for being a man, they might be embarassed, but I can't remember any of them doing so in my hearing—well, you & Chip were going to be read out of that Symposium thing because of your sex, but that fell apart of its own stupidity anyhow, thank goodness. This is that same Jeff Smith, isn't it? By the way, is it necessary that your cover be blown? Do you want it to be, are you ready or if he hadn't ferreted about would you have just gone on? He sounds like a decent sort, if you asked him couldn't he just not say anything? I assure you that I wouldn't. Or, having even one person "know," does that sort of end the game. If you don't <u>want</u> the game to end, I don't see why it should.—About Raccoona, by the way, there some of your truelovers did kind of suspect something. Vonda and I have wondered if Raccoona wasn't Tiptree, several times in the past. However, I will tell you stranche ting: I really & truly don't like any of Raccoona's stories I've read (only 2 I think, or 3) as well as most of Tip's. They <u>are</u> different. Whether I, & the beercan-putting-down editors, are right, I don't know; but we are responding to a difference in kind, if not perhaps in quality. Raccoona, I think, has less control, thus less wit and power. She seems a good deal younger than Tip.—There is no reason of course why she shouldn't grow up. Though a first name like Raccoona is a very heavy burden on a growing girl... but hell, if Margaret Drabble can make it... Anyhow, to descend precipitously to mundane details for a minute, if _any_ of you people there in MacLean will send me a story for my anthology, I will be purfickly delighted! You can all collaborate on it, or anything—if there are any more of you, they are welcome—Currer, Acton, Ellis—George—Tip, Raccoona, Alli—Don't let this worry you either, by the way. I won't mention it again. There is NO HURRY. So far the "anthology" consists of—nothing—except one 2-page story by Avram Davidson, about Simon Magus, which I did not understand at all but found extremely funny, & sent off to Virginia saying Hey, how about this? and I haven't heard from V. yet but Avram told me at once that she saw it years ago and loathed it. How's that for a merry start? I may have lost my Friend & Agent anyhow. She got up a contract for me for a book of non-fic. which I thought I had told her not to do, but I guess I didn't tell her clear enough, & probably she feels really out on a limb now because I simply cannot sign the contract. Oy gewalt. Never mind. ANYHOW again I think all your friends will be as childishly pleased with you as I am—and as for what the Sf World says, my God, Allitree, who cares? what does it matter? I hope their little eyes widen & their little mouths fall open. By God I just wish Stanislaw Lem was a woman too! —I am not feeling very kindly towards the Sf World jut now, as you may have gathered; at least not the ones who represent us via SFWA etc. Anything that might shock their tiny complacency is Grist, baby, Grist.—Hey, can I ask you now what it is you teach? & where?—And how on earth you get all over the Tristes Tropiques all by yourself (despite little adventures like heart-stoppage)?

Tip can say goodbye to me but I bloody well won't say goodbye to Tip, why do I have to? can't I just say hello to Alli, Oh Welcome, Alli! I only wish all my friends were like you! And love to Ting and health and luck—

And love
Ursula the Bear

Dearest Starbear, Oh, thank god!

Your wonderful letter collapsed me I was so damn scared.

Oh you thrice-blessed soul.

I guess you know how I feel. The fear of disappointment that all the fuss finally devolved into one aged suburban matron having a joke. Of course all the rest—th adventures of the past—is true; I'm told I've had an exciting/glamorous/ whatnot life, but it just felt like a lot of hard work and scared at times. But "secret master of the CIA"—my foot, she says expurgatedly.

Let's see, you ask can't the secret be held awhile. It can as far as you and the other few other pros I yesterday felt I had to tell— Vonda and Quinn and Joanna, plus Fred Pohl who helped me so, plus Craig Strete whom I kind of love, the blinding ass. But this fan—yes, Jeff Smith—says Harlan is broadcasting his guesses around. I don't know how that will work out… If he's just guessing, it may die down. If not, we'll have a grand Unveiling in Jeff Smith's KHATRU in April. So for the time let's just sit tight and see.

By the way, Raccoona sold another one to Ben Bova yesterday, with Tip's help—I said I was hijacking it for his eyes en route to her usual non-paying markets. It isn't quite so minor. Say about Tip's B level. The fact is, I palmed off oldies and weakies on poor Raccoona, I had to with my low production. But I do stand by the one in AURORA; outside of the jerky p.o.v. business, which

is instrinsiceto the story, I think it stacks up. Not really? Ouch...
(But it's deeply me.)

And as to flirting, don't be too sure, Madam. Certainly you can't flirt with Alli, who forty years ago may or may not have been a lesbian manquée, but somewhere behind my left shoulder hovers a thin figure in tropical whites with a faded vermillion cummerbund and totally unrealistic dreams of strolling with you, as I said, amidst the Madagascar moonlit where the lemurs weave their ring-tails.

You see I am of that last generatuon where <u>people</u> still flirted with <u>people</u>, flirted mindwise, the spark of soul on soul, the laughing excited tension of mind sparking mind, the curious effect of—maybe momentary <u>total</u> attention, admiration, bedazzlement. Without todays sequelae of the inevitable motel room, or Plaza Hotel dimness, the dropping clothes, the fumbling—and then the realisation that it hadn't really been about that at all, that in fact the spark has been, unless one was lucky, killed.

So if the occasion comes up I beg leave to flirt my peacock-tail at yours,—funny how "flirting" really involves showing off, knowing the other is looking, admiring totally. Despite the total physical gulf of possibility, despite everything but that extraordinary recognition of some mutually fascinating moment, the lucky instant of the unknown being seen by the private eye, the—ah but I do wamble.

[handwritten] You know—you always know. Bless you my
Starbear

10XII76

Allitree,

Thank Goodness you went & told Vonda. She was down here this past weekend, I had a lovely time with her (and reading her first-typed-draft novel—more about Snake, Mist, Sand, et al.—it is a lovely book, full of genuinely amiable people and some marvelous bits of Pure Creation) but when she said Have you heard from Tip lately? I was standing on a chair balanced precariously on a cot trying to reach down books from the top shelf of my study-shelves and I went <u>hlp</u> and nearly fell off which with the chair, the books, and self would have been rather a large-scale disaster as the study is only about 8 ft. wide and Vonda was in the direct line of Descent. So I got down and said hlp hlp, oh yes, he's fine (She, Them, and It having rapidly flashed into my brain and almost onto my tongue—honestly) but has been a bit depressed lately, and then told her rapidly about the 40,000 African mole skins (wasn't it?) and then changed the subject. It will be a great relief not to have to! Vonda is the only person I had any desire at all to TELL (other than Charles and Caroline: I figured you knew that to tell me anything meant to tell Charles, & Carlie, who is a Tiptree fan, was there; they were both delighted and we sat around snortling about it.) By the way, Harlan has announced at least once before that He Knew Who Tiptree Was but wasn't telling. I love Harlan madly, but pay <u>no</u> attention to him—unless he has really put Facks together like Jeff Smith. Last time he Knew, I think you were, indeed, in the CIA; he had Inside Information.

Mindflirtation is precisely what I meant. I can do it easier with men than women & enjoy it immensely. Probably because of growing up w. 3 older brothers & genial father, also watching examples of my Indescribable Mother making grouchy & pompous Professors of This and That come smiling to ear sugar out of her hand, and be witty instead of overbearing—oh what a bore-tamer she was—She has strong elements of the Great Goddess, which I did not alas inherit, but was grand to grow up with! Anyhow, I always tend to play Bright Little Sister: which at 47 is pretty damn grotesque—but damn if it didn't work just as well as ever with that Welshman! Somewhere I read Auden saying that all his life he felt that he was the youngest person in the room, which "has very seldom been the fact for the past forty years," and I have felt kindly towards Auden ever since.

I bin reading a book about Hinduism (several, but Zaehner's is the only good one so far.) Because I did a sort of Hindu short story, & then decided I better find out if I had got it right (I did; sort of.) Shiva is far out. Shiva is Shakti (male & female) and he-she-they-it dances—I knew that much—but I didn't know that sometimes Shiva dances the world into being, and sometimes Shiva dances downhill, with animals all around, and dances the world right to hell. I find Shiva a God worth trembling at. Shiva has a peacock tail.

Alli, I have to keep calling you Tree, at least at times, because of all the tree-metaphors & connotations that have grown about you in my head; Tip joins the many other Figments I have, and do, love(d) you know, like Darcy & Heathcliff! but I have to keep hold of my Tree, the Tree the Bear leans on, is that all right? YOU ARE the tree you know.

Love
The Bear

Dearest Bear,

Forgive the pallour of this type; by a quirk Tiptree's faithful old typer collapsed a week after he did, and I must make use of this feeble Olivetti.

Your beautiful THE WATER IS WIDE arrived. I have read it twice, and I understand it on a—you should forgive—gut level, while not yet understanding the overstory. "Gut level?" no; say rather that dreamy denied craving somewhere in the medulla which murmurs sadly & forever, "This can't be all."

Thank you for the lovely gift.

I wish I could understand the window in your soul. Mine has none such, but I believe in others'. It is as though mine says to me, You alone are damned. To you the daylight, to you the reality of what appears; for you the dead of Carthage will be dead forever, the pain everywhere the overmastering reality, the skull beneath the fairest skin always visible under the blue-veined temples, in the laughing teeth. To you, the lone and levels sands covering human endeavor, the ephemerality of laughter. .... Only for others, the reality of human life, the game worthwhile as it is being played. Only for others, any kind of hope. Only for others, the window from the closed room. —or closed galaxy, it makes no difference.

I was always like that. Where you grew up with young people I grew up with older people whom I felt as death- and time-obsessed, although they were superficially merry. I first tried to cut my wrists at 12, I was so stupid I didn't know which side they were on and bear the hash-marks under my wristwatch today.... Later I found out, and I can still recall fitting a razor-blade into a five-pound history book and sawing, sawing. Nothing happened except that I woke up tied by ropes of blood to the carpet and got up and cleaned up the mess and went to class. (I was in boarding scoools all my early times.) That was fourteen. Then the engines of sex, the conviction of excitement and reality Out There just beyond me somewhere gripped me, and I never tried again. But now as I age the process reverts itself. I have been there, seen and tried it all, and what I haven't personally experienced I have shared from friends or seen the results of. And the old Futile-futile has gripped me again. For a time it seemed important and satisfying to find out how to scream out my sense of trapped-ness in stories; now that too is fading, and I have been in such a terminal mood, waiting in good health for a death which seems overdue, that I am reluctant to communicate my real feelings to anyone lest I contaminate them. But I suffer horribly from a kind of anomie, an anhedonia of the soul. I bless all the active ones, the cheery scramblers, but there is nothing on earth I would reach out a hand for—except to throttle the devil that is blinding my deep friend, my husband, who be the way is called, if I haven't said it before, Ting (for Huntington, which no one ever pronounced since his christening.) ... But of course all this is false too, or I should not be writing you. Somewhere an engine will start again. But they better not set up Vonnegut's Euthanasia parlors while I can get to one.

Bear, I never planned on being trapped by a Relationship, by someone who needs me and whom I can't bear to leave alone. I always planned just to go. Is this femaleness? Procrastination, more likely. At any rate I am stuck, and you better get that anthology off the ground as doing my thing for it is the only secret engine in my life right now. I daren't start, just savor the fact that there is <u>something</u>. Ahead.

Of course selfish isolation enters into it. I am a natural hermit, the only sharing I've done with others is things like joining the Quaker vigil outside the White House. (They were having trouble keeping going from midnight to six, and it was 22 with a wind on the pavement—and the bastard was in Florida.) ... Which I get back from Yucatan (and drafting SLOW MUSIC) I think I'll get indoctrinated in how to be helpful in our local Rape Crisis center. Maybe my outward appearance of a stern suburban matron with a tongue in my head can intimidate cops and help kids get adequate treatment. Ting might join, too. With his sturdy bearded—white—presence and his upper-class Etonian background he could be very helpful with small tyrants.

When I write you and share by osmosis all the cello-playing and England-walking I feel hopeful. As my therapist says, there is nothing wrong with me except a morbid outlook. Like Eeyore in A. A. Milne—remember?

Now Bear because I have confessed my dreary soul do not come all over life-giving and maternal, because (a) that would falsify our genuineness and (b) it doesn't work. I have been life-guv by experts, all that happens is that the life disappears into my ambience like light down a black hole. Just accept me as old Gloomy Gus who enjoys a good laugh with the desperation only gloomy gusses know. In fact when we meet you'll find a disconcertingly hearty, cheery object who will make you feel like a delicate embodiment of Otherworldly Considerations. I shall be arranging pillows for you and bringing you glasses and generally putting on an impersonation—genuine—of a mere mortal trying to entertain the Spirit of Aesthetics. Are you sure you aren't too cold? —too hot?—is the gravity right? —would you care for a ring of candles around you?—should the fire be green and the leaves pink? ... And bringing you glasses of distilled snow while you would probably prefer earthly wine. Or scotch.

(I have no idea when this will be but believe devoutly in Organic Chronicity—things happen when they must.)

Now back to mortality, it being 5:30 AM. I was disappointed in Quinn, I felt obliged to tell her and she felt no obligation not to tell Gordon Dickinson, whom I do not know. What is he like? And what is Liz Lynn like, who seems to want to teach my stories—the feminist one—at her courses?

Well, I should have known. Quinn is a disciplined person in some ways, but has not the life discipline of keeping secrets without making it personal. While Tiptree was going I didn't even telll Mother. Just, "Sorry," but no." That No takes hard years to learn. Quinn's a softie.

[handwritten] Olivetti & page gave out together. I love you.
bear, scratch.

245

Dearest Allitree,

don't worry, mother bear will not smother you in vast furry embrace smelling slightly of raw antelope & mothballs. Mother bear will merely lean against the tree & scratch a bit. Tree has deep roots which go down into dark places (it has been observed that trees which do <u>not</u> have deep roots which go down into dark places, fall over very easily.) Bear has also been known to hibernate in extremely dark unpleasant deep places, but apparently is only a visitor there, not rooted. The Water is Wide was written in such a cave; and if the end of it is Hopeful, it is not a hope I understand when I come out of the cave. Nor do I understand the cave when I am not in the cave (nor do I understand the sunlight when I am in the cave), so I cannot be of use to you as I wish I could; except for words, words; little thin cobweb ropes spun between us; sometimes they are surprisingly strong. Your profound depression illuminates for me the strength of your writing. There are times your stories are so bitter to the taste that I flinch away, not wishing to admit what you are really saying, but it is a mere body-flinch, the soul says O yes, yes. Quite right. There are very few writers going who have this power to force acceptance & agreement; it is the power of truthfulness, of course. Writers of despair, woe, pain, fear, apocalypse etc. are a dime a dozen & to most of them my response is Yeah big deal, or Aw poor itta bitty fing did it hurts its itta head on the hard nassy world? We are in a Jeremiacal age & nothing is easier than despair, any twit can learn to howl. The howl, of course, generally comes out as a feeble whine, when you really listen; like our American Jewish school of novelists, or nine modern British writers out of ten. There is a strong element of mere chic in the howling, it does not come from the depths, & indeed the violence, vulgarity, stridency, & seeming acceptance of incoherence and ugliness and misery actually reveal, I think, a total noncomprehension of real misery, real pain, real loss of meaning; they haven't been there at all; they write about it comfortably from outside, just playing the game of Kafka. In sf, poor old Harlan has all the worst mannerisms of this school, & I don't really like most of his stories—but I do sense in them a streak of the real bacon, a lode of the true ore of pain, no faking. And Phil Dick has indubitably been there, & sometimes he makes it back with a message (sometimes not.) And Compton. And nobody else: but you, who hit on a deeper level of the spirit than any of them, & bring back not the ore, but the heavy heavy gold.

Have you read Rilke's Duino Elegies? maybe you read German, I don't, I have to read it in MacIntyre's translation & look over on the left hand side & see the poetry glimmering there in unattainable splendor, but Mac. is very good, anyhow, when I have been deep in the cave it is one of the few books that shine brighter the darker it gets. Nothing quite seems to put it out.

I have met Gordon Dickson once or twice, and have a vague impression of an amiable commonplace man—I have a terrible, utterly non-novelist's memory for names-faces-personalities—I had read only one of his things, something awfully Military in Space (indeed, irritation at it was the seed that produced "Vaster Than Empires," with its crew of undisciplined & argumentative Mad Scientists, come to think of it!) and recall being surprised at what a very unmilitary mild friendly fellow… stupid I am, expecting soldier-worship books to be written by soldiers! Anyhow, I don't know whether Quinn's telling him is equivalent to shouting it from the housetops, or not. I can't understand why she did. I don't know her; met her once, I think, but do not remember her at all. Oh yes, it was years ago she was very young and trying to take photographs or something. Vonda is fond of her is all I know. And she is the one in that horrible Round Robin on Feminism who said women can't possibly be friends with women, isn't she. That threw me so hard I asked my Sunday afternoon Recorder and Viol Playing Group (the Thurman Street Terminal Philharmonic) —which consists of me 47, Natalie 47, Harriett 47, Inge ca. 38, and sometimes Prue ca. 45—<u>why</u> would any woman <u>say</u> such a thing? and Harriett said at once, with total certainty, "she grew up in the suburbs somewhere…" which turns out to be true (I asked Vonda.) All the same it is a stupid horrid thing to say & as when she said it my friend Jean was in the process of dying of cancer I somehow hold it against Quinn as a kind of blasphemy or desecration, isn't that odd. Projecting guilt or impotence, I suppose.

Oh Lord it is snowing. Good Lord, clever Lord, to have invented snow! —I don't expect you feel this way, come to think of it, it's a terrible winter in the East isn't it? and you escape to places like Yucatan—If I am very very bad in this life I expect to be reborn in Yucatan! —but the thing is, we had a mild winter & then the endless drought in England; came back home to the worst drought in 86 years and a mild winter—and now at last it is Doing What it is Supposed to Do and manna is descending from heaven and the forest begins to look like a Christmas card. Snow is incredibly exhilarating when you don't get it very often.

Don't know Liz Lynn, she wrote me too. Sounded nice, & earnest, & young.

Caroline (17) just emerged from the basement singing a Christmas Carol and her brother (12) kicked her and it went like this, "Quem pastores laudavere screw you!" Ah, the Holiday Spirit! Home Life among the Cannibals.

I don't know that I quite believe what you say about not reaching out a hand for anything on earth, when on the next page you contemplate working in a rape Crisis Center. Or is that a social conscience thing separate from spiritual activity? I'm not sure the distinction is valid (she says thus dismissing 5 centuries of arguments on Salvation by Works). Seems like if you do it you do it. And if you don't (like me) you don't.

I am reading Virginia's letters Vol. II ("I saw Mrs Flower at the Library. We spat at one another.") and the Mahabharata, alternately (abridged—to say the least—this version is 1/20th of the original I believe) —both lovely—though they haven't very much superficially in common to be sure—Bloomsbury & the ancient

Hindus—But surely that is one of the grand things about our age, you can make these improbable mixtures! Since we have lost purity we might as well enjoy confusion. On this feebly aphoristic note I shall depart to make lunch for the Cannibals (eldest cannibal leaves tomorrow DAMN through snowy mountains towards earth-quake-threatened San Francisco, taking boom of cello and sweet giggle away DAMN) wishing you a long steadily softly rising new year into the sunlight, and leaves on all your branches dear Tree,

[picture of a bear and a tree]

Dear Allicampane Raccoona Gerbilia Tippo Sempervirens,

WHY do you always go to bloody Yucatan just when I need you most? Well, as usual, I am going to pretend you are in Box 315, not dehydrated in some narsty jungle, and write you anyway—have been wanting to for weeks—indeed, happy thought! perhaps you are home?

I just talked to young Jeff Levin (when I am 87 and he is 65 I will be calling him Young Jeff Levin) and I gather from him that you have written a sort of second round of letters to various people about Tip & Raccoona and Alli and all. I am glad because once Quinn whatshername blabbed it was obviously going to filter all over the place & people like Jeff & Vonda & me feel strongly we'd rather have you filtering it. I just wish you'd announce it pronto in Jeff Smith's mag. or somewhere, and beat people like Charlie Brown of Locus to the draw. This is a mean nasty petty feeling, but still, it would be satisfying. Nothing is more satisfying than the satisfaction of a truly mean nasty petty feeling, what?

I have been reading a bio. of George Elio (Ruby V. Redinger, G.E.: The Emergent Self) and it is, besides being a nice honest thoughtful book, fascinating in a certain relevance to my friend Miz Alli. Mary Ann Evans's relationship to the George Eliot name/persona: how it freed her; how she handled the identification when it came; and (this is just Redinger's theory but it sounds very sound to me) how "George Eliot" because a certain <u>voice</u> in the novels—the rational, moral, judging, distanced voice that speaks so often <u>about</u> the people & the things that are going on in the story. Speaks wisely & fascinatingly, too. <u>But</u> it was Mary Ann that made up/lived the people/story. <u>But</u> she could not have done it, perhaps, without having been George Eliot... Well, it is fascinating, if you like the novels particularly: I had just discovered The Mill on the Floss, which I do think is absolutely first class, a very very great work of art. I had started all wrong with her long ago, with Romola which I couldn't stand, Deronda which irritated me, & Marner which is sort of too neat. But the Mill, by God, is right up there with the Brontes... I am saving Middlemarch & Adam Bede, with restraint so uncharacteristic as to be uncanny, for this summer, when we hope to have two long, absolutely empty months in the old house in the Napa Valley. Anybody could write The Mill deserves some clear space around them!

I want to write you about some stuff that has been troubling me, but I really don't know how because it is far too close to me & I am all churned up exactly like a 17-year-old. It also has to do with Male & Female inside the Woman. See I have been getting an increasing lot of static from the women's movement about how I always write about men. Used to be people would ask questions and I would say Well look I don't <u>know</u> why I do this, aside from some obvious things like growing up with an impressive father & three older impressive brothers and so introjecting a lot of male values, but that doesn't explain it all because I also had an impressive mother who managed to turn me out—once the bluejeans and Horses stage was over—a woman who was really quite pleased to <u>be</u> a woman; and so I don't understant it either, so let's talk about it, and then we would. But now a lot of virulence is coming at me about it & the talking stage seems to be over with. Joanna wrote me ten pages telling me how all my women are Aunt Toms and all my men have no balls anyhow—which I was totally unable to answer. And some similar stuff has been coming. And the thing is, whether they are right or not does not concern me particularly, but they are hitting something unresolved, unsolved, painful inside me…

[There is more to this letter, but the next page appears to be missing.]

Dear Tree,

You sound as if you are feeling a little trapped. I spose this is inevitable but, but it OUGHT to be evitable—Well; all this is about <u>real</u> life. I have never believed in real life; have you, honestly? What they mean is quantifiable. Alli S. is 61 (is it) and weighs 112 (160, 386) lbs and lives at 6037 Ramshorn Pl. 22101 etc. etc., hell, these days you can do it <u>all</u> in digits, the Social Security number will do. So there is quantifiable life, & I ain't knocking it; 1500 calories a day is the first thing you ask God for. But why does only it get called real? Are you trying to tell me there is no such person as James Tiptree Junior, that he isn't real? I've got 5 years of letters from him, and I <u>know</u> the man. He has written some excellent fiction. If he hasn't got a Soc Sec No he isn't real? Come on!

To tell you the truth, I have so cherished & valued my friendship with the fellow that I am somewhat jealous of his close association, his intimacy as you might put it, with Alli Sheldon. If Alli is going to get possessive & domineering now, just because she has a lousy Soc Sec No, and not let James T. say anything (on paper, of course; he always was a quiet sort of man), I shall be very disappointed, and I really shouldn't wonder if James T. didn't get resentful. He and Raccoona might league together, and escape, disguised as a horse—J.T. will have to be the back legs, because he's taller, and THEN what are you going to do when you look out the window and there on your lawn is a ridiculous horse whose back knees bend wrong cavorting around and eating the roses and trampling the herbaceous borders in fits of joie de vivre and whinnying I'm real! I'm real! —Eh?

I wish Jung had known you. He would have had more damn fun with this magnificent imbroglio of extravert-introvert-animus-persona-self you have achieved; I think he would have admired it wholeheartedly, and invented a new & rare aspect of the Self, which, when it occurs, is called the Anomalous Function, & causes everybody considerable delight.

I'll tell you where I'm at, if it's any help. I learned I could do active fantasy a couple years ago & every now & then when more than usually confused I do one; it's always the same one, I mean it takes up where the last one left off even though months ago—typical goddam one track mind novelist.—Anyhow for weeks & weeks I was walking through this endless desert called The Sand Levels, carrying under my armpit an egg, which a dragon gave me, & trying to forget what she told me to do with the egg, which was "Take a stick & break it." When I finally obeyed orders, I became the dragon's daughter, & there I was back in her cave—she is a VERY large, frightening, & disagreeable dragon—& she was telling me impatiently to sharpen my claws. Because I have to go out and eat knights.

I still resist this. I keep saying I don't WANT to eat knights. Knights are brave and noble & not very well armoured, etc., it isn't fair. But I have eaten one, with considerable pleasure, I must admit. I was thinking about something or other I'd written, and suddenly this voice, a young male voice, most self-assured and snotty, said with a sneer, "You didn't do that, you know." And I lost my temper, I said, "I did too!" —and ate him. Snap.

If I meet many more like that one I may end up a pretty fat dragon.

I guess what I am now engaged in is the Search for the Inedible Knight.

[Ursula]

Ah yes, Beloved Starbear:

I was reflecting on your remark about how we know less about each other now we meet as women—or parts thereof. (Oh but hoe we really knew each other, the mind's unimpeded radar.)

Had Tiptree been—no, if Tiptree was—my outer persona, so that I met you in the flesh as old-man-to-young-woman—or rather, to woman at that best of ages, I can just picture it. How I would have swept off my hat, bowed low over your hand, with a look expressive of Oh Queen and Had-I-but-Forty-Years-ago—and then stept back and let off a carefully contrived firework (obtained in Hongkong) which would have filled the sky with falling dragons featuring Hearts Entwined, and writ over all in letters of green fire to the zenith, URSULA K. LE GUIN...And then we would have strolled and chatted of the habits of English versififers and you would have let out carefully edited of your internal family life, which would have filled me with pangs of gallant awe, fascination and love. And I would be so careful, so careful, because you are in fact tho thenshitive. And then ... what but more strollings and chats, an uncly friend whom Charles would never resent. Dodgson to your Alice.

But when we meet as women, there is the strange come-down of reality, myth lost... And I conscious that I come on too strong, a leathered veteran of the wars, yet whiningly vulnerable, my chest visibly open to all the same domestic concerns (bar young, which nature forbade) (or rather, a bloodily inept gynocologist—a detail James would never have permitted to intrude)—plus a wild long biography, complete with aroma of twice-told tales of exploits found remarkable in the female—but very female—it is all different... But it is not, it is the same. Only I hang back, hiding my great paws behind my back, afraid to step too closely into what I know is a field of exquisitely sensitive radar, afraid to damage invisible tentacles. Maybe it's all summed up as, for a woman I come on vigorous (except for the invisible endless times of lying doggo with a cold cloth on my head in a dark room, my sensors overloaded, my heart longing for oblivion. Self-pity—to which Tip would never admit.) Whereas as a man I came on gentle.

Another woman...woman-to-woman...we are all untrained. We have no art at "real" meetings, we start talking about how hard our stoves are to clean... It gives me marvellously to think and ponder.

Since I have become a woman to my correspondents, I am shattered daily by confidences of woe; as Tiptree I knew the woe was there, I tried—buoyed up by myth—to help. I think I helped. As a woman, another depressed one, I can do little but murmur Oh my Oh my, my dear. And it doesn't help as much.

(Maybe I am over-influenced by a recent bout of long hours on our County Rape Crisis hotline, in which I have had to learn more that I wanted to know about my sex.)

Anyway, Ting is snatching me away early to Yucatan, under the impression that (a) my doctors, (b) the telephone, and (c) the mail are killing me. He may be right. We leave 7 Nov., so this may be the last for awhile as there is truly no mail out of there.

> [handwritten] *This was just to write you.*
> *Had a long talk about you with Dave Hartwell.*
> *He says, she has wildness in her*
> *that she won't let out.*
> *Love, rockets*

Dear Joanna,

To say that this is a hard letter to write would be the understatement of some time.

How will you react when I tell you that the person you have been corresponding with as Traptroop is really Raccoona Sheldon, aka Alli Sheldon, aka Dr. Alice B. Sheldon—the doctorate being merely in a behavioural science, not the kind that does anybody any good?

The thing is, the last thing poor Mother did was blow Tiptree out of the water, I had no idea her obituaries would be splashed around. So Jeff Smith wrote me that Harlan had latched on to one, or something, giving me as sole survivor, and was busy telling the fans. So Jeff looked it up forhimself and wrote me the question direct.

I don't lie, except for the signature—which has grown, over the years, into just another nickname—so I had to tell him yes. (That was good, actually, because I had always promised him he would be the first to know. I left a letter telling the truth in Bob Mill's safe, to be opened if Tiptree i.e., me, died; but I'm morally sure he hasn't opened it.)

The letter says that James Tiptree Jr. was born in late 1967 in the Import Food Section of Giant, when I was looking for a name that editors would forget rejecting. It never occurred to me that everything would sell. So then everything just snowballed from there. I love the sf world, and I couldn't resist Jeff Smith's request for an interview—figured I could skip over the bio details quickly without lying, because my curriculum vitae does sound male—and start waving Hello to all the people I've loved and admired for so long.

But then the epistolary friendships grew—especially with women, if you noticed Raccoona you understand I am deeply committed to women; and I thought in my innocence that this prank would help. (There are anthologists who have sharp inquiries from Tiptree as to why no women contributors.) But the friendships got real. But I never wrote calculated stuff or lies, what I've written you—or anyone—is true, true true. All of it.

So now it is time for me to stop being a brand of marmelade and painfully write those of you who have befriended Tiptree what the facts really are: A 61-yr-old woman—past adventures, I guess, life said to be "exciting" and "glamorous", but it just seemed like a lot of work at the time—6 ft 8 ½ [sic], wt. 135, hair brownish going greystreak, incurable open childish stare, lumpy writer's face, as I said, once said to be good-looking but really only animated; mostly wears jeans and cords, and worried sick that my much more aged husband of 30 years is going blind.

Jo, can you take it? God, the number of times I've wanted to cry out, dear Sister, how well I know, how well I know what you mean. But I am different, by reason of age and time of upbringing, from the feminists today. Maybe more pessimistic, more aware of the male power structures in which I've struggled for long years. (With their Queen Bees.)

Have I done anything evil? It didn't feel evil, it was just a prank that dreamed its way into reality. I think were beginning to "see through", too.

Can I ask you to hold this "secret" a awhile longer, at least until Ballantine's stop sitting on that damn novel and decide to publish? I don't think they want an ersatz Tiptree.... I had planned to establish Raccoona better and then kind of slide over, but with my low production and this damn novel I've only been able to give her minor stories. Funny though; editors screaming for Tiptree stuff return Racoona with beer-can stains on the pages—not really that bad but almost.

(If you take this in the true spirit it happened in, there are quite a few laughs to share.)

The funny thing is, Tiptree has taken on a kind of weird reality; I'm beginning to believe something was awaiting incarnation in the gourmet food section. Tiptree for instance insisted of "Tip," would not be called "Jim." And he has shown himself a spiritual uncle to quite a few depressed people, mostly fellow pros. Alli Sheldon almost had to give up teaching for the same reason—all the outsiders, green monkeys, tearful young girls, spotted me at once and made me into a kind of crying-shoulder or hot-line for troubles. I can't resist. I know too well how things hurt.

For your information, in addition to Jeff Smith, I wrote Ursula at once because of our long friendship, and then Quinn and Vonda because of ditto. Since we met later, I waited two nights to write you; it takes a sleepless night to write this. So you are the only ones who <u>know</u>, pace Harlan.

How I admire you who have made it openly as women.

I think I would have if I'd thought it through, but I was finishing my PhD orals at the time I wtote my first 4, and I wasn't thinking anything through except the evidence for and against rat learning—I'm a behavioural or "rat" psychologist. So I just tagged on the first male name that came handy and let it go. And then was stuck. You see, I am extremely shy and recessive.

I guess that's all the brute facts. If I should have put in more, let me know, if your still speaking to your friend

Tip

Alli

Raccoona

PS one thing I noticed, Tip was going to write you about. Have you noticed that we have always discussed writers not as technicians or the "art of writing"—but as their ethical, moral, political messages? Fascinating. Of course maybe you didn't want to discuss writerly points with me because neither Tip nor I really know <u>how</u> to write.

PSS Another point; all of Tiptree is me; Ting (my husband) is a non-reader, hasn't a clue what I really do. An old friend, really; at 61 and 75 that becomes more important than gender.

Oh, Joanna, will I have any friends left?

Dear Allie,

Just a short note.

A red squirrel was running across the snow only ten minutes ago. Temperature at 9AM – 10 degrees F. They never seem to hibernate here; they only get fatter and fatter. Therefore the Doberman next door never stops having intermittent hysterics.

Merilyn Hacker wants to take you to task about the story, "Your Faces, O My Sisters" and since she's currently reading 80 poetry mss. for her next-term class, I said I'd rely [sic] the message. She says that the present-day (i.e. non-crazy) women in that story are all presented as not helping or being enemies of the one free (mad) woman and in several cases the man is the one who wants to go to the aid of the woman and the woman with his doesn't. The couple on a date, for example (or was it husband and wife) – my experience has been that the woman might very well urge the man to get involved and he make some kind of excuse.

Anyway, she says (and I agree) that one ought to make clear why or how the other women have been made so traitorous and so reluctant to help. And I don't think it'll wash that the policewoman refuses to go help. After all, that's her job.

Otherwise: I've just written an enormous Bloof! to Ursula, with the anguish of three years' silence in it, and basically begged her to write about herself. But of course she won't. If as Suzy says, she really thinks she's got a man in her who does her writing.

I'm tired, having caught up with three weeks' correspondence in two days, and half forgotten how to type. So I won't say anything else, but wanted to relay Marilyn's message to you. I've got to go out & buy things and pick up parcels at the P.O. and generally prepare for real life, a task that's beginning to seem less and less interesting. I also have to try to get some money from the health insurance on campus (every year!) and go hire—if I can—a cook.

Love,
Joanna

Dearest Joanna,

I hope you got the cook and the health insurance and found the strength to immerse again in real (ugh) life.

At present I'm immersed in it and coincidently in the blackest phase of depression (I keep dreaming I'm dead and spending eternity in hell with a collection of failed financiers and Tupperware salespeople.) There being nothing interesting to write about depression, I shall refrain.

Thanks for the stimulating argument from Marilyn Hacker and you about FACES. Yes, of course it was horrible how the women failed to help the girl. But I couldn't stop the flow of her narrative to explain why, part of the point was that there really is such a sorry host of such women. (And by the way, there may have been two girls in the story, one inadvertently reliving the past of a ghostly twin—I mean, the courier may have been real too.)

The point is, I suspect I have spent a great deal more time among women of the sort you—and maybe Marilyn—never see. They're THERE. Of course there's reasonswhy they are like that—reasons we all know all too well; the trivialised, the man-identified, the too-private-souled (Rebecca West called it the woman's sin of "idiocy", in the Greek sense). When I see them I amsick, I lose all hope. (There's still something wrong with this typer.) But you know I am paranoid. I am hideously depressed about the difficulty of a real joining of force among women. There are so very many who cling to, pride in their deformity of soul. Fear freedom, hate the free. Tell Marilyn that, tell her I wanted to contrast the (possibly real) world of sisters with the horrible actuality of today. That it was very bitter in my mouth. And tell her also I let them speak for themselves to those who understand, that technically I couldn't put in their upbringing... As to the "compassionate" man, he was a professional compassionater, a doctor, and his impulse was only a fleeting one of "protecting a girl." The reporter at the end who is dismayed by the policewoman's indifference is simply me, speaking my paranoid heart about how I had believed women really always help women. To that policewoman, her job in the male world was all-important, she had absorbed the callousness toward female vagrants.

You—and maybe Marilyn—have found the small network or community of the feminist world. I have, too, peripherally, I belong to two chapters of NOW, but I "live" among women who are untouched by it, who don't even care about—or know about—ERA (Which Virginia has failed to ratify.) I wanted to show them in all their varied ghastliness... After a point, who cares how Eichmann got that way.

That Marilyn Hacker must be quite somebody, by the way.

Now I'll go back and cut my throat some more. I'll be gone to Yucatan when you get this, but my affection & admiration star with you.

[handwritten:] Back end March
Alli

Dear Allie,

It's such a pleasure to write you that I can't resist. After making the bed, doing the laundry, shopping, sharpening pencils, &c. &c. everything I should've done yesterday and couldn't because I spent 10 hours writing a 22-page article about my sexual history, merely to get it together in my own head. It now looks almighty dull and I will have to go back and sparkle it up a bit. This, by the way, is for a novel which will come out under a pseudonym and is a dark deep secret, like Tiptree. I'm not even going to tell you what it is. It's my Lesbian Novel (somehow everybody who's gay ends up writing one Gay Novel like Forster).

The cook hasn't emerged. Every time the phone rings, I pick up to find it's somebody from Oshkosh who wants to give a talk or it's telephone solicitation (of which there's a lot) or a student who must get into a class or die, and I'm going to have my number unlisted, damn it.

This week has been a zoo, incredibly emotionally demanding. I end up with 62 people in my s.f. class and people trying to get into the writing class and general screaming and confusion. It gets so that I can be polite <u>only</u> in class or in my office and at home I merely snarl.

About Marilyn's comment about (&c.) I've been hassling that question, i.e. how does one deploy the story so that you <u>don't</u>

have to stop and EXPLAIN (ugh). I re-read it and there's more splitting of pov between the women that Marilyn remembered. And your one male doctor really does come out as unbearably patronizing & not really interested. I would still question the policewoman—if she's been recruited recently into the force, she's probably a feminist herself, since it apparently takes a rhino hide and a portable flamethrower simply to get in, for a woman.

[handwritten in margin] These ideas are not for re-writing of course, just thinking about.

Why not make the reporter at the end a woman? (Especially since you say that is where your soul lodges.) He is "bald"! so I guess that's not a woman. A woman's paranoia about women changes the whole thing. There must be, I think, many ways of doing this sort of thing quickly without impeding the narrative. I tried in TWO to make sure that there's a few saving-grace moments for everybody, even my villain. I mean just as you decide that X or Y is hopeless, they say "Everybody knows that. Even Dr. Blank in his book says...." and you see them absorbing the information that women have raging hormones or whatever. I think the point is to force some kind of shorthand as to where the pov comes from. Chip has been at me about this until I finally did absorb it and say: OK, not so much "why" is so-and-so like this, but what are the social forces operating and can we have a dramatic glimpse of them. I admit it's a LOT easier in a novel. There must be some way of indicating, for example, that the policewoman is uptight about her job, and that she's right because the Dept.'s trying to get rid of her or whatever.

May I ask you for some information, s.f. wise? I'm writing a story called "The Woman Who Kept Her Medulla in Her Handbag" —you can see subtle little echoes of "The Girl Who Was Plugged In"—for some cracked reason I've thought up the idea that if someone's cerebral cortex and even whole brain were rotting slowly away from a localized viral infection, the person might be saved (if the thing was caught early) by excising the brain after having made a computer analogue of it. You then put a transceiver of some kind where the brain used to be and hook it up via a special wavelength (FM? AM?) to the computer, so that (without any time lag to speak of) this woman is doing her thinking by renting computer time in the city's central computer. Since the medulla is essential for various life-support stuff, she carries an analog to that in a shoulder bag or backpack. It would be possible to beam a very strong signal for at least a few miles, but I would imagine she couldn't get too far away from the computer, since the time-lag would begin to matter on the other side of the world, say, and because reception might get staticky. Imagine having static in your thought-processes!

How far away does she have to go to get effectively out of range of an ordinary FM signal? A tighter microwave beam might do, but they're both line-of-sight, aren't they?

Do you know anything about this besides what you put in "The Girl Who Was Plugged In"? Which I will re-read.

This image won't go away. There is obviously a story attached to it, but nothing else has come clear. I really like the idea that if she happens to find herself completely surrounded by metal (as on a bridge) and her cerebral cortex suddenly is disconnected, as it were, the medulla keeps her going. She just faints and somebody drags her into the open—because they all know her. She would probably wear a Medical Alert necklace! (What would it say!) Anyhow I keep seeing her in a black leather coat with the handbag. Sort of the ultimate prosthetic. I suppose it's really about existential freedom and suchlike, i.e. that we are free to be "unnatural".

This may not follow you to Yucatan. I wonder… is there an alien outpost there? Do you really—Never mind. But it will be waiting when you return. I'm tired and rather harried at the moment, having been through the first week hysterickals all week. I really come out of school feeling that people have been trying to nip me in hordes and drink my blood. They don't really mean to, actually. But why they think a class in s.f. will be easy to get into… !

Back to the 22-page essay on my love life, squalid and dull as most of it was. But I'm beginning to get an idea why it was that way. And it will have gossip-value if nothing else.

[handwritten] Good health to both of you in Yucatan!

Love,

Joanna

Dear Allie,

Your name was taken much in vain in <u>Locus</u> today—as usual it was the Jan. 30 issue out in mid-March (!) and by now you must've seen the little box. I'm waiting with bated breath to see how many fans "knew all along" and how many "suspected that style was a man's" and how many voices are lifted to tell us that somehow, looking back at what you've written, it isn't, after all, <u>that</u> good.... I don't think much of the last will happen, actually, but I suspect that fans' writings about you are going to get a shade less chummy.

This is a dreary evening—mostly my own fault, as I spent the day happily whizzing about, cleaning house and doing errands, and am now paying for all that sense of purpose and activity by the usual Workaholic slump. The movies on TV are terrible; my TV itself is beginning to need treatment (and will have to go to the shop some week when I'm not here or I shall die of withdrawal pangs), and I <u>refuse</u> to watch Westerns. Or even Carol Burnett, though in a bemused way I like looking at that channel because it has a good picture.

...[1]

Anyway, I am sick of writers' egos (except yours and mine and Suzy's, of course).

Actually my classes seem to be going well, although there's

---

1 Discussion of Russ' work omitted.

6 weeks of the term still left, very odd because I am <u>quite</u> sure I have been teaching for about 12. But no. A few days ago suddenly the sun reached that height in the sky where there is a genuine middle to the day. Until now (since November) it's been early morning suddenly becoming early evening. Now it's obviously spring—which here has nothing to do with the temperatures. You can tell it's spring because it <u>snows</u> in the spring.

It hasn't snown enough, though. We're hoping for lots more.

I have the remains of 10 violet-colored crocuses in my front yard. ...[2]

Anti-intellectualism is the bane of every radical movement, I suppose, at least in the U.S. and the 20th century. I am really sick of "women's movement" women (<u>they</u> think) who have no sense of history (other than melodrama), who believe the world can run on yoghurt and astrology, and who in general put the name of feminism to their very ordinary lack of brains, knowledge, common sense, realism, and so on. It is very Los Angeles, somehow. Everybody in her own little back yard, shutting out the world.

Do you remember seeing anywhere a Mack Reynolds story (I think it was) in which women were divided into two kinds: the "sexless" office workers who dressed in gray and were considered by men to be genuinely physically sexless, and the "others" who had breasts and desire, and in general looked like Dolly Parton, wig and all—they had sort of night clubs where they belly-danced (one to each woman) and men came to watch them. The dancer-

---

2 Discussion of Russ' work omitted.

women had padded bosoms and fake eyelashes and makeup, and the official biological theory was that at puberty some women developed naturally like this. It was an obvious attempt to embody something of the same kind of division as we have in folklore today and expose that superheated "sexy" image. I did, by the way, see Dolly Parton on TV for the first time, and she is to the nth degree that extremely artificial female image—to the point that she's genuinely eerie: hair nobody could really have, terribly long and impossibly wavy and blonde and thick, eyelashes ditto, a mask of a face (with heavy makeup), and breasts that are simply very improbable. She scared me.

If you can remember seeing this story, please tell me. I don't know if it's ever been published. Somebody showed it to me in manuscript (I don't remember how that happened or why) some years ago, say five or six, and it was quite good. I think it was Mack Reynolds and I think he'd never had it published, fearing to, I suppose.

(And by the way, about Dolly Parton—one of those sweet, little-girl voices. Though obviously anybody who's made it as she has must be built out of titanium steel.)

I wonder sometimes what sort of man could be fixated on that body type that nobody has, and what on earth he can do with his sexuality if he is.

An excellent article on sexuality came from KNOW, Inc. I'm going to try to make copies of it and send it around; it's really first-rate and says some of the things that nobody has talked about yet, not really, though some discussions of (say) rape fantasies do touch on the subject. In brief what the article says is that women are to some degree (from mildly to very much, I suppose) conditioned so that our sexuality is structured in a male dominance/female submission model which, if a woman has any kind of strong desire for personhood, involves her in the most awful and hideously painful conflicts. In short, you must sell your soul for a good fuck—which I have always refused to do, and suffered endlessly thereby. I'll try to get it to you.

Marilyn has been away too long. I've turned around a fixated myself on somebody else. Right now it looks impossibly difficult just because everything does; in fact, she's a good friend whose company is worth a lot more to me than "sex"—whatever that is. Our erotic vocabulary is ridiculous and designed to mystify and befuddle; I refuse to use it. Like Rita Mae Brown's new book in which the two characters meet, bed, and instantly achieve a zillion orgasms apiece—which is going to leave many readers wondering what is wrong with them. ·

I seem to have about ten head-trips that turn me on—all different and all equally mysterious. I give up. So I won't understand it, so what!

Really by tomorrow (when I've stopped working for a day or so) I should feel reasonably human. And when school ends, a lot of people will have time for sociability and fun, which nobody seems to now. Solaris is in town, so one of the things this next week must be seeing it.

I really don't see anyone from week's end to week's end sometimes—my own fault largely for not arranging contacts. This whole country suffers from the Sunday neurosis. I'm just crabbing about tonight and must go shopping tomorrow & work out new notes on <u>1984</u> (that fake) and that will put me in good humor.

Love, Joanna

Dear Allie,

...[3]

"I never planned to live this long." My dear, my dear, you're not old! And do you know how many people would mourn you? I hear a suicidal ring to that letter which disturbs me mightily. It may amuse you to know that your very description of your "aging body" turns me on! I like old women with a very special feeling and get all dreamy and erotic about them (an indecent proposal by letter!). Honest. If you only could locate yourself in some youthful Lesbian feminist community (you would soon be bored to death by them, but never mind) they would all crowd round you (in overalls, with shaved heads and multiple earrings) and coo softly, patting you in all sorts of places and saying admiring things about you until you got embarrassed. Truly. So don't run yourself down, or at least recognize the feeling for your own and no objective fact whatsoever. I wish I we could actually meet in the flesh some time some where—we would probably be all prim and stuff and proper unless I had the chutzpah to throw my arms around you and kiss you, which at the moment I would rather like to do!—anyway, perhaps we can, soon, someday?

Consider yourself well and truly propositioned. I was in love with you when you were "James Tiptree, Jr" and have been able

---

3 Russ' discussion of her relationship with her parents has been omitted.

to transfer the infatuation to Allie Sheldon, who is, after all, the same person. So if you ever decide to inhabit the same Con or the same MLA meeting , we can <u>at the very least</u> have a good, long, hearty talk together, if not much more.

ARE you a frustrated Lesbian? I know that for me the scene with men was also mostly pure havoc, with sometimes lots of affection for a particular man but basically everything going wrong. But many women were getting along perfectly well in an erotic fashion with men and then decided to be gay, and there are straight women who have even more trouble with men than I do. Did, that is. I know that my mother also (when I was getting divorced) intimated that she had these weird erotic feelings about me (she said so in a restaurant, in front of my father, and I almost crept under the table in sheer embarrassment). I would suspect that it happens, more or less, in every family to every daughter, except in families where (1) mother is too busy and/or ground down to have erotic feelings for anybody, and (2) there's such a lot of hatred between mother and daughter that they're perpetually flinging things at one another. I don't know. But I don't think it's rare or even that odd.

Did I tell you about my own horrible depressions, which vanished once and for all, when I decided I WAS gay? It's like cutting off part of one's personality; the cut-off part begins to rot and poison one. It's odd; it's not a matter of not actually having some good, on-going love thing actually happening; it's rather a matter of one's own internal economy. Have you told this to your shrink and your MD and what do they say? You know, it's not disloyalty to Ting; it's not that at all. But to live, knowing that you can never be yourself, that's a very tough thing and enough to make life seem pointless and hopeless. I only say all this tentatively, having lived through something like that myself. I am hazarding a guess at venture. Venturing a guess? No, I won't go on yarning out that phrase in every possible permutation!

"Also, I didn't know how." Oh, nobody knows how. You make it up. You know. People aren't so simple. I remember looking at a Playboy cover and thinking that I couldn't be a Lesbian because the cover didn't excited me (in fact, I loathed it) and getting very upset because I wasn't a Lesbian. Something silly going on with guilt feelings and impossibility feelings. As my friend, to whom said her shrink, "You know, you're the only patient I ever had who was afraid she might be heterosexual!" I felt like that for several years.

Are you ready to have mad adventures in your waning years?

Marilyn Hacker, who is up here for a month with her three-year-old daughter (a royal pain, who talks ALL THE TIME) says admiring things about you & thinks that James Tiptree, Jr,. is the best literary impersonation ever and a splendid achievement. So I'm relaying that to you. Don't feel you have to live up to it! You have already done it.

You sound absolutely in the depths of despair. I wish I had a 2000-mile-long crowbar to lift you out! If anything s.f.-al ever happens near McLean, Va., I'm going, but only on the provision that we can have a quiet visit together. I have this absolute horror of hearing (from someone else, naturally) that you've been found hanging from a lamp post or with your head in the oven. Dear God! Promise me: if you decide to commit suicide, call me up first on the telephone, OK? ...[4]

Another book is coming on and I'm holding it off at arm's length. If I'm lucky, I can have six months before I get started. It'll be all hideously narcissistic, splendid adventure and maybe plus life in the 1950's.

May I give your address to Marilyn? She'd like to write you. Maybe if enough of us keep writing you, you'll be too busy writing us to get quite so low. At any rate, to me the thought of you reaching 85 (handsomer all the time; that's one of the advantages of being a Lesbian) is delightful and heartening and I hope you do.

At a venture: depression is real. I don't believe it's all in the head, &c., some sort of thing that needs autoplasty to cure. Depression is having what you think you ought to want but not getting what you really truly want. Yes, it can go on and on and on. I get bored, angry, irritated, sad, everything now, but that hopelessness and sense of absolute despair is gone. It has been gone for a year and a half, which I consider long enough to figure it's gone for good. At least I've repossessed my own head, if nothing else.

Lesbianism isn't sleeping with women; it's loving women. Can't define more. Never mind Yeats; why don't you write out what you want? Daughters, Inc. can publish it under ANOTHER pseudonym.

---

4 Russ' personal details omitted.

Must go now. I've been washing floors and vacuuming all day (house guest with dog just left; never again!) and putting through endless washes.

...[5]

You MUST write me.

Much love,
Joanna

---

5 Russ' personal details omitted.

Dear Alli,

I <u>do</u> read your letters. I don't answer anything in them unless I have something to say about what's in them—which strikes me as fairly reasonable, frankly. And maybe I go in for "banal whining," <u>but that is me, too.</u> I don't come in "flashes of Joanna" but Joanna all through, banal or otherwise. That in your letter offended me (see, I read it), though now I'm more tired than offended & probably am getting the flu. Either that or a simple menstrual headache. I have a 4-day-a-week schedule and am being slowly ground into nubbins by it—I haven't anything like my full strength back yet.

I don't want to be angry, but did have to say something! When I whine about the miserableness of life, it's because <u>I can't cope</u>—for whatever reason—not because the things themselves are so awful. I know that. But that's how I feel, damn it.

Enough.

I'm trying to imagine you growing a beard.

Wish someone could build you not just a new clutch of pills, but a new body—something with jets in—so we could look up, about midnight, and watch Alli scooting about in interstellar space, gathering material for a novel.

...[6]

There's an article you ought to read in <u>Conditions Four</u>. Do

---

6 Personal information about Russ omitted.

you get Conditions? If not tell me & I'll send it you for a birthday present. One of our (writers') problems is that we can't measure out lives by ordinary standards: Successful Children, Nice House, etc. —even if we have these, we're so apt to measure everything sub specie aeternitatis (sp?) that nothing is unequivocally O.K. Which feeds all sorts of despair.

I am teaching your story "Houston, Houston" (in Star Songs) to the frosh—few of whom will read the intro. & find out who you are. They'll get it at the end of the quarter, when they trust me... !

The article in Conditions is about a shelter for homeless women, the bag ladies, and what is the dynamic of their self-hatred. Basically it's the necessity of living for the needs of others, the guilt at having needs of their (her) own, the terror and rage of not being able to fill these needs. It sounded like me. I wondered if it would sound like you to you.

...[7]

Love,
Joanna

---

7 Personal comments from Russ about work and life omitted.

29 Sept. 1980

Dear Tip,

Never mind about the story. That will take care of itself. So will your dear heart, dear heart, I hope, and the crumbling oral cavity—which we all have. The real payment for art & literature is <u>dental work</u>. Cats have arthritis, but only humans have bad backs & lousy teeth! (My teeth are being fixed WELL.)

Your letter was lovely. I know just what you mean: I like some men a lot, too, even lust after them (as Adrienne Rich has written), but they don't light me up. That's a lovely phrase.

I've been reading your letter and crying, on & off. I'm very moved. No, you never told me. I always wondered, though—first of all because I find you very beautiful in your photographs, in that high-handed sort of way I love in women. I mean you look <u>real</u> and full of Tiptree-ness. As well as, objectively, quite lovely, something I know you'll never believe. Second was your amazing facility at male impersonation—except that "Tiptree" was That man Who Is On Our Side, which means he was never real. He was a freed Us. I was madly in love with him & sensed uneasily that this was odd, since no real man, & no real-man-as-truly-revealed-in-literature has ever had that effect on me of intimacy and "I know <u>you</u>"! Though I kept trying to persuade myself over & over that Such Men Existed. But even the nicest have been, at best, interesting, even attractive aliens. Third was your depression. I think I asked you once point-blank about the connection between Lesbianism and depression & you said Mmfp wmpf murble yes no never mind.

The terrible thing is how all this is <u>hidden from us</u>—what <u>is</u> a Lesbian, anyhow? It's unthinkable, invisible, ridiculous, Somebody Else, duck-tail haircuts & leather jackets, all that nonsense. As Rich says.

Dear Tip, have you any IDEA of the women all over the U.S. of A. who would trample each other into mulch just for a chance to kiss your toes?

Listen, idiot, you're not UGLY.* Old, yes—and with various awful ills that mean you can't go gallivanting about. But <u>ugly</u>? Say that again and I'll HIT you! It's so Goddamned writerly: <u>I</u> think <u>I'm</u> ugly. Vonda thinks <u>she's</u> ugly. (I had all I could do for several years to avoid squeezing her, as she is so cute!) Writers are impossible people. And I suspect that Lesbians manage a decent love life—as perhaps <u>women</u> do—only if we're prepared to sacrifice in some other area. And since writer women aren't prepared to do so, other parts of our lives suffer. It's a bad, bad world!

...[8]

Love,

Joanna

*I think you just wanted a compliment

---

8 Personal information and comments from Russ omitted.

Everything
But
The Signature
Is Me

Introduction to *Star Songs* of an *Old Primate*

Ursula K Le Guin, 1978

When the author of this book requested me to write an introduction for it, I was honored, delighted, and appalled. Omitting the civilities and apologies customary between old primates, and which went on for about a week, the request appeared in these terms, and I quote: "Write a two-line introduction saying, Here are some stories."

I have been trying to obey these instructions ever since. Various versions have been tested; for example:

Here
Are some stories.

Here are
Some stories.

Here are some
Stories.

Since none of these efforts seemed entirely satisfactory, I took the liberty of expanding upon the basic instructions, at the risk of offending the profound and authentic modesty of the author, and arrived at this:

Here are some superbly strong sad funny and very beautiful Stories.

That seems a little more like it. I may return to this problem later, with renewed vigor. There must be some way to do it.

I have known James Tiptree, Jr., for several years now; known him well, and with ever-increasing trust and pleasure, and to the profit of my soul. He is a rather slight, fragile man of about sixty, shy in manner, courteous; wears a straw hat; has lived in, and still vacations in, some of the more exotic parts of the world; has been through the army, the government, and the university; an introvert, but active; a warm friend, a man of candor, wit, and style. He always types with a blue typewriter ribbon, and the only question I have asked him which he has always evaded is, "Where do you get so many blue typewriter ribbons?" When he himself is blue, he has told me so, and I've tried to cheer him up, and when I have been blue I've been turned right round into the sunlight simply by getting one of Tiptree's preposterous, magnificent letters. Tiptree has introduced me to the Clerihew; Tiptree has pulled me from the slough of despond by means of a single squid drawn (in blue ink) on a postcard. The only thing better than Tiptree's letters is his stories. He is a man whose friendship is an honour and a joy.

The most wonderful thing about him is that he is also Alice Sheldon.

Recently I've been hearing from people who have friends who say, "I knew all along that Tiptree was a woman. I could tell it from the prose style," or "from the male characters," or "from the female characters," or "from the Vibrations." I don't know any of these people who knew all along; they didn't say much about it; never even happened to mention that they knew, for some reason, until all the rest of us knew. We (the rest of us) knew rather suddenly and utterly unexpectedly. I don't think I have ever been so completely surprised in my life—or so happily. All I can say is I'm glad I didn't know all along, because I would have missed that joyous shock of revelation, recognition—that beautiful Jill-in-the-box.

Quite a lot of us did, however, suspect the short-story writer Raccoona Sheldon of being either an invention of Tiptree's or his natural daughter, and we were quite right; only what is right? What does it mean to say that "Tiptree is Sheldon," or that "James Tiptree, Jr., is a woman?" I am not sure at all, except that it's a fine example of the pitfalls built into the English verb *to be*. You turn it around and say, "A woman is James Tiptree, Jr.," and you see you have said something quite different.

As for *why* Alice is James and James is Alice, that is still another matter, and one where speculation very soon becomes prying and invasion of privacy. But there are fascinating precedents. Mary Ann Evans was a Victorian woman living with a Victorian man to whom she wasn't married; she took a pen-name to protect her work from censure. But why a male pen-name? She could, after all, have called herself Sara Jane Williams. It appears that she needed to be George Eliot, or George Eliot needed to be her, for a while. She and she together got past certain creative and spiritual deadends and morasses that the woman Mary Ann alone was in danger of getting stuck in. As soon as she felt herself free, she admitted and announced the George Eliot/Mary Ann Evans identity. George's name continued to appear on the title pages of the great novels: as a practical matter, of course—the name was a best-seller—but also, I should guess, in gratitude and in sheer, and characteristic, integrity.

Dr. Alice Sheldon isn't a Victorian, nor are we, and her reason for using pen names may be assumed to be personal rather than social; and that's really all we have any right to assume about the matter. But since she did use a male persona, and kept it up publicly with perfect success for years, there are some assumptions that we ought to be examining, gazing at with fascinated horror, revising with loud cries and dramatic gestures of contrition and dismay: and these are our assumptions—all of us, readers, writers, critics, feminists, masculinists, sexists, nonsexists, straights, gays—concerning "the way men write" and "the way women write." The kind of psychic bias that led one of the keenest, subtlest minds in science fiction to state, "It has been suggested that Tiptree is a female, a theory that I find absurd, for there is to me something ineluctably masculine about Tiptree's writing. I don't think the novels of Jane Austen could have been written by a man nor the stories of Ernest Hemingway by a woman." The error was completely honest, and we all made it: but the justification and the generalization—even with such supposedly extreme examples as Austen and Hemingway—that bears some thinking about. We ought to think about it. And about all our arguments concerning Women in Fiction and why we have them; and all the panels on Women in Science Fiction (omitting, of course, James Tiptree, Jr.). And all the stuff that has been written about "feminine style," about its inferiority or superiority to "masculine style," about the necessary, obligatory difference of the two. All the closed-shop attitudes of radical feminism, which invited Tiptree out of certain inner sanctums because, although his stories were so very good and so extraordinary in their understanding of women, still, he was a man. All the ineffable patronization and put-down Sheldon is going to receive now from various male reviewers because, although her stories are so very good and so extraordinary in their understanding of man, still, she is a woman. All that. All that kipple, gubbish, garble, and abomination which Alice James Raccoona Tiptree Sheldon, Jr., showed for what it is when she appeared, smiling a little uncertainly, from her postbox in McLean, Virginia. She fooled us. She fooled good and proper. And we can only thank her for it.

For though she stood us all on our heads, isn't it true that she played her game without actually lying—without deceit?

The army, the government, the university, the jungles, all that is true. Mr. Tiptree's biography is Dr. Sheldon's.

The beautiful story "The Women Men Don't See" (oh—now

that we know—what a gorgeously ironic title!) got a flood of nominations for the Nebula Award in 1974. So much of the praise of the story concerned the evidence it gave that a man could write with full sympathy about women, that Tiptree felt a prize for it would involve deceit, false pretences. She withdrew the story from the competition, muttering about not wanting to cut younger writers out of all the prizes. I don't think this cover-up was false, either: the truth, if not the whole truth. She had had a Nebula in 1973 for "Love Is the Plan the Plan Is Death," and a Hugo in the same year for "The Girl Who Was Plugged In." These prizes sneaked up on her and caught her by surprise, I think. Her 1976 Nebula for the powerful "Houston, Houston, Do You Read," in this volume, came so soon after the disclosure of her name that she didn't have time to think up a good excuse for withdrawing it; so she went off and hid in a jungle instead. She practises that "low profile" which Carlos Castenada, standing in high profile on the rooftops, preaches. The cult of personality, prevalent in art as in politics, is simply not her game.

Yet she did fool us; and the fact is important, because it makes a point which no amount of argument could have made. Not only does it imperil all theories concerning the woman as writer and the writer as woman, but it might make us question some of our assumptions concerning the existence of the writer, per se. It's idiotic to say. "There is no such person as James Tiptree, Jr." There is. The proof that there is, which will incidentally outlast us all, is these stories. But, because James wrote them, is Alice now to be besieged by people asking impertinent questions about her family life, where she gets her ideas from, and what she eats for breakfast—which is what we do to writers? Can anyone explain to her, or to me, or to himself, what all that has to do with the stories, and which is more real: the old primate or the star songs?

Again, there are lovely precedents; this time the one I'd choose is Woolf's novel *Orlando*. Alice Sheldon has quite a lot in common with Orlando, and, like Orlando, is an unanswerable criticism of the rational and moral fallacies of sexism, simply by being what and who she is. She also provides an exhilarating criticism of what real life, or reality, is, by being a fictional character who writes real stories; here she surpasses Orlando. On the edge of the impenetrable jungles of Yucatan, on the beach, the straw-hatted figure stands, dapper, fragile, smiling; just before vanishing into the shadows of the trees he murmurs, "Are you real?" and Alice, in a house in far Virginia, replacing the blue ribbon in her typewriter, smiles also and replies, "Oh yes, certainly." And I, who have never met either of them, agree. They are real. Both of them. But not so real, perhaps, as their stories. This book you hold in your hand, this is the genuine article. No fooling.

Here are
Some real stories.

Introduction to *Her Smoke Rose Up Forever*

Michael Swanwick, 2004

A stream ran through the living room of the house in McLean, Virginia, and there were pet tarantulas as well and a tank of Siamese fighting fish atop the toilet. But strangest of all were the three writing desks, each with its own distinct typewriter, stationery, and color of ink. One belonged to James Tiptree, Jr. A second was used exclusively by Raccoona Sheldon. The third was for Alice Sheldon, a sometime scientist, artist, newspaper critic, soldier, businesswoman, and retired CIA officer, who on occasion moved to one of the other desks to write science fiction in the persona of Tiptree or Raccoona. Those stories established her firmly as one of the finest short fiction writers the genre has ever produced.

But who was Alice Sheldon?

That question has hung over the science fiction community since long before anybody in it knew her real name. In the late 1960s, during a period of considerable stress and for reasons she could never adequately explain, Sheldon began writing fiction as James Tiptree, Jr., a nom de plume plucked from a jar of marmalade.

Tiptree's first four stories, published in 1968, attracted little or no attention, and deservedly so. But then came "The Last Flight of Dr. Ain."

What a knockout! It's told backwards, in a flat documentary voice, like the forensic recreation of a crime. But who's compiled this information? To whom is it being reported? Formally, this story is like Goya's *Los Caprichos* etchings, whose figures exist in an uneasy grey zone that bears no identifiable relationship to background and horizon as we know them. And it has a stinger in its tail, in the revelation that it is not Dr. C. Ain but his companion who is the true criminal, and that this is not her first offense.

"The Last Flight of Dr. Ain" placed on the Nebula Award ballot, a surefire attention-getter for a previously unknown writer. It was followed by other works, equally startling, equally original. Continuing in order of publication, "And I Awoke and Found Me Here on the Cold Hill's Side" introduced one of Tiptree's great themes, the destructive force of cultural contact when one culture is far richer and more technologically advanced than the other. It also made explicit another theme, already present in "Dr. Ain," that of individual human beings caught in the grip of biological imperatives they are helpless to resist. Moreover, it was a classic example of an artist biting the hand that feeds him. The very xenophilia and sense of wonder that fuel the science fiction enterprise are portrayed as negative forces leading to the destruction of human culture, and possibly the species as well. "And I Have Come Upon This Place by Lost Ways" is almost a zen koan, simple and clean but lending itself to several interpretations. I would argue that it's about responsibility and that callow young Evan (callow young men are recurrent in Tiptree's fiction) dies in a state of grace. But if you care to read it as a parable of scientific integrity, that's there too. "The Man Who Walked Home" is another koan-like tale, and one that became talismanic for Tiptree, after a critic pointed out that it was the distilled essence of his work: a lone protagonist desperately striving to reach home, whatever the consequences, however improbable his chances of success. By now the fact that the story begins with its conclusion and proceeds backwards into the future, relating the future history of humanity through furtive glimpses along the way, until understanding is achieved and the tale can end, was no more than we expected from this brilliant, brilliant writer.

"On the Last Afternoon" is about communication, of course. Communication between Mysha and the *noion*, between the old man and his wife and daughter, between the individual and the community at large. Most importantly, it's about communication with one's self. Tiptree thought that it was a miracle people were able to communicate at all. No surprise, then, that communication must so often fail.

Meanwhile, Tiptree had begun corresponding with fans and other writers, and contributing occasional pieces to the fanzines. From these letters and articles a portrait emerged of an elderly WASP, born into privilege and possessed of shadowy connections with the American intelligence community, who was a habitual globe-trotter and had spent much of his childhood in colonial India and Africa. More significantly, his writings established him as a man of rare sensitivity and possibly even wisdom. "When you're old enough," he wrote, "you're *free*. Your energy is not only less, it is different. It's in—if you've done it right—a different place. Your last, hottest organ." And elsewhere, "You know as well as I do we all go around in disguise. The halo stuffed in the pocket, the cloven hoof awkward in the shoe, the X-ray eye blinking behind thick lenses, the two midgets dressed as one tall man, the giant stooping in a pinstripe, the pirate in a housewife's smock, the wings shoved into sleeveholes, the wild racing, wandering, raping, burning, loving pulses of reality decorously disguised as a roomful of Human beings. I know goddam well what's out there, under all those masks. Beauty and Power and Terror and Love."

Here was a rara avis indeed and, understandably, everybody wanted to meet him. Yet meet people Tiptree would *not* do. He didn't give talks, show up at conventions, accept awards in person, or drop by a correspondent's house for coffee. Given his gregarious and confiding personality, his admirers could only conclude that he was hiding something. There were rumors that he was a government spook, a Native American, black, even (but most people scoffed at this one) a woman.

The stories kept coming. "The Girl Who Was Plugged In" is yet another tour de force, a rude, jeering narrative that leads with the chin, sets up a horrible and inevitable human tragedy, and as good as lays the blame at the reader's feet. Even with the tacked-on and perfectly unconvincing happy ending, it remains one of Tiptree's key works. In "Love is the Plan the Plan is Death," the loving, optimistic Moggadeet leads an emotionally rich and intellectually self-examined life, which all leads to... well, nothing more than our own lives do. Here is the distilled essence of Tiptree's darkest pessimism. "A Momentary Taste of Being" extends this sense of individual futility in the face of biological determinism to its logical extreme. A dispassionate reader might even conclude that there is nothing inherently tragic in this tale at all. Alas, we are human, and cannot afford to be that dispassionate.

"The Women Men Don't See" was the story that established Tiptree as a feminist. Had it been the only such in his career, it would have done the trick. From the concept embodied in its title to the final six words, it was the work of somebody who understood the predicament of women in our society in a clear-eyed and visceral way. Morever, it was written (we thought) by a man. There was hope!

Well, as it would later turn out, in a very Tiptree-esque way, perhaps there wasn't. But, whether taken as feminist SF or simply straight up, it was an instant classic.

Tiptree came perilously close to giving his secret away in the title of "Her Smoke Rose Up Forever." Many autobiographical elements, particularly the Fox CE shotgun that was his obsession for three teenage years, were familiar to his fans. But who else could the female pronoun refer to but Alice Sheldon? This story explores everything she feared most, inadequacy in particular. Sheldon had astonishing parents: an attorney, naturalist, and explorer for a Dad, an explorer and two-time O. Henry award-winner for a Mom. Prior to science fiction, her many accomplishments were, in her own eyes anyway, not equal to such a heritage.

"Houston, Houston, Do You Read?" was another feminist fable, this one positing a familiar thought-experiment, that possibly the only way to ensure the survival of humanity and the Earth is to kill all the men. But Tiptree, never one to settle for a revenge fantasy when something deeper and more disquieting could be achieved, went on to demonstrate its wrongness. When Lady Blue says "Why, we call ourselves ... the human race." the note of complacency is horribly familiar. Humanity, despite all final solutions, remains what it has always been. Similarly, "She Waits for All Men Born" may well be the history of the battle between Life and Death that it sets itself up to be. But the outcome of that battle reflects Tiptree's antipathy for all ultimate resolutions, whether imposed by human beings or by something greater and more basic.

Because Alice had stories to tell that Tiptree could not, she created a second persona, Raccoona Sheldon—named after the raccoons which occasionally wandered into her house by the same entryway the stream did—to write them. One of these, "Your Faces, O My Sisters! Your Faces, Filled of Light!" (she had a particular genius for titles), is the story of the only free woman in the world and what inevitably becomes of her. Its dark beauty is enough to make you weep for a way of life that can only be imagined, never achieved. This belongs right up there with the best of Tiptree's works and yet, ironically enough, because it was published under a woman's name, it got nowhere near the attention it deserved.

But while Sheldon was industriously working away, the fans were closing in on Tiptree. One of them actually staked out his post office box. Another got as far as Sheldon's door, only to be turned away by a lie. Nevertheless (and in retrospect, one has to wonder if this were deliberate), little autobiographical hints kept popping up in Tiptree's letters and nonfiction. Until one day a woman died whose obituary perfectly described the career, books, and remarkable life of the mother that Tiptree had so often reminisced about. Her name was Mary Hastings Bradley and her sole surviving child was a woman named Alice B. Sheldon.

Sheldon professed to be delighted at being outed. "How great," she wrote. "At last it's out." But she got very little in exchange for the Tiptree glamour. She met only a handful of her fans and compeers, and a certain fraction of her male readers fell away. In the aftermath, she wrote, "After this only the feminists would remain delighted, but on a different basis, having nothing to do with the stories. Tiptree, by merely existing unchallenged for eleven years, had shot the stuffing out of male stereotypes of women writers. Even nonfeminist women were secretly gleeful." The problem with this being, as she later lamented, "No one talked about the *stories* anymore at all."

Perhaps they didn't talk about the stories to Sheldon herself. But everybody was talking about "The Screwfly Solution," when it came out the following year, as by Raccoona Sheldon. This one had everything—hard science, engaging characters, and a truly terrifying premise. The plot could only be read literally; but it had a symbolic weight as well. It forced the reader to think. It proved that the woman who was no longer Tiptree was still one of our best.

Being discovered, however, precipitated Sheldon into a crisis. In some way, she needed Tiptree—as a mask, as a buffer, as a liberating excuse, the reason doesn't matter. The sad truth was that after she became herself, the truly first-rate stories were much slower in the coming.

One strategy she employed to work around this was to write wide-screen, galaxy-spanning space opera. "We Who Stole the *Dream*" is an excellent example of its kind, the tale of a terrorist hijacking as seen from the viewpoint of some of the most engaging aliens Sheldon ever created. This was science fiction of a rather old-fashioned sort, with military hierarchies, captains whose power was absolute, and more than a whiff of the 1940s about it. Sheldon was perhaps the last major writer to work this territory with a straight face. But that doesn't mean she couldn't make magic with it. As witness "With Delicate Mad Hands," wherein a woman who has been horribly mutilated, both physically and spiritually, is called outward and in her brief freedom discovers both love and death. It's a sentimental story on the surface; but on reflection, the question inevitably arises: Was CP ever truly free?

Slowly, a new picture of the author was emerging. She was a handsome and impressive woman. Her beloved husband was retired intelligence officer Huntington Sheldon, an aristocratic man who had been her commanding officer in WWII and looked, one admirer said, like Commander Whitehead in the old Schweppes ads. She was paralyzingly shy. She was fiercely, blazingly feminist.

"Slow Music" is an elegiac tale of the rediscovery of death. Ignore the protagonists, the callow Jakko and the marvelously named Peachthief, and keep your eye and ear instead on the dying old, poetry-spouting man-woman who midwifes the attempt at a new beginning. It's hard not to read him/her as Sheldon/Tiptree making a cameo. It's hard not to read her/his words as prescient.

On May 19, 1987, at 3:30 a.m., Alice Sheldon took a shotgun and killed her husband, "Ting," and then herself. Huntington Sheldon was blind and terminally ill at the time of his death. Police found their bodies in bed together.

Dear God.

An embarrassed silence fell over the field. Nobody could reconcile this act with sweet old Uncle Tip, who dispensed kindly advice from afar and wrote to editors urging them to buy more work from struggling young women writers. Nor was it the work of the flinty, tough-minded Alice Sheldon we were all coming to know. We thought we'd learned the lessons we were supposed to take from her life. And now this. What did it *mean?*

Which was, of course, nonsense. Sheldon had suffered for decades from clinical depression so bad that she once said it was like having a vulture perched on either shoulder. Depression is a literal illness. She died of it as surely as she might have of leukemia or a car crash.

In the aftermath, Tiptree's name has been kept alive chiefly by an award given annually in Sheldon's honor for science fiction or fantasy that expands or explores our understanding of gender. But, in part because of her death and in part because short fiction doesn't stay in print the way novels can, her stories sank into an undeserved obscurity.

You hold in your hands a partial corrective.

This collection was originally put together by the late, lamented, and intensely valuable Jim Turner—I picture him a little pleased, like a child, to be briefly the center of attention, while simultaneously scowling with embarrassment and disapproval because he believed an editor should, like a ninja, be both anonymous and invisible—and he assembled the Tiptree volume we all wished for. It can never be the perfect collection, of course. We all have our favorites and blind spots, and if you want to stay up half the night arguing why Story X should have been left out in favor of Story Y... well, that sounds like good clean fun to me, and exactly the sort of tribute that Alice B. Sheldon would have most savored.

Read. Enjoy. These are the works that will remain long after the woman who was Tiptree, the mystery that was Sheldon, are forgotten.

They will endure.

The Battle of the Sexes in Science Fiction

Justine Larbalestier, 2002

eminist accounts of science fiction are as much a part of the historical moment in which they occurred as the texts they were engaging with, as we see from James Tiptree Jr.'s "The Women Men Don't See" and the ways in which the story has been discussed. First published in the December 1973 issue of the *Magazine of Fantasy and Science Fiction*, the story is one of the best known battle-of-the-sexes texts of the 1970s. John Clute, in *The Encyclopedia of Science Fiction*, calls it Tiptree's "most famous single story" (Clute and Nicholls 1993:1231).

At the time of publication, its author was not known to be Alice Sheldon by anyone in the science fiction community. The story is told in the first person by the middle-aged Don Fenton, presumably some kind of government operative, which is what many speculated that the "real" Tiptree was:

Because Tiptree lives jut a few miles from the Pentagon, or at least uses a mailing address in that vicinity, and because in his letters he often reports himself as about to take off for some remote part of the planet, the rumour constantly circulates that in "real" life he is some sort of government agent working in high-security work. His obviously first-hand acquaintance with the world of airports and bureaucrats, as demonstrated in such stories as "The Women Men Don't See," gives some support to this notion. ... Tiptree's admission to one of his editors that he spent most of World War II in a Pentagon subbasement has contributed to this myth. (Silverberg 1975: xii)

"The Women Men Don't See" received a rapturous response and was nominated for both the major science fiction awards, the Nebula and the Hugo. Tiptree, however, withdrew the story from consideration. At the time "he" said it was because he wanted to give the younger writers a turn; however, it has been argued that Tiptree was reluctant to win an award for the "masculine" feminism it supposedly displayed (Le Guin 1978).

...

"The Women Men Don't See" can be read as addressing the notion that women can only be represented in science fiction in discourses of romance of the domestic. In the story, Don Fenton, the narrator, can only see women sexually. He describes Mayan women thus: "[T]he little Maya chicks in their minishifts with iridescent gloop on those cockeyes [are]... highly erotic. Nothing like the oriental doll thing" (Tiptree [1973] 1990: 122). When Fenton first encounters the two women, Ruth and Althea Parsons, on the flight from Cozumel Airport, they are merely a "double female blur... registering nothing. Zero" (121). On the chartered light Fenton "see[s] the girl has what could be an attractive body if there was any spark at all. There isn't" (121). The women become visible to him when they crashland together. Fenton's perceptions of the women change when they are the only women present: "[M]y eyes take in the fact that Mrs. Parsons is now quite rosy... with her hair loose and a sunburn starting on her nose. A trim, in fact a very neat shading-forty. ... Miss Parsons is even rosier and more windblown. ... A good girl, Miss Parsons, in her nothing way" (128-29).

Fenton's perceptions of the women echo the long-running debate within science fiction about women's place within the field. In that debate, a woman is only visible when she is a potential love interest. He misreads what is happening around him because he can only think of women within such a narrow perspective. Women exist for the convenience of men like himself. They exist within a chivalric order: there for him to desire, or for him to rescue. They exist so that he can see his "real" manliness reflected back at him. In "The Women Men Don't See," neither of the Parsons will respond to his desire, and when the opportunity arrives for him to achieve the rescue, he accidentally shoots Ruth Parsons in the arm (143). When it becomes plain that Fenton does not matter to either of the Parsons, a "mad image" of a female conspiracy "blooms" in Fenton's mind, and he imagines "generations of solitary Parsons women selecting sires, making impregnation trips. Well, I hear the world is moving their way" (138). This scenario of a secret conspiracy of women against men is straight from the pages of texts like Jerry Sohl's *The Haploids* (1952), James Gunn's "The Misogynist" (1952), and Sam Merwin's *The White Widows* (1953). "The Women Men Don't See" shifts the terrain of the battle of the sexes away from images of "mad" conspiracies of women against men to that of women "surviv[ing]... liv[ing] by ones and twos in the chinks of your world-machine" (Tiptree [1973] 1990: 140).

Robert Silverberg, in his introduction to the Tiptree collection *Warm Worlds and Otherwise*, "Who is Tiptree, What Is He?," was also struck by the way this story inverts earlier science fiction. He characterizes the story's ending thus: "The thematic solution is an ancient s-f cliche—Earth-women carried off by flying-saucer folk—redeemed and wholly transformed by its sudden shattering vision of women, stolid and enduring, calmly trading one set of alien masters for another that may be more tolerable" (Silverberg 1975: xvi). Nevertheless, he claims, the story proves that men can "do" feminism, because "The Women Men Don't See" is a "profoundly feminist story told in an entirely masculine manner, and deserves close attention by those in the front lines of the wars of sexual liberation, male and female" (xvi).

Terry Carr makes a similar argument in his 1975 editorial "You've Come A Long Way, Baby." In it, he writes that "there are some male writers in the field today who are able to show some insight into the female point of view" (Carr 1975: 125). He cites Tiptree as one of these writers. Carr gives his own summary of the plot of "The Women Men Don't See": the story's resolution, he claims, with the mother and her daughter getting into the "alien's ship and tak[ing] off for spaces unknown" is a sign that "[w]e really have come a long way, people" (125). Carr's sign of the most spectacular "progress" of science fiction is that "The Women Men Don't See" was written by a man. A woman writing a "profoundly feminist story" would not be such a revelation. Carr also discusses Joanna Russ's "When It Changed" (1972) as a sign of the progress of science fiction. However, this story signifies for Carr, not so much because the story inverts battle of the sexes tropes, but because the story won a Nebula: the story was accepted and lauded by the once "almost... exclusive province of male readers" (Carr 1975: 5).

By the mid 1970s, the men who constituted the field of science fiction had grown up and were able to welcome women into their midst. Tiptree's story demonstrated for them not only that men can recognize women's talent but that they can even *understand* women. The revelation in 1977 that Alice Sheldon "was" James Tiptree Jr. undid this sense of progress and caused the story's feminism to be read differently. The uniquely sensitive, though very masculine male author had become a woman. The story's feminism had shifted and was no longer a proof of the adulthood of male sf writers.

"The Women Men Don't See" is frequently referred to in more recent work on feminist science fiction.... For some critics the story has become an "exemplar for feminist science fiction" (Cranny-Francis 1990: 26). Once again, this reading seems to be largely dependent on the perceived sex of the story's author—Amanda Boulter, in her 1995 article "Alice James Raccoona Tiptree Sheldon Jr: Textual Personas in the Short Fiction of Alice Sheldon," argues that once Tiptree became Sheldon, readings of "her" stories were caught up with the story's authorship by a writer whose writing life has come to embody a feminist lesson, "demonstrat[ing] that there was no inevitable connection between biology and writing, the penis and the pen." Boulter argues that "[t]his gender deception has made Alice Sheldon a particular exciting figure for feminist critics of science fiction" (Boulter 1995: 6).

Sarah Lefanu, in her 1988 book-length study of feminism and science fiction, *In the Chinks of the World Machine*, discusses "The Women Men Don't See" in conjunction with Robert Silverberg's now-famous introduction to *Warm Worlds and Otherwise* in which he had written, "It has been suggested that Tiptree is female, a theory that I find absurd, for there is to me something ineluctably masculine about Tiptree's writing" (Silverberg 1975: xii). In his later postscript to the introduction to *Warm Worlds*, Silverberg writes: "She fooled me beautifully, along with everyone else, and called into question the entire notion of what is 'masculine' or 'feminine' in fiction" (Silverberg 1993: 5). Lefanu agrees with Silverberg's postscript: "The notion of what is 'masculine' or 'feminine' fiction must indeed be questioned; it is too simplistic to say that male writers of science fiction concern themselves only with technology or 'hard' science at the expense of development of character and the consequences in social terms of technological development. Such a distinction not only posits a crude sexual dualism—masculine is hard, feminine is soft—which anyway is anathema to Tiptree, but it also denies the connections between the different 'hard' and 'soft' sciences, connections that in good science fiction should be made" (Lefanu 1988: 123-24).

This split between "hard" and "soft" science has its equivalence in "hard" and "soft" science fiction. "Hard" science fiction is frequently portrayed as "real" science fiction because it is more "scientific" than "soft" science fiction. "Hard" science fiction is predominantly mapped on to the male, and "soft" sf, on to the female. Sheldon/Tiptree's authorship of "The Women Men Don't See" makes explicit the fragility of this opposition of "masculine" to "feminine."

References

Boulter, Amanda. 1995. "Alice James Raccoona Tiptree Sheldon Jr: Textual Personas in the Short Fiction of Alice Sheldon." *Foundation* 63 (spring): 5-31.

Carr, Terry. 1975. "Guest Editorial: You've Come A Long Way, Baby." *Amazing* 49, no. 3 (Nov): 4-5, 122-25.

Clute, John, and Peter Nicholls, eds. 1993. *The Encyclopedia of Science Fiction*. London: Orbit.

Cranny-Francis, Anne. 1990. *Feminist Fiction: Feminist Uses of Generic Fiction*. Cambridge: Polity Press.

Lefanu, Sarah. 1988. *In the Chinks of the World Machine*. London: Women's Press.

Le Guin, Ursula. 1978. "Introduction." In *Star Songs of an Old Primate* by James Tiptree Jr., vii-xii. New York: Del Rey Books.

Merrick, Helen. 2009. *The Secret Feminist Cabal: A Cultural History of Science Fiction Feminisms*: 264-274

Silverberg, Robert. 1975. "Who is Tiptree, What Is He?" Introduction to *Warm Worlds and Otherwise* by James Tiptree Jr., ix-xviii. New York: Ballantine Books.

Silverberg, Robert. 1993. "Reflections." *Amazing* 67, no.12 (Mar.): 5-6.

Tiptree, James Jr. [1973] 1990. *Her Smoke Rose Up Forever*. Sauk City, Wisc: Arkham House.

Reading sf feminisms from Tiptree texts

Helen Merrick, 2009.
Excerpts from The Secret Feminist Cabal:
A Cultural History of Science Fiction Feminisms
(pp264-274)

The dialogues and interactions of community participants in sites such as the Tiptree Award actively contribute to the discursive formation and mediation of "feminist sf" and indeed sf feminisms in general. ... [The] award is continually in the process of being re-invented, in that each year each jury must decide for themselves what its parameters are. ...The award thus provides an interesting case study of the changing meanings and constitutions of "feminisms" and "gender" in the science fiction field. The parameters of this discussion can be inferred from the set of texts that win or are short-listed for the award, as well as from the jurors' comments on these texts. Also forming part of the dialogue are published reflections from past jurors... .

In concert with sf criticism, book reviews, and events such as conventions and author readings, the Tiptree Award helps to delineate a shared set of texts that define and produce the object feminist sf. Since its inception, the Tiptree Award has become a significant site of—and just as importantly—a *focus* for such debates. Interestingly the Tiptree Award itself and the texts it recognizes do not necessarily equate with or map directly onto "feminist sf." As Larbalestier points out, people now refer to "tiptree texts," a term that has taken on rather complex meanings, invoking as it does texts nominated (or even potential nominees) for the award as well as the oeuvre of sf author James Tiptree Jr. (Larbalestier 2002: 202, 218). Either way, within the sf field the very name "Tiptree" signals a nuanced and complex history of engagement with gender, sexuality, postcolonialism, and feminism that does not always map neatly onto normative feminist genealogies.

In this context, it is useful to view the award as a continuation of the kind of dialogues and processes ongoing since the early 1970s in fanzines, letters, and forewords to collections like [Pamela] Sargent's *Women of Wonder*: the identification of potential "feminist friendly" authors, the ever popular fannish activity of constructing reading lists, and of course reviewing and commenting on recent publications. Although not all jurors would agree, and the award is officially "branded" as feminist (other than its association with the secret feminist cabal), I would argue that the very existence of the award, its processes, and associated dialogues are all central to feminist production and practise in sf.

...

The question of [the] slippery relation between gender and feminism can be examined more closely through the juror commentaries on Tiptree winners and short-listed works, which often explicitly address why—or why not—a work is considered "Tiptree worthy." A variety of identifiable and often repeated themes emerge, some of which are specific to sf, others of which are related to central concerns of the feminist movement/s. Approaches dominated by the latter tend to downplay the notion of gender bending and instead implicitly (and sometimes explicitly) invoke a relationship to feminism as the primary basis of judgement.

For many of the juries, an important facet of the award is the part it plays in the ongoing transformative relation of feminism and sf. Thus a number of works are identified as meriting short-listing because they constitute feminist reworkings of, or replies to, traditional sf tropes and themes. The 1991 jury, for example, posits both Karen Joy Fowler's *Sarah Canary* and Gwyneth Jones' *White Queen* as a "feminine reply" to the masculine endeavour of cyberpunk (TAC 1991, SL). Other examples emphasize the award's role in advancing feminist conversations in sf by acknowledging texts the build on earlier works. Tess Williams' story "And she was the Word," for example, is read in terms of its connections to earlier works by authors such as Merril and Bradley. Le Guin's winning story, "The Matter of Seggri," is also marked as being part of a dialogue with earlier feminist texts: "The world of Seggri invites comparison with Gethen and Whileaway and Women's Country without being an imitation or a simple answer to any of them" (Attebury TAC 1994).

Other texts are singled out for the ways in which they reveal or deconstruct normative gender roles and, in particular, how this opposition has impacted notions of woman and female sexuality. A central theme running through feminist sf has been the challenge to the idea that the human is normatively represented by man, a theme identified in the 1993 winner, Nicola Griffith's *Ammonite*, about a "community of people, all of whom happen to be women" (Gomoll, TAC 1993). As Le Guin comments, "it answers the question 'when you eliminate one gender, what's left?' (a whole world, is the answer)" (Le Guin, TAC 1993). Other texts are recognized for their investigation of the role of reproduction and sexuality in the maintenance of normative gendered binaries....

Sexuality is of course central to feminist understanding of gender. A recurring issue in the juror comments is whether or not portrayal of non-heterosexual characters or even economies is enough to qualify as gender bending. Thus one year Gomoll questions whether Griffith's story "Touching Fire" qualifies: "does the fact that the lovers are lesbians make this gender-bending?" (TAC 1993 SL). Yet the following year, in the commentary on *Larque on the Wing* (joint winner), Susanna Sturgis notes that "Lesbian characters, erotic love between women: these are still out on the gender-bending frontier" (TAC 1994). Over a decade later, however, it would appear that the ground has shifted, with Notkin observing that,

> [a] leading editor got very angry when a book from his list
> with a lesbian protagonist didn't get much attention from

*that year's jury. He ... seemed unable to understand the
jury's response, which was that having a lesbian protagonist
is no longer an exploratory or expansive auctorial decision.
(Notkin 2005)*

In contrast... explorations of masculinity seem to be very
Tiptree-worthy, featuring in winning texts such as John Kessel's
"Stories for Men," Matt Ruff's *Set This House in Order*, and Harrison's *Light*. Michael Blumlein's "Fidelity: A Primer," for example,
is recognized as being "one of the rare stories that explored gender
issues by examining male body issues, and the choices they involve
(TAC 2000 SL).

...[A] central and recurring source of jurors' approval [is] the use
of alien cultures and races to provide a distancing and oppositional
perspective on contemporary gender norms. That is, where the
social, cultural, and political systems mapped onto our normative
gender systems are exposed, often through parody, role-reversal,
or exaggeration. Thus Eleanor Arnason's *Ring of Swords* is noted
for creating "an alien race whose assumptions are just enough
different than ours to bring ours into high relief" (McHugh TAC
1993 SL). Similarly James Patrick Kelly's "Lovestory" is to provide
a "wonderful example of how depicting an alien way of being
'normal' can make our own 'normal' society look weird" (Tuttle,
TAC 1998 SL). This is the area where sf is seen to offer unique
possibilities for re-examining gendered constructions, "by creating
a society that has different assumptions than ours, thus forcing us
to examine our own" (Murphy, TAC 1994).

The Text of this Body: "Reading" James Tiptree Jr. as a Transgender Writer

Wendy Gay Pearson
Originally presented at the International Conference on the Fantastic in the Arts, Ft Lauderdale, March 1999

Prologue

This article was originally written to be presented at ICFA in 1999, so it has somewhat of a historical valence. Certainly, things have changed in Tiptree scholarship, most notably due to the publication of Julie Phillips' exhaustively-researched biography, *James Tiptree, Jr.: The Double Life of Alice B. Sheldon*, in 2006, but also due to changes in the ways we have come to think about the relationship of both feminist and queer theory to science fiction (1999 was also the year that *Science Fiction Studies* first published an issue devoted to science fiction and queer theory). I had some correspondence with Julie around this time, so was privileged to read some of her work in advance not long after I wrote this piece. We certainly know more about Sheldon and especially about both the process and the reasons that Sheldon became Tiptree—although many questions still remain unanswerable. Even more has changed in trans theory, a field that can be said to have begun with Sandy Stone's response to Janice Raymond's anti-trans diatribe (*The Transsexual Empire*): "The *Empire* Strikes Back: A (Post)Transsexual Manifesto," first published in 1991. This was followed by works by Kate Bornstein, Judith Butler, Leslie Feinstein, Susan Stryker, and others. By the late 1990s, there was starting to be recognition that trans studies was a field in its own right, not entirely congruent with queer theory (despite having both feminist and postmodern roots in common) or with queer studies. Butler's 1993 book *Bodies That Matter* (which I cite here) articulated a theory of gender performativity that has remained immensely useful. However, Butler's discussion of drag queens and Jenni Livingstone's documentary, *Paris is Burning,* was criticized by many trans people for treating transgender issues as an allegory of gender, rather than recognizing the materiality of people's lived experience; for disallowing the specificity of trans oppression and reading it merely as a form of heterosexism; for conflating transness with a gender subversion whose primary objective is to deconstruct heterosexual gender performance; for reading drag queens as subversive, but relegating transsexuals to "an uncritical miming of the hegemonic" (*Bodies* 131); and for locating "transgressive value in that which makes the subject's real life most unsafe" (Prosser 275; for critiques of Butler's early work on transgender see, in particular, Namaste [13-14] and Prosser). All of which is to say that, were I writing this today, I would approach trans issues in Tiptree's life and texts somewhat differently—but even so, I think this piece continues to have some historical validity as a way of witnessing how it was possible to think about the transgender body/text at the time.

We begin in Montreal in the year 1971:

As usual, my class has let out just sufficiently late that I've missed the bus, which also means I've missed my train home. Walking through the wind-swept canyon that is Dorchester St., on a fine October afternoon, I turn into the lobby of the Queen Elizabeth Hotel. Downstairs in the train station, it's crowded, smoky, noisy in the way that only the cavernous Victorian maw of a train station can be. Up here, the chairs are comfortable and I sit with my psychology textbook in a haven of peace and quiet that will last just as long as it takes the hotel staff to realize that I'm not a paying customer, nor am I meeting one.

A middle-aged man sits down beside me, suit, tie, one of those ugly briefcases businessmen favour. He's wearing too much cologne and a wedding ring, but I'm not paying much attention because I'm engrossed in what I'm reading. He says, 'Hi there, son,' and I look up long enough to say 'Hi' back. I'm used to being taken for a boy, know that I look about fourteen rather than seventeen.

This man's persistent, though, with his soft Southern accent that doesn't seem to go with his loud voice. 'What're you studying there, son?' 'Where do you go to school?' And on and on. And I give him brief, polite answers and wish he'd go away and let me get back to my book. I've still more than an hour until the next train. The man's a pest, but it doesn't occur to me that he's looking for anything more than a conversation to relieve his boredom until his hand falls on my knee. He's got beer in his room, apparently—with a knowing look because he's offering alcohol to the underage—and would I like to come up and have a drink with him. Son. The hand creeps up my thigh. We'll have a good time, he says. Son.

For a moment I'm almost tempted, just to see the look on his face when I take my sweatshirt off. But I say no, thank you, acting like I've no idea what he's on about, and eventually he goes away. I go back to my psychology book and don't think much about it, but later I tell the story to a heterosexual but impoverished classmate who supplements his official part-time work by giving blowjobs in the train station toilets when the rent is due. He points out that if I'd kept my sweatshirt on, I could have made ten bucks—a whole month's train fare. By the time I reach university, I'm used to being propositioned by men who call me 'son.'

In 1971, James Tiptree, Jr., a man who was starting to make a name for himself in the sf world, published a number of short stories, one of which was entitled "And I Awoke and Found Me Here on the Cold Hill's Side." The narrator of "And I Awoke..." is an overeager cub reporter, on his first visit to the space station Big Junction. Unwillingly, because it's distracting him from his quest for the aliens for whose convenience Big Junction has been built, the young newsman finds himself listening to another man's story, a story which, like the one I've just read you, is about sexuality and gender and the alien—and about making mistakes, about being mistaken.

Inevitably, given the largely pessimistic mode of Tiptree's story telling, the narrator ignores, as both author and storyteller know he will, the warning to avoid the siren-like seduction of the alien. There are a number of ways in which "And I Awoke" can be read. Veronica Hollinger, for example, reading Tiptree in the context of queer and feminist theory, suggests in the most recent issue of *Science Fiction Studies* that in both "And I Awoke..." and the 1973 story "Love is the Plan, the Plan is Death,"

> *human (hetero)sexuality is both instinct and damnation. Human sexual desire for the "other" results only in pain, as our objects of desire become increasingly, and sometimes literally, alien to us. Sexuality is the failed attempt to know the irreducibly alien. From this perspective Tiptree's stories are modern tragedies of gender difference. (27)*

While I agree, of course, that "And I Awoke..." is a story about the incoherence and, perhaps, impossibility of human sexuality as a means towards knowledge of the desired other, I would like to suggest that the story, like much of Tiptree's work, is also about the incoherence and impossibility of knowledge, in general—about making mistakes and about being mistaken. Characters, in Tiptree's stories, particularly the narrators, read and interpret wrongly. The body itself is a particular focus—or, perhaps, a particular locus—for Tiptree, of this disconnection between the sign and its meaning, between reading and "reality."

The year 1971, with which I have begun this paper, was, of course, a time relatively early in Tiptree's illustrious career—and a full six years before the revelation, in 1977, that Tiptree—described as "the most masculine of all science fiction writers" (Boulter

5)—was, in "reality," a woman named Alice Sheldon. The news of Tiptree's "real" sex brought into sharp focus the relationship of gender to writing. As Amanda Boulter has pointed out, "Tiptree's reputation demonstrated that there was no inevitable connection between biology and writing, the penis and the pen" (6).

Like my seventeen year old self, James Tiptree was (mis)taken for a male. Unlike my seventeen year old self, Tiptree made an effort: chose a name and, perhaps, a nickname (Tip), kept up a masculine persona ("real" or otherwise) in correspondence, refused personal meetings of any kind.[1] The verisimilitude of Tiptree's impersonation, the persuasiveness of his performance of the male as sf writer, certainly serves to highlight the performative nature of gender roles; at the same time, however, it also raises certain questions about the purpose and degree of intent of Tiptree's performance as male. Was Tiptree (mis)taken for a male—or does the persona of Tiptree have a certain existence in its own right, separable from the persona of both Alice Sheldon and of her female writer creation, Raccoona Sheldon? And, finally, what effect must our (various) answers to these questions have on our readings, retrospective as they inevitably are, of the writings of James Tiptree and Raccoona Sheldon?

In attempting to answer, however partially, these questions about

---

1   We know a great deal more about this since the publication of Julie Phillips' excellent, indeed extraordinary, biography, *James Tiptree, Jr.: The Double Life of Alice B. Sheldon,* although it still cannot entirely clarify the relationship between Tiptree and Sheldon. So many questions remain, about intentionality, about playing with revelation, about whether Tiptree was, in some ways, a more "authentic" expression of who Sheldon felt she was.

the relationship of the body or bodies of the author (Tiptree/ Sheldon)—specifically, the *sexed* body of the author—to the body of the text and to the bodies in the text, I will be taking a somewhat different trajectory from that traced by Boulter. Instead of focusing on the feminist recuperation, the feminisation, of Tiptree's writings to reveal the possibilities of reading Tiptree beyond gender, I want, instead, to examine the possibility that Tiptree can also usefully be read through the lens of current work on the body and, especially, on the transgender body. I will thus be reading Tiptree primarily through Judith Butler's work on performativity and drag.

Before I attempt this, however, I want briefly to note the possible confusions and particular ambivalences that adhere to the terms "transvestite," "transgender," and "transsexual."[2] In popular parlance, these terms are often rendered interchangeable; "transgender," in particular, has a tendency to slippage in both directions, being variably used to indicate those who cross-dress (the transvestite) and those who have undergone sex reassignment surgery

---

2   In the years since this was written, trans studies and trans theory have both become established academic disciplines while the terminology has both proliferated and been contested in many ways. "Trans" covers a proliferation of terminology that includes *trans**, *trans woman*, *trans man*, *FTM*, *MTF*, *genderqueer*, *agender*, *boi*, *dragboi*, *transdyke*, *transexion*, *transnatural*, *translesbigay*, *transsissy*, and a host of others. These terms, of course, run alongside "man" and "woman" for—generally post-op—transsexuals who see themselves as their new gender and don't embrace any type of trans identity. People whose gender identity sits comfortably and normatively with their perceived biological sex are referred to as "cisgender." Pre-op, post-op, and non-op are terms for trans peoples' relationship to sex reassignment surgery, which many transgender individuals don't want at all or want only aspects of—but which also may be reflective of economic status in the US, where SRS is rarely covered by medical insurance, assuming the individual has insurance, and in some Canadian provinces (some provinces include SRS costs, wholly or partially, under provincial health insurance plans).

(the transsexual). However, even the latter term is unclear, since its usage includes those who have had complete genital conversion surgery, those who have had partial surgery (as, for example, the FTM who opts to have a mastectomy, but not to undergo genital surgery), and those who use hormone therapy. In this paper, I am using the word "transgender" to indicate those who, deliberately or otherwise, are (mis)taken for the "opposite" sex.[3] In this sense, no matter how female or feminine (or unfeminine) Alice Sheldon may have been, James Tiptree himself was a transgender sf writer. What consequences Tiptree's 'transgendering' has for his understanding and depiction of the body are thus central to this paper.

In "Gender is Burning: Questions of Appropriation and Subversion," Judith Butler makes the point that the subjects of Jenny Livingstone's film *Paris is Burning* (1991), who are primarily black and Latino drag performers, aspire to an effect of "realness." Butler notes that

> *what determines the effect of realness is the ability to compel belief, to produce the naturalized effect... Significantly this is a performance that works, that effects realness to the extent that it cannot be read. For "reading" means taking someone down, exposing what fails to work at the level of appearance*

---

3   I realize that "(mis)taken" is somewhat of an awkward shorthand for the many levels of identification and mis-identification that plague systems of gender. While many transsexuals want to be taken for their new sex (and, perhaps, long-time gender identity), many other transgender people do not or are ambivalent about it or simply resent the category of gender itself. Yet others identify with their biological sex yet are routinely taken by other people for the "opposite" sex. These issues often coalesce around the choice of which public toilet to use and the remarkable insistence of some cis-gender people that they get to police the gender of others.

*... For a performance to work, then, means that a reading
is no longer possible, or that a reading, an interpretation,
appears to be a kind of transparent seeing, where what
appears and what it means coincide. On the contrary, when
what appears and how it is "read" diverge, the artifice of the
performance can be read as artifice; the ideal splits off from
the appropriation. But the impossibility of reading means
that the artifice works, the appropriation of realness appears
to be achieved... (129)*

In treating the performers at the drag balls in Harlem as men
who do drag, rather than as transgender, Butler may be effacing
the difference, even as she tries to draw out some of the complexities and ambivalences of drag performance more generally. In
the standards of house culture, the drag performance is judged
according to a standard of "realness." If a performer can be
"read"—that is, if the performance in any way indicates that the
performer is male—then it has failed to achieve a requisite level of
realness. Interestingly, this remains the case when the performers
compete in military garb, but the index of realness in this case is
hegemonic masculinity, as opposed to hegemonic femininity (Butler
does point out that not all the categories in the competition take
white American culture's gender ideals as their standard). The
point, for Butler, then becomes that drag *can* be "subversive to the
extent that it reflects on the imitative structure by which hegemonic
gender is itself produced and disputes heterosexuality's claim on
naturalness and originality" (125).

In the terms that Butler has appropriated from the film *Paris
is Burning*, Tiptree's decade of passing as a male sf writer is

successful precisely because he cannot be "read." In literary terms, however, it is hard to avoid noting the peculiar paradox inherent in the terminology: passing "unread" is not often the goal of a writer! Two things need to be noted here: first, that Tiptree's avoidance of being "read" as inauthentically masculine had positive benefits to Tiptree beyond, or perhaps in lieu of, the psychic benefits that accrue to the black and Latino drag queens, a fact that was made ineluctably clear by the difficulty Raccoona Sheldon had in getting her stories published, despite their having very much the same subject matter and style as Tiptree's stories (Boulter 14-15). Second—and most importantly for this paper—the problem of "reading" or misreading the transgender body is echoed by the importance in Tiptree's works of reading and misreading, of making mistakes and of being (mis)taken.

A few examples should suffice, I hope, to demonstrate the way in which Tiptree lays out the problem of "reading" the body and its identity. In "The Milk of Paradise" (1972), the story begins with a mis-take that, significantly, involves sex, the body, and the question of human/alien identity. The protagonist, the one who is not-Timor although he is called Timor, is having sex with Seoul and ends up vomiting. Seoul is unable to discern, that is to "read," either not-Timor's alienness or his lack of desire. As a male, he should desire her; as a human, he should think himself superior to all others. Yet, not-Timor was born on Paradise and sees himself as hideous; he compares himself, and Seoul, to the Crots, the ugly "subhumans" (*Warm Worlds* 25) who are the only alien lifeform the other humans acknowledge. The story continues through a proliferating series of mistakes and misunderstandings until the ironic resolution, the point at which not-Timor is returned to the planet of his birth and the sublimely beautiful beings he has disparaged himself against are revealed as

> [g]ray rotten little things ... lumps ... dove-gray like himself, but it was hide, not silk, that bloated at elbows and knees. Gray splayed feet, and between them, under the bags of belly, the giant genitals ... leaving triple furrows in the soft mud. (Warm Worlds 35)

And not-Timor himself is not a human rescued from a dying planet, but rather one of them.

> ... he heard his name in the music. His true name, the name of his babyhood under the soft gray hands and bodies of his first world. The bodies that had taught him love, all in the mud, in the cool mud....

> And then they were down, tearing and rolling in the sweet mud, gray bodies with him. Until he found that it was no longer fighting but love—love as it always had been, his true flowing ... flowing together in Paradise in the dim ruby light. (36)

Not-Timor is also not human. Reunited with his own people, he leaves behind the shell of a "dead or dying thing," (36) the clothing of flesh that has allowed him to be (mis)taken for human. His true nature is revealed by the naming of names and is manifested as love; that that love is sexual in nature is made apparent by Tiptree's earlier use of the word "flow" to describe sex between humans (sex in which, unsurprisingly, Timor does not flow) and by the emphasis on the genitalia of his alien race.

For Tiptree, occupying the position of the transgender writer who is successfully not "read" as, i.e. is (mis)taken for, male for almost a decade, the emphasis on both "the true name" and on the sexual identity of the protagonist, who is also the alien, can be seen as either—both—playful and psychologically revealing. Tiptree's role as male emphasizes not only the performative nature of gender itself, but the alien-ness of being the "wrong" gender, or no gender; at the same time, Tiptree's "prevailing masculinity" (to quote Silverberg [xv]) requires, particularly in the heteronormative world of sf in the 60s and 70s, that Tiptree be "unread" as not only male, but heterosexual.[4] Tiptree and Sheldon thus share a (hetero)sexual identity, yet differ in the presumed object of their desire, a desire in Tiptree's case which is literally, but not necessarily psychologically, disembodied.[5]

Bodies are problematic things in Tiptree's work. They are almost always misread—that is, they are "read" performatively and the artifice of that performance is rarely exposed until it is too late. This is very much the case in the 1973 story "The Girl Who Was

---

4 Gender performativity is a postmodern approach to gender that sees gender as something produced by culture, not inherent to the body. All gender is thus performed, although the performance is required, not optional. I work within a theoretical model that regards the self as fluid, not fixed, and would dispute the notion that there is such a thing as an "authentic self."

5 Thanks to Phillips' biography and her extensive citation of Tiptree's diaries and correspondence, we now know that Sheldon/Tiptree's sexual identity was more complicated and that, in spite of having sexual relationships predominantly with men (including two heterosexual marriages), Sheldon's primary drive was probably towards women. She wrote to Joanna Russ saying, "I too am a Lesbian" (Phillips 431). This aligns Sheldon even more with Tiptree, who was positioned in correspondence as a cisgender, heterosexual man.

Plugged In." As with "The Milk of Paradise," "The Girl Who Was Plugged In" is not a literal rendering of Tiptree's own transgender state into fiction. Yet the same issues apply, however exaggerated they may be by the hyperbole of this supremely ironic story. Lethal consequences ensue from the young lover Paul's failure to read the beautiful Delphi's duplicity (in this case, her literal duplicity, since she has, in fact, *two* bodies, even if one is kept discreetly in the basement—a psychological metaphor, if there ever was one). P. Burke, the extraordinarily ugly young woman who is the mind behind Delphi's beautiful but mindless flesh, likewise fails to read Paul's love for Delphi as an infatuation with her beauty, rather than with her self. Furthermore, Paul Isham, buoyed up by having acquired a little knowledge of his father's business, mistakes a PD (Placental Decanter—a mindless modified embryo who cannot function without the neural impulses of a Remote Operator like P. Burke) for a PP (a human with a pleasure-pain implant that allows him or her to be controlled by someone else). And P. Burke, who knows all about Delphi, but nothing else about GTX's corporate affairs, cannot interpret Paul's reactions other than in the context of Delphi's entirely fantastical life. As the narrator says, "How can she guess that he's got it a little bit wrong?" (112) In the end, both P. Burke and Delphi die, Paul turns into his father, and the narrator, whom the reader discovers to be the sharp-faced and none too ethical lad whose schemes misfire so badly and who mistakes his value to the corporation, ends up a guinea pig in a time travel experiment that doesn't quite work "—and wakes up lying on a newspaper headlined NIXON UNVEILS PHASE TWO" (121), talking about the future that is the life and death of P. Burke and Delphi.

"The Girl Who Was Plugged In" highlights the failure to read the emptiness of Delphi or to see anything at all in P. Burke save an ugliness that is also all about gender (women must, after all, be beautiful in order to be desirable, ie. useful, to men). Particularly when it comes to issues of sex, gender, and otherness, the signs do not signify, the cues are opaque, the people involved are (mis)taken. Delphi/P. Burke's performance of "the girl" (sometimes also referred to in the story as "the girl-body") cannot fail to highlight the artifice of gender. It is not only drag queens, but also women who seek to perform the feminine so as to pass unread.[6]

Similarly, the storyteller in "And I Awoke..." unwittingly reveals to the reader the artifice of heteronormativity. Although the human sexual drive is defined in the story as always focused outward, toward the other, the other in the story is the alien, that which can only be read as non-human. Everything else is irrelevant. The storyteller tells the newsman,

---

6 This is the crux of Judith Butler's theory of gender performativity, in which gender is a required citational performance, one whose embedded anxieties (because no citation can quite match the "original") enforce its normative power. Butler's idea of performativity has often itself been mis-cited in the assumption that it's reducing gender to an optional performance or form of theatrical play—but that could not be further from what Butler is actually arguing. In relation to trans issues, see in particular Butler's recent issue with *Transadvocate* (Cristan Williams. "Gender Performance: The *TransAdvocate* Interviews Judith Butler." *TransAdvocate*. May 1, 2014. http://www.transadvocate.com/gender-performance-the-transadvocate-interviews-judith-butler_n_13652.htm).

> *The first Yyeir I saw I dropped everything and started walking after it like a starving hound, just breathing. You've seen the pix, of course. Like lost dreams. Man is in love and loves what vanishes.... It's the scent, of course. I followed until I ran into a slammed port. I spent half a cycle's credits sending the creature the wine they call star's tears.... Later I found out it was a male. That made no difference at all. (14)*

In the human pursuit of the alien, nothing it seems makes any difference, neither biological sex (if the alien has one—or two) nor the fact that the only aliens who'll condescend to sex with lowly humans are the perverts nor the probability of damage or death. Just as the peculiar cyber-construct that is P. Burke/Delphi reveals the artifice of our cultural assumptions about gender, the depiction of human sexuality in "And I Awoke..." reveals the deeply artificial nature of our contemporary understanding of sexuality as a binary opposition based on the biological sex of the object of desire. Furthermore, Tiptree's portrayal of sexuality in this story only serves to showcase the extent to which we mistake and are mistaken by the objects of our desire. Like the married man mistakenly trying to pick up the teenaged boy who is "really" a girl, the humans in "And We Awoke..." fail to read the artifice of both human and alien appearance. Thus, while I read "And I Awoke..." as being about more aspects of human sexuality than gender difference *per se* (just as Tiptree's own sexuality is about more than simply constructing a heterosexual cover story), I agree with Hollinger's contention that sexuality, for Tiptree, "is the failed attempt to know the irreducibly alien" (27).

Earlier I asked what readings might result from seeing the "body" of Tiptree in the text as transgender. In attempting to answer this question, what has become most visible to me is the focus within the stories on the probability, indeed the inevitability, of reading the artifice, of failing not only to know the alien but to see it/her/him. And the consequences of being mis-taken are complex and multifarious, sometimes tragic, sometimes comic (as in "All the Kinds of Yes"). However, these (mis)takes, like Tiptree's transgender "body," invariably throw light on the artifice of our systems of thought, our attempts to know the alien, the other, even when it/she/he is us.

I want to end, briefly, with another story, one that occurs a quarter century after the first.

> *It's 1996 and Veronica Hollinger has asked me to give a guest lecture on Marge Piercy's* Woman on the Edge of Time *to her Utopian Literature class. I stay for the discussion, which includes not only Piercy, but also Raccoona Sheldon's "Your Faces, O My Sisters, Your Faces Filled of Light." In the course of that discussion, someone says, apropos of the "real" world death of the protagonist, that every woman has experienced what it means to be afraid to walk alone at night. For some reason, though I've heard such blanket statements many times before about what it means to be a woman, I experience a moment of radical discontinuity. It occurs to me, for the first time, that if the statement is true, then I am not a woman. If gender is, as Butler argues in "Critically Queer," a compulsory performance that all of us are forced to negotiate, it is, for all that, a performance that can be made to reveal its own artifice, that can be read, that can be (mis)taken. The transgender body is all too apt to make these (mis)takes evident.*

Works Cited

Bornstein, Kate. *Gender Outlaw : On Men, Women, and the Rest of Us*. New York: Routledge, 1994. Print.

Boulter, Amanda. "Alice James Raccoona Tiptree Sheldon Jr: Textual Personas in the Short Fiction of Alice Sheldon." *Foundation* 63 (Spring 1995): 5-31. Print.

Butler, Judith. *Bodies that Matter: On the Discursive Limits of Sex*. New York and London: Routledge, 1993. Print.

Feinberg, Leslie. *Transgender Warriors: Making History from Joan of Arc to RuPaul*. Boston: Beacon Press, 1996. Print.

Hollinger, Veronica. "(Re)reading Queerly: Science Fiction, Feminism, and the Defamiliarization of Gender." *Science Fiction Studies* 26.1 (March 1999): 23-40. Print.

Namaste, Viviane. *Invisible Lives: The Erasure of Transsexual and Transgendered People*. Chicago: U of Chicago Press, 2000. Print.

Phillips, Julie. *James Tiptree, Jr.: The Double Life of Alice B. Sheldon*. New York: St. Martin's Press, 2006. Print.

Prosser, Jay. *Second Skins: The Body Narratives of Transsexuality*. New York: Columbia University Press, 1998. Print.

Silverberg, Robert. "Who is Tiptree, What is He?," Introduction to *Warm Worlds and Otherwise* by James Tiptree Jr. New York: Ballantine Books, 1975. ix-xviii. Print.

Stone, Sandy. "The *Empire* Strikes Back: A (Post)Transsexual

Manifesto." *Body Guards: The Cultural Politics of Gender Ambiguity*. Ed. Kristina Straub and Julia Epstein. New York: Routledge, 1991. Print.

Stryker, Susan. "My Words to Victor Frankenstein Above the Village of Chamounix: Performing Transgender Rage." *GLQ* 1.3 (1994): 227-254. Print.

Tiptree, James. "All the Kinds of Yes." *Warm Worlds and Otherwise*. New York: Ballantine Books, 1975. 1-23. Print.

--------. "And I Awoke Here on the Cold Hill's Side." *Ten Thousand Light Years from Home*. New York: Ace Books, 1973. Print.

--------. "The Girl Who Was Plugged In." *Warm Worlds and Otherwise*. New York: Ballantine Books, 1975. 79-121. Print.

--------. "The Milk of Paradise." *Warm Worlds and Otherwise*. New York: Ballantine Books, 1975. 24-36. Print.

--------. "Love is the Plan, the Plan is Death." *Warm Worlds and Otherwise*. New York: Ballantine Books, 1975. 173-193. Print.

Everything but the Signature Is Me.

Revised version first published in Meet Me at Infinity.
James Tiptree, Jr., 2000

How great. At last it's out, and you're the first to know, as I promised long ago you would—although I didn't expect it to happen through your own initiative. But at least you're the first I can write to in my own persona.

Yeah. Alice Sheldon. Five-feet-eight, sixty-one years, remains of good-looking girl vaguely visible, grins a lot in a depressed way, very active in spurts. Also, Raccoona.

I live in a kind of big wooden box in the woods like an adult play-pen, full of slightly mangy plants, fireplace, minimal old "modern teak" furniture strewn with papers, hobbies, unidentifiable and unfileable objects; the toolroom opens off the bedroom, there are six doors to the outside, and it's colder than a brass monkey's brains in winter, except when the sun comes out and shoots through all the glass skylights. We've added on porches (which turned into libraries), other excrescences—as somebody said, all it needs is a windmill on top. Not so ridiculous now. Ting (short for Huntington, my *very nice* more aged husband of thirty years who doesn't read what I write but is happy I'm having fun) used to raise thousands of orchids before he retired and stated traveling; he gave them to the nation, i.e., the National Botanic Gardens, who wanted hybrids. So now in the middle of the living rooms sticks this big untended greenhouse I am supposed to be growing things in. What I'm growing is mealy bugs—must get at it. We built the place very modestly in 1959, when it was all woods here. Now houses, subdivisions, are creeping toward us. No more stags on the lawn—real ones. But lots of raccoons. Still private enough so you can sneak out and grab the mail or slip a cookie to a raccoon in the buff if you want to.

If you'd asked me any time from age three to twenty-six, I'd have told you, "I'm a painter." (Note, not "artist"—painter. Snobbism there.) And I was. Oh my, did I draw, sketch, model, smear oils, build gesso, paint-paint-paint. (Age three I drew pictures of our bulldog, with lollipop legs.) I worked daily, whether I was supposed to be listening to lectures on Chateaubriand, whether my then-husband was shooting at me (he was a beautiful alcoholic poet), whether sheriff was carrying our furniture out, whether Father was having a heart attack, whatever. And I wasn't too bad; I illustrated a couple of books in my early teens, I had a one-man show at sixteen, I exhibited in the All-American then at the Corcoran—and the painting, which used me as model, sold. Somewhere my naked form is hanging in a bedroom in North Carolina, if it hasn't been junked. I bought a shot-gun, a Fox C-E double-barrel 12-gauge full choke, with the money. (Those were the three years when I was a crazy duck hunter, before I shot one too many cripples and gave it up never to kill another living thing, bugs excluded.) I believe the Fox is now far more valuable than anything I ever did.

The trouble was, you see, I was just good enough to understand the difference between my talent and that rare thing, *real* ability. It was as though I had climbed the foothills high enough to see the snow-clad peaks beyond, which I could never scale. This doesn't stop some people; it did me. What's the use of adding to the world's scrap heap? The reason people thought me innovative was that I was good enough to steal mannerisms and tricks they had never climbed high enough to study. But I knew where it was coming from.

And then came the dreadful steady unstoppable rise of Hitler—a great spreading black loin chop on the map—and I found out something else. There are painters who go on painting when a million voices are screaming in terminal agonies. And there are those who feel they have to Do Something about it, however little.

So I came back to Chicago—I'd been living in San Angel, near Mexico City, mucking around on the fringes of the Diego Rivera/ Orozco/Siqueres crowd—and took a job as the *Chicago Sun*'s first art editor, while waiting for the Army to open female enlistments. (I wasn't one of the famous first group of female potential officers; for some reason it was important to me to go in as an ordinary G.I. with *women officers*.) Besides, I was having a great time discovering that Chicago was full of artists, who had to exhibit in NYC before they could sell to their Chicago neighbors. Chicago then had two art critics; one was a lethal, totally politicized Marxist (female), and the other was an elderly gent who knew art had died with Cezanne, and whose feet hurt. So when people sent works to Chicago shows they didn't get reviewed—or it was worse when they did. Anyway, I rooted out about forty producing groups, started what was then a new thing, a *New Yorker*-type calendar, told people interesting things to look for in shows. (One Art Institute guard, coping with a host of people with my "guide" clipped out, demanding to know which was the east room, asked me, "Did *you* do this?" Nobody had asked him anything but "Where is the toilet?" for twenty years.)

But this was all waiting, while the paper shortage cut me from a page to a half and then to a quarter. And then the great day came, and I trotted down to U.S. Army Recruitment Station Number 27 in three-inch heels and my little chartreuse crepe-de-chine designer thing by Claire somebody, and my pale fox fur jacket, and found a drunken second lieutenant with his feet on the desk. And when I said I wished to enlist in the Army, he caught an imaginary fly and said, "Ah, hell, you don't want to go in *that* goddamn thing." And I said if it was all the same to him, I did. And so—but that's another, five-year-long, fairly hilarious story.

People tell me I've had an exciting or glamorous or whatnot life; it didn't feel like much but work and a few adventures. A few, *ah oui...* All I write is really from life, even that crazy duck-shooting boy breaking the ice naked at ten degrees below zero on the Apache reservation was me, once ("Her Smoke Rose Up Forever").

As to science fiction: Well, you see, I had all these uncles, who are no relation at all, but merely stray or bereaved or otherwise unhappy bachelors whom my parents adopted in the course of their wanderings. (That sort of thing happened much more in the old, old days. The fact that Father was an intensely loveable man of bewildering varied capabilities, and that Mother was a blazing blue-eyed redhead of great literacy and gaiety didn't hurt, of course; and in their odd way they were both secretly lonesome— having nothing but peculiar me for family.) This particular uncle was what used to be called a Boston Brahmin, dean of a major law school and author of a text on torts so densely horrible that I still meet lawyers who shudder at its name. In short, he was dignified and respectable to an extreme—on the surface, as it turned out.

The summer when I was nine we were up in the woods of Wisconsin as usual, and Uncle Harry returned from an expedition to the metropolis of one thousand souls thirty miles away with his usual collection of *The New York Times*, *The Kenyon Review*, etc. (There was a funny little bookshop-hole there that ordered things for you.) Out of his bundle slipped a seven-by-nine magazine with a wonderful cover depicting, if I recollect, a large green octopus removing a young lady's golden brassiere. We all stared. The title was *Weird Tales*.

"*Ah*," said Uncle Henry. "Oh. Oh yes. I, ah, picked this up for the child."

"Uncle Harry," I said, my eyes bulging, "I am the child. May I have it, please?"

"Uh," said Uncle Harry. And, slowly, handed it over.

And so it all began. He would slip them to me and I would slip them back to him. Lovecraft—Oh, God. And more and more and more; we soon discovered *Amazing* and *Wonder Stories* and others that are long forgotten. We never discussed them; it was just Our Secret. But I'll tell you one thing: You haven't read fantasy or SF unless you have retired, with a single candle, to your lonely little cabin in the woods, far from the gaslights of the adult world, and set your candle stub up in a brass basin and huddled under about sixteen quilts—the nights were cold and drafty, the candlelight jumped and guttered, shadows everywhere. And then, just as you get to where the nameless *Thing* starts to emerge, the last shred of candle gutters out, leaving you in the dark forest. And a screech owl, who has silently taken up position on the roof above, lets loose with a nerve-curdling shriek.

That's Tales of Wonder as they should be read, man.

Well, of course I was hooked, from then on, permanently. By the time World War II came along, I had about 1300 mags and paperbacks stacked in that cabin alone. (I gave them all to the county library, despite the sneers of the librarian, who doubtless used them for doorstops. Alas, alas; rubies, pearls, emeralds gone to the gravel crusher.)

With the war came a break, after which I started all over again (having discovered the magic of subscriptions). I now have about forty running feet of them double-stacked, plus head-high shelves bulging in all bathrooms, plus miscellaneous deposits. In addition, there's another forty feet of philosophy and politics and history, sixty feet of my old professional specialty (experimental psychology), twenty feet of math, astronomy, and miscellaneous, twenty feet of fiction by dead authors and another twenty of same by live ones (horrible how quickly one seems to have to shift them), twenty feet of women's studies and related material, and twenty feet of mostly poetry. And *something* has got to give. (Oh well, who needs *Das Kapital* anyway?)

The painful part of starting like that is that you read, read, read—without, in most cases, noticing dull stuff like the author's name. Until I started to write it myself, of course; then names become acutely important. But I am still in the embarrassing position of not knowing who wrote some fantastic scene that is forever engraved on my liver. And then finding out, Oh my god, yes of course—*he* or *she* did that! (Worse yet, finding it out in his or her presence, whether in the flesh or in one of my Victorian correspondences.)

Now maybe this is the best place to lay to rest one last ghost—the business of the anonymity and the male pseudonym. First, the important part: *Everything I've ever told you or anyone else is true*, with one exception. David Gerrold came looking for me and I told him he was on a different street. If he'd waited before ringing the bell he would have seen through the glass a solitary figure staring at a *Star Trek* re-run in the dark, and I'm sure the jig would have been up. Other than that I have never told a lie or modulated my natural voice—I was very careful about pronouns, things like "child" instead of "boy," etc., etc. But it wasn't calculated. (I'm lousy at that.) All my letters have been just first draft typed as fast as I can go with my one finger. I can't help what people think sounds male or female.

You see, when I started, I was in rather a stuffy job atmosphere. A university. And I was something of a maverick; I kept having ideas that didn't jibe with the official academic outlook of my department. And when I started my own research it got worse. ("In this department we do feel rather strongly that recent PhDs do best when their work fits in with or amplifies some of the ongoing lines of research here.") Well, I wasn't about to fit in with or amplify anyone else's line; I had my own long-held ideas, and I kept citing research nobody else had read, or had read and dismissed, and with great pain and struggle I set off on a totally independent tack, which had the ill grace, after four agonizing years, to pay off. (I still keep getting requests for it from obscure Europeans universities, or behind the Iron Curtain.) With this background, the news that I was writing *science fiction* would have destroyed my last shreds of respectability and relegated me to the freak department, possibly even to the freak-whose-grant-funds-should-be-stopped division; those familiar with older academe will get the picture. Anonymity seemed highly desirable. The name "Tiptree" started by seeing it on a can of marmalade in the Giant; I was looking for a forgettable name so editors wouldn't remember rejecting my manuscripts. The "James" was one more bit of cover—and my husband threw in "Jr." for whimsy's sake. I was shocked when the stories all sold and I was stuck with the name. What started as a prank dreamed its way into reality.

You have to realize, this never was run as a real clandestine operation with cutouts and drops and sanitizing and so on. The only "assets" were one P.O. box, a little luck, and the delicacy and decency of some people who decided not to pry. Namely and chiefly one Jeff Smith.

When you wrote asking for the *Phantasmicom* interview was the first time I was approached personally by anyone, and I told myself, Dammit, say no. But then this business of really loving the SF world and wanting to say so welled up, and I thought I could kind of race over the bio without telling lies and start waving Hello. You'll note what I put in there about masks... So that's how it all started.

Then, from about the second year, when things began to get serious, "James" started to feel more and more constrictive. It was as if there were things I wanted to write as me, or at least a woman. (I still don't know exactly what they are, that's the odd part.) Meanwhile Tiptree kept taking on a stronger and stronger life of his own; if I were superstitious I'd say Something was waiting for incarnation there in the Giant Foods important section... maybe I do anyway. This voice would sneak up from behind my pancreas somewhere. *He* insisted on the nickname, he would not be "Jim." And as to "Uncle" Tip—maybe I'm a natural uncle. See, I have no family, nobody ever called me Sis or Mom or even Aunt Alice.

And his persona wasn't too constricting; I wrote as me. Maybe my peculiar upbringing—where values like Don't-be-a-coward and Achieve! and Find-out-how-it-works and Fight-on-the-underdog's-side were stamped in before they got to the You're-a-young-lady stuff (which was awful)—maybe this resulted in a large part of me being kind of a generalized Human being rather than specifically female. (I am very pro-woman, though; once when dabbling in NY politics I had the opportunity to personally thank one of the original suffragettes, then a frail but vital eighty, for the privilege of the vote. It was a beautiful moment.) But still I wanted to write as a woman. By this point it became obvious that killing Tiptree off, say by drowning him out on the reef here, wasn't going to be that simple. He—we—had all these friends, see. So all I did was rather feebly set up Raccoona Sheldon with a Wisconsin P.O. box and bank, and I confess to giving her some of Tip's weaker tales to peddle. (Except for the one called "Your Faces, O My Sisters! Your Faces Filled of Light!" in the anthology *Aurora* by McIntyre and Anderson. Nobody much mentions that one, but I consider it as good as I can do.) Anyway, the upshot of all this was that where I lived I wasn't, and I didn't live where I was, and things were reaching some kind of crescendo of confusion. Frankly, I had no real plan. So I was really relieved as well as traumatized to have Mother's ghost do Tiptree in. But it left me with an extraordinary eerie empty feeling for a while; maybe still does.

One problem caused by having a male pseudonym was that there was a desire to rush (by mail) up to many female writers and give them a straight sisterly hug. (And to some male writers, too; especially those I knew were feeling down. I guess I wrote some fairly peculiar letters here and there.) Another problem that may seem trivial, wasn't to me; people kept saying how lifelike my female characters were, while all the time I was perishing to find out if the *male* characters were living!

Things like being hooted at in the Women in SF Symposium really didn't bother me at all, because I doubtless would have done the same myself. And also I am used to being hooted at for unpopular ideas—the struggle I mentioned in the university was just one of a lifelong series. And then, too, I'm a feminist of a far earlier vintage, where we worked through a lot of the first stages all by our lonesomes. There are stages in all revolutions of consciousness where certain things are unsayable, because they sound too much like the enemy's line. Then after some years, when everybody is feeling more secure about unity on the facts and the wrongs, those "unsayable" things can be looked at objectively again, and new insight gained. I refer, of course, to my real interest in why people are mothers. (I just saw an article in *Psychology Today* that triumphantly claims that Fathers Do It Too—but turns out on reading the data that what they "do" is quite different. They play with baby; mother takes care of it.) There were, of course, a lot more things I felt like saying in the Symposium, but I thought that one was safe for Tip. As indeed it was—typical "male" nonsense.

I've been amazed at the warm, kind, friendly reaction I've been getting, even from the most unlikely people. I worried deeply about what had unwittingly become a major deception. I wrote at once to everyone I could thing of who might feel I'd let them go out on a cracked limb. They couldn't have been nicer. If someone does feel griped, they haven't gotten it to me. The only problem seems to be that now I'm expected to produce something somewhere grander, more insightful, more "real." Well, if I knew how, I would—the trouble is that the Tip did all I could in that line. If there is something—other than "Sisters" —which is going to burst forth from my liberate gonads, it hasn't peeped yet. In fact, I may be written out for a while. With each story I dug deeper and deeper into more emotional stuff, and some of it started to hurt pretty bad. "Slow Music" reads like a musical fadeout or coda to Tiptree's group of work.

Now, I've got one more thing to add to this terrible monologue. In a funny way, I found that as Tip I could be useful to my fellow female writers. There were times when Tiptree (male) queried anthology editors on why nothing from this or that female writer was being used. And as an old gent I may have been more helpful to sisters who were fighting depression than another woman could. They had to brace up and respond to my courtly compliments—Tip was quite a flirt—and they knew somebody quite different valued them. Whereas just another woman coming in with sympathy and admiration tends to dissolve in a mutual embrace of woe.

Now, adieu, dear Jeff and Ann. Outside the Caribbean is in roaring high tide, storms are chasing themselves overhead, the palm trees lit up olive and white by great bursts of lightning. And the generator is, as usual, failing. May you never be the same.

Oh Joanna,
Will I Have
Any Friends Left?

Dear Tip

and

Dear Alli,

O Alli, I wish you knew how many friends you have left.

I'm writing this after reading something like thirty-seven letters written to you in 2015, and numerous letters from Ursula Le Guin and Joanna Russ, too, from the 1970s and 80s. So I don't really feel like I can say anything original; so much has been said, and so well, from so many different perspectives. And I'm not an author myself, to be inspired by your titles to write my own; I've not questioned my gender identity nor my sexuality; I've only read your works since knowing you were a woman writing with a man's name. (I've been crowing about the phrase "ineluctably masculine" since before I knew who wrote it or where.)

Anyway. Still. I love your work, so that's something I hope you'd like to know. "Your Faces, O My Sisters! Your Faces Filled of Light!" horrifies me whenever I think of it. So does "With Delicate Mad Hands," and "The Girl who Was Plugged In." "Houston, Houston, Do You Read" makes me gleeful—and I've got the double, paired with Joanna Russ' "Souls", a fact which is now very funny to me (I didn't get it when I first bought it years ago). And of course there's "The Women Men Don't See"—I don't remember whether I read Karen Joy Fowler's "What I Didn't See" before or after, but they are inherently tangled in my mind now, and have made a lasting impression. In fact I just reread that story and I am floored anew by what you're saying about society via both Don and Ruth.

But short stories are not my first love; I'm relatively new to liking them at all. What I like are novels. And *Brightness Falls from the Air*? I love it. Who knew that a book that includes adolescents involved in pornography could hold any appeal for me? I think this is one of the things that made you distinctly *you*: you took difficult issues, and didn't make them palatable or agreeable—didn't come over all moral and indignant—instead you were sympathetic, and realistic, and blunt. And of course there's so much more to the novel than that—there's an Agatha Christie-type plot, a range of interesting characters, a fascinating world, and the beginning of a post-colonial tilt that lifts the novel from *just* being a fun science fiction novel. So thank you for writing it—even after the world discovered that you were *just* an old lady in MacLean.

When Alisa asked me to co-edit a collection for your centenary—a tribute to your work and contribution to the field—I was thrilled by the idea of acknowledging you in such a way. I was also excited and daunted by the idea of adding something to The Conversation. You know, that conversation that's been going on for longer than many in my generation give it credit; the one where we think about Women in Science Fiction and Fantasy. The one that sometimes has to go back over old ground to say WE WERE ALWAYS THERE in every facet of the science fiction world, we've just been overlooked and forgotten. The one that strives to have

more women than just Ursula Le Guin (your Bear) remembered—
and yes, even more women than Le Guin plus Joanna Russ and
James Tiptree Jr. (maybe Octavia Butler if we're lucky). And the
authors who responded to our call have gone beyond my dreams
for how they engaged with your work, with your identity, and what
you personally and fictionally mean for the twenty-first century.

After reading the letters you wrote to "Starbear" and Joanna…
I mean, I'd read Julie Phillips' biography, so I had an idea of some
of your life and all. But those letters where you are (re)introducing
yourself to these long-time friends: they tear at my soul. You are
the sort of doctor who "doesn't do anybody any good"? Oh Alli!
I am so sad if that's how you really felt! Perhaps you were so deep
in self-deprecating mode, because you weren't "actually" Tiptree,
that you felt you had to apologise for it all? I wish I could have
known you to chastise you about running yourself down. Even
though I know you wouldn't have wanted it. Because oh, how much
good you have done so many people—and I'm sure that's also true
within your professional fields, as a teacher and researcher, as well
as an author. After all, you talk about those young women who
sought you out to pour out their soul, and how you volunteered
in a rape crisis centre.

How I wish you could have known how much an Australian in
the twenty-first century loves your work.

With deep appreciation,
Alex

Dear Alice Sheldon/James Tiptree Jr./Raccoona Sheldon,

Sitting down to finally write my own letter to you, I'm suddenly aware just how difficult it is to know to whom to address it. You're an enigma; for all the words written to you and about you and by you, there's still so much left to know. I never know which pronouns to use, which you truly preferred. I wish I could know how much of the Tiptree persona was defiance in the face of patriarchy and how much something far more cynical, or hopeful, than that? For all the words written, I wish I could know more about you.

You left such an indelible mark on this field. For all the tribute books and collections and non-fiction about our great writers, you, I'm guessing, would not be surprised to know that not a lot of them are written in tribute to female authors. We wanted you to have one for your hundredth birthday.

I think the best way to remember someone is to tell and retell the stories about them—the things they did that inspired you, made you laugh (or cry) or altered the way you thought about life. When we embarked on compiling work for this book, I had hoped that the stories and letters we gathered might shed light on a few things. You know, ask a bunch of smart people to tease apart a mystery and hopefully the think tank will explain it.

I've left writing my piece for last, hoping that reading all those written before this one would solve the riddle of just who was Alice Sheldon/James Tiptree Jr./Raccoona Sheldon? One of the resounding themes in this collection is that we just don't really know. Where I had hoped there was an answer, each letter takes us down another wormhole, with yet more questions that will never, can never, be answered.

Alex and I were also given the opportunity to read many of your personal letters. Thank you for leaving them to be archived—the experience of reading your thoughts and feelings as you wrote them felt both intrusive, as though we'd snuck into your private study and rifled through your desk drawers, and utterly inspiring. Our genre has spent much of this year debating and discussing what it means to be Good, and Successful, and Award-worthy. Reading your personal letters resoundingly answered that for me—you were brilliant, incisive, and exceptional. You demonstrated that the kind of science fiction *I* want to read can be written and by a woman at that! You showed that we can invoke change, we can ask the hard questions, we can demand better of ourselves and society. (Even if you were totally bleak about the outcomes, you never lost your empathy, and maybe then we are never truly lost?) You were brilliant, Alice Sheldon/James Tiptree Jr/Raccoona Sheldon. You stood head and shoulders above almost everyone, and continue to do so now. You are what we can only strive to be in the quality of our prose, the depth and breadth of our imagination, and the exploration of the Great Questions in life: what it means to be human, what it means to be ourselves (both as individuals and collectively).

My heart breaks that you never felt free to be who you truly wanted to be—and I don't know that we will ever know who that person was, or even if you ever did. I'm also so sad for the way your "true identity" was revealed, without your consent. You wanted your privacy; you deserved to have it. It's not our right to know all of your business. So, after reading all these letters, and realising that we can't ever answer all our questions about you, what I do know is you were complex, complicated, and brilliant. People are, and should be, complicated. We are more than one characteristic, and perhaps more than one identity. We are always performing. Choosing which parts of our authentic selves to share and which to keep private. We are all inconsistencies, incongruencies and complexities. We're human.

We may never see a star burn as bright as yours again. It will certainly never burn across our sky the same way. But we are so blessed to have been able to still stand in your light.

In the end, this collection of letters to you is united by the themes of identity and acceptance. And, really, aren't they the underlying themes of all human journeys? And the most traditional epic fiction? To find out who we really are and seek out those who accept us for it.

Thank you for your story, and for your fiction.

Happy 100th birthday, Uncle Tip.

Alisa

About the Editors

Alexandra Pierce has been inhaling science fiction and fantasy for as long as she can remember. She writes a monthly column for Tor.com, Aurora Australis, rounding up the interesting happenings in the Australian and New Zealand speculative fiction scene, and blogs at Randomly Yours, Alex. She has won Chronos and Ditmar awards for her reviews and interviews. As co-host of the Galactic Suburbia podcast she shares the Peter McNamara Award from 2011 and four Hugo Award nominations. With the rest of her life Alex teaches history and English, knits monsters, bakes cakes, and indulges in visual astronomy. She's a Christian and a feminist and a big Led Zeppelin fan.

Alisa Krasnostein, as the founder of Twelfth Planet Press, has been editing and publishing books for nearly a decade. In 2011, she won the World Fantasy Award for her work with the press, and Twelfth Planet books and stories have won the Locus, Shirley Jackson, WSFA Small Press, Aurealis, Ditmar, Chronos and Tin Duck awards. Alisa is also a four times Hugo nominee, and winner of the Peter McNamara Award in 2011, as co-host of the Galactic Suburbia Podcast. Twelfth Planet Press has championed under-represented voices from the very start. Previous projects include the acclaimed Twelve Planets series of twelve short collections of short fiction by Australian women and *Kaleidoscope*, an anthology of diverse YA fiction, published in 2014.

Copyrights

The Female Factory

Lisa L Hannett & Angela Slatter

In The Female Factory, procreation is big business. Children are a commodity few women can afford.

Hopeful mothers-to-be try everything. Fertility clinics. Pills. Wombs for hire. Babies are no longer made in bedrooms, but engineered in boardrooms. A quirk of genetics allows lucky surrogates to carry multiple eggs, to control when they are fertilised, and by whom — but corporations market and sell the offspring. The souls of lost embryos are never wasted; captured in software, they give electronics their voice. Spirits born into the wrong bodies can brave the charged waters of a hidden billabong, and change their fate. Industrious orphans learn to manipulate scientific advances, creating mothers of their own choosing.

From Australia's near-future all the way back in time to its convict past, these stories spin and sever the ties between parents and children.

aurealis
awards
FINALIST

Secret Lives of Books

Rosaleen Love

Secret lives, replete with possibilities.

Elsewhere exists as a better place, in a better time, for a better life. The trick is how to get there from here. These stories give the answers. Share in the secret lives of books. Fly to Mars, the first stage, perhaps, in the onward journey to elsewhere. Hear the music of the heavenly spheres and be forever changed, providing the bad guys don't hear it first. Discover Gaia may not be quite who we think she is.

Discover the universe is a rather big place.

Embrace Utopia for women too, if only...

Secret Lives of Books is the much anticipated all new original collection of short stories from one of Australia's most respected and loved science fiction writers. Winner of the Chandler Award for outstanding achievement in Australian science fiction, Rosaleen Love's previous collections Total Devotion Machine and Evolution Annie were published by the Women's Press alongside classic works by Joanna Russ, Suzy McKee Charnas and Octavia Butler.

What do a disabled superhero, a time-traveling Chinese-American figure skater, and a transgender animal shifter have in common? They're all stars of *Kaleidoscope* stories!

Kaleidoscope collects fun, edgy, meditative, and hopeful YA science fiction and fantasy with diverse leads. These twenty original stories tell of scary futures, magical adventures, and the joys and heartbreaks of teenage.

Featuring New York Times bestselling and award-winning authors along with newer voices: Garth Nix, Sofia Samatar, William Alexander, Karen Healey, E.C. Myers, Tansy Rayner Roberts, Ken Liu, Vylar Kaftan, Sean Williams, Amal El-Mohtar, Jim C. Hines, Faith Mudge, John Chu, Alena McNamara, Tim Susman, Gabriela Lee, Dirk Flinthart, Holly Kench, Sean Eads, and Shveta Thakrar

"*Kaleidoscope* is one of the best anthologies I have read for a very long time.... engaging and thoughtful and brilliant..." — *Tehani Wessely*

CPSIA information can be obtained at www.ICGtesting.com
Printed in the USA
BVOW08s0482403l6
441549BV00002B/31/P